T0212487

Lecture Notes in Computer Science   10264

Commenced Publication in 1973
Founding and Former Series Editors:
Gerhard Goos, Juris Hartmanis, and Jan van Leeuwen

Daniel Archambault · Helen Purchase
Tobias Hoßfeld (Eds.)

Evaluation in the Crowd

Crowdsourcing and Human-Centered Experiments

Dagstuhl Seminar 15481, Dagstuhl Castle
Germany, November 22–27, 2015
Revised Contributions

Editors
Daniel Archambault
Department of Computer Science
Swansea University
Swansea
UK

Tobias Hoßfeld
Modellierung adaptiver Systeme
Universität Duisburg-Essen
Essen
Germany

Helen Purchase
University of Glasgow
Glasgow
UK

ISSN 0302-9743   ISSN 1611-3349   (electronic)
Lecture Notes in Computer Science
ISBN 978-3-319-66434-7   ISBN 978-3-319-66435-4   (eBook)
DOI 10.1007/978-3-319-66435-4

Library of Congress Control Number: 2017954909

LNCS Sublibrary: SL3 – Information Systems and Applications, incl. Internet/Web, and HCI

Printed on acid-free paper

This Springer imprint is published by Springer Nature
The registered company is Springer International Publishing AG
The registered company address is: Gewerbestrasse 11, 6330 Cham, Switzerland

Preface

During November 22–27, 2015, a seminar entitled "Evaluation in the Crowd: Crowdsourcing and Human-Centred Experiments" (no. 15481) took place at the International Conference and Research Centre for Computer Science, Dagstuhl Castle, Germany. The centre was founded by the German government to promote computer science research at an international level and quickly became established as a world-leading meeting centre for informatics research. It seeks to foster dialog within the research community, to advance academic education and professional development, and to transfer knowledge between academia and industry.

Human-centred empirical evaluations play an important role in the fields of human-computer interaction, visualisation, graphics, multimedia, and psychology. Researchers in these areas often involve users in their research to measure the performance of a system with respect to user comprehension or the perceived quality or usability of a system. A popular and scientifically rigorous method for assessing this performance or subjective quality is through formal experimentation, where participants are asked to perform tasks on visual representations and their performance is measured quantitatively (often through response time and errors). When evaluating user perceived quality, users undertake tasks using the system under investigation or complete user surveys. Other scientific areas like psychology use similar tests or user surveys. A common approach is to conduct such empirical evaluations in a laboratory, often with the experimenter present, allowing for the controlled collection of quantitative and qualitative data.

The advent of crowdsourcing platforms, such as Amazon Mechanical Turk or Microworkers, has provided a revolutionary methodology to conduct human-centred experiments. Through such platforms, experiments can now collect data from hundreds, even thousands, of participants from a diverse user community over a matter of weeks, greatly increasing the ease with which we can collect data as well as the power and generalisability of experimental results. However, when running experiments on these platforms, it is hard to ensure that participants are actively engaging with the experiment, and experimental controls are difficult to implement. Also, qualitative data is difficult, if not impossible, to collect as the experimenter is not present in the room to conduct an exit survey. Finally, the ethics behind running such experiments require further consideration. When we post a job on a crowdsourcing platform, it is often easy to forget that people are completing the job for us on the other side of the machine.

The focus of this Dagstuhl seminar was to discuss experiences and methodological considerations when using crowdsourcing platforms to run human-centred experiments to test the effectiveness of visual representations. We primarily target members of the human-computer interaction, visualisation, and quality-of-experience research communities as these communities often engage in human-centred experimental methodologies and have already deployed crowdsourcing experiments. We also engaged researchers who study the technology that makes crowdsourcing possible. Finally, researchers from psychology, social science and computer science who study the crowdsourcing community brought another perspective on this topic.

The inspiring Dagstuhl atmosphere fostered discussions and brought together the researchers from the different research directions. This book is an output of Dagstuhl Seminar no. 15481, and will provide information on (1) crowdsourcing technology and experimental methodologies, (2) comparisons between crowdsourcing and lab experiments, (3) the use of crowdsourcing for visualisation, psychology, QoE and HCI empirical studies, and (4) the nature of crowdworkers and their work, their motivation and demographic background, as well as the relationships among people forming the crowdsourcing community.

We would like to thank all participants of the seminar for the lively discussions and contributions during the seminar. The abstracts and presentation slides can be found on the Dagstuhl website for this seminar[1] and an online document reports on all activities during the seminar[2]. We are grateful to all the authors for their valuable time and contributions to the book. The seminar and this book would not have been possible without the great help of the Schloss Dagstuhl team. We would like to thank all of them for their assistance.

Last but not least, we would like to thank John Hamer for his help in editing and polishing the final version of the book.

May 2017

Daniel Archambault
Helen C. Purchase
Tobias Hoßfeld

---

[1] Dagstuhl seminar website: http://www.dagstuhl.de/15481.

[2] Report of the Dagstuhl seminar: http://dx.doi.org/10.4230/DagRep.5.11.103.

Contents

Evaluation in the Crowd: An Introduction

Daniel Archambault[1]([⊠]), Helen C. Purchase[2], and Tobias Hoßfeld[3]

[1] Swansea University, Swansea, UK
d.w.archambault@swansea.ac.uk
[2] University of Glasgow, Glasgow, UK
[3] University of Duisburg-Essen, Duisburg, Germany

Human-centred empirical evaluations play an important role in the fields of human-computer interaction, visualisation, and graphics. The advent of crowdsourcing platforms such as Amazon Mechanical Turk has provided a revolutionary methodology to conduct human-centred experiments. Through such platforms, experiments can now collect data from hundreds, even thousands, of participants from a diverse user community over a matter of weeks, greatly increasing the ease with which data can be collected as well as the power and generalisability of experimental results. However, such an experimental platform does not come without its problems: ensuring participant investment in the task, defining experimental controls, and understanding the ethics behind deploying such experiments en masse.

This book is intended to be a primer for computer science researchers who intend to use crowdsourcing technology for human centred experiments. It focuses on methodological considerations when using crowdsourcing platforms to run human-centred experiments, particularly in the areas of visualisation and of quality of experience (QoE) for online video delivery. We hope that this book can act as a valuable resource for researchers in fields who intend to run experiments on crowdsourcing for the purposes of human-centred experimentation.

1 Focus of the Book

In areas of computer science involving interactive and visual elements, it is often necessary to understand the performance of such systems with respect to user experience. A popular and scientifically rigorous method for assessing this performance is through formal experimentation, where participants are asked to perform tasks on visual representations and their performance is measured quantitatively (often through response time and errors) or through quantitative subjective ratings. In the past, such empirical evaluations were conducted in a laboratory setting, often with the experimenter present, allowing for the controlled collection of quantitative and qualitative data. Such formal experiments can collect information on the advantages/disadvantages of a visual representation for visualisation or the perception of video quality in our fields.

The principal limitation of the formal experiment methodology is that it often takes weeks, sometimes even months, to collect data from a sufficient number of participants. Also, the diversity of the user community tested is often restricted,

D. Archambault et al. (Eds.): Evaluation in the Crowd, LNCS 10264, pp. 1–5, 2017.
DOI: 10.1007/978-3-319-66435-4_1

consisting mainly of a sample of university undergraduate and graduate students. Crowdsourcing platforms can address these limitations by providing an infrastructure for the deployment of experiments and the collection of data over diverse user populations and often allows for hundreds, sometimes even thousands, of participants to take part in an experiment in parallel over one or two weeks. However, such platforms are not free of limitations. When running experiments on crowdsourcing platforms, it is hard to ensure that participants actively engage with the experiment. Also, experimental controls are difficult to implement. Qualitative data about the experimental conditions is difficult to collect as the experimenter is not present in the room to conduct an exit survey. Participants are drawn from a more diverse community of users, but this itself introduces limitations. Finally, and importantly, the ethical issues associated with running such experiments require further consideration. When we post a job on a crowdsourcing platform, it is often easy to forget that people (rather than machines) are completing the job for us on the other side of the machine.

In this book, we have collected chapters from experts in a variety of fields that use crowdsourcing in order to run human-centred experiments. In particular, we we have contributions from experts in the human-computer interaction, visualisation, and the quality of experience (QoE) communities who often engage in human-centred experimental methodologies to evaluate their developed technologies and have used crowdsourcing platforms in the past. We also have contributions from researchers who are interested in the technology that makes crowdsourcing possible, as well as researchers in the social sciences and computer sciences that study crowdsourcing community, that is the people performing the microtasks behind the scenes.

In this book, we focus on a variety of perspective in the area of crowdsourcing. In particular, we consider the following:

1. *Crowdsourcing Platforms vs The Laboratory.* The laboratory setting for human-centred experiments has been employed for decades and has a well understood methodology with known advantages and limitations. Studies performed on crowdsourcing platforms provide new opportunities and new challenges. A cross community discussion over the nature of these technologies as well as their advantages and limitations is needed. When should we use crowdsourcing? More importantly, when should we not? What are the right incentives to use to engage the crowd participants and ensure the quality of the output? Moreover, how can we retain the top contributors over the time? How do we design the tasks and when are complex, orchestrated tasks appropriate?

2. *Scientifically Rigorous Methodologies.* As human-centred crowdsourcing experiments are relatively new, our communities have the opportunity to better understand the strengths and limitations of the platform to better refine our experimental methodologies. When running between-subjects experiments, what considerations do we need to make when allocating our participant pools that are compared? Are within-subjects experiments too taxing for crowdsourced participants? How do we effectively collect qualitative

information beyond free text boxes? Is there any way to better ensure engagement in the experiment or easily detect non-engagement via data analysis means?

3. *Crowdsourcing Experiments in Human-Computer Interaction, Visualisation, and Quality of Experience.* Each of these fields has unique challenges when designing, deploying, and analysing the results of crowdsourcing evaluation. We are especially interested in the experience and best practice findings of these communities in regards to these experiments. What sorts of methodological considerations need to be taken into account when considering each of these communities? Are these considerations different for our communities?

4. *Getting to Know the Crowd.* While understanding how research communities use crowdsourcing technologies is important, no less important is consideration of the people themselves that accept and perform the jobs that we post on these platforms.

5. *Ethics in Experiments.* Even though the participants of a crowdsourcing study never walk into the laboratory, ethical considerations behind this new platform need to be discussed. What additional considerations are needed beyond standard ethical procedures when running crowdsourcing experiments? How do we ensure that we are compensating our participants adequately for their work, considering the nature of microtasks?

We explore these broad questions in the following chapters of this book after introducing common terminology and some preliminary definitions.

2   Terminology and Definitions

Crowdsourcing is a new technology developed for purposes that were not originally intended for human-centred experimentation of visualisations and video quality assessments. Therefore, the terminology of two areas, mainly that of human-centred experimentation and crowdsourcing, need to be combined into a single set of cohesive terms for the purposes of this book. These overarching terms are used throughout the book unless otherwise specified by the chapter authors.

In this book, we use the term *microtask* to describe a single task performed by our participant as it is divorced from any particular commercial product. However, at the time of writing, many crowdsourcing experiments have been run on Amazon Mechanical Turk (AMT): if the microtask is implemented in AMT, we use the appropriate term, HIT (Human Intelligence Task), to describe it.

The term *stimuli* has the same meaning as in human-centred experimentation research. A stimulus is the visualisation or video shown to the participant during a microtask. *Experiment* or *test* indicates the broad assessment activity consisting of the full set stimuli. In particular, *experiment* will indicate assessments that are performed in the lab without the use of a crowdsourcing platform. A *test* is an assessment in a crowdsourcing environment.

In our experiment, we have a group of people that undertake the experiment or test. A group of people that undertake an experiment (thus, a lab-based assessment), will be referred to as *participants*. If the experiment is conducted online using a crowdsourcing platform, the people undertaking the crowdsourcing test will be referred to as *workers* or *crowdworkers*.

Task will refer to the complete set of actions that participants need to perform to complete an experiment. A *campaign* refers to group of similar microtasks. Every campaign consists of the description of the tasks and requirements (e.g., the number of quality ratings required, the number of workers are needed, etc.). A campaign can be a subset of a test as multiple campaigns may be needed to cover a large set of stimuli in a crowdsourcing environment.

3   Outline of the Book

Each chapter of this book examines crowdsourcing and human-centred experimentation from a different perspective.

Chapter 2 provides a comparison of crowdsourcing experiments to those conducted in the laboratory. It begins by discussing the limitations of laboratory, crowdsourcing, and crowdsourcing platforms for use in human-centred experiments. It then discusses the goals and requirements of laboratory experiments and how to adapt these to crowdsourcing platforms. It concludes with methodological considerations and the future of crowdsourcing in human-centred experiments.

Chapter 3 presents an overview of the participants who undertake crowdsourcing experiments and the ethics behind deploying human-centred experiments on these platforms. The chapter begins by presenting an overview of the community. It then discusses their motivation for performing microtasks and how the workers organise and perform their work. Given these considerations, the chapter discusses how we should use crowdsourcing platforms for experiments in our research. Legal and ethical considerations are discussed before the conclusion of the chapter.

Chapter 4 provides a discussion of the technological considerations and how they can best support academic research. The chapter provides an overview of existing platforms along with their benefits and limitations. With this information in mind, it discusses features that would be beneficial for academic research.

Chapter 5 presents an introduction to information visualisation and how crowdsourcing platforms can be used to support experiments in this area. It considers all elements of human-centred information visualisation experiments including: participant selection, study design, procedure, data, tasks, and what to measure. The chapter also presents four case studies on the successful deployment of crowdsourcing technology for human-centred experiments.

Chapter 6 discusses how crowdsourcing experiments can be used in the field of psychology. It presents an overview of the field and how information visualisation and HCI research has influenced it. The chapter discusses the possibilities and potential pitfalls of using crowdsourcing as an experimental platform in psychology.

Chapter 7 presents how crowdsourcing can be used in quality of experience (QoE) experiments in video streaming. It describes the nature of experiments in this area and how to transfer methodologies from the laboratory to the crowd. It provides an overview of existing frameworks and a discussion on the lessons learned from moving experiments to crowdsourcing platforms.

Given the diverse set of topics in this book, we hope that the chapters of this book can provide inspiration for readers to develop and deploy their own crowdsourcing experiments.

Crowdsourcing Versus the Laboratory: Towards Human-Centered Experiments Using the Crowd

Ujwal Gadiraju[1]([⊠]), Sebastian Möller[2], Martin Nöllenburg[3], Dietmar Saupe[4],
Sebastian Egger-Lampl[5], Daniel Archambault[6], and Brian Fisher[7]

[1] Leibniz Universität Hannover, Hannover, Germany
`gadiraju@L3S.de`
[2] TU Berlin, Berlin, Germany
[3] Algorithms and Complexity Group, TU Wien, Vienna, Austria
[4] University of Konstanz, Konstanz, Germany
[5] Austrian Institute of Technology, Vienna, Austria
[6] Swansea University, Swansea, UK
[7] Simon Fraser University, Burnaby, Canada

1 Introduction

The notion of '*crowdsourcing*' was born nearly a decade ago in 2006[1], and since then the crowdsourcing paradigm has been widely adopted across a multitude of domains. Crowdsourcing solutions have been proposed and implemented to overcome obstacles that require human intelligence at a large scale. In the last decade there have been numerous applications of crowdsourcing both in research and practice (for example, [25,34]). In the realm of research, crowdsourcing has presented novel opportunities for qualitative and quantitative studies by providing a means to scale-up previously constrained laboratory studies and controlled experiments [44]. By exploiting crowdsourcing we can build ground truths for evaluation, access desired participants around the clock with a wide variety of demographics at will [31], and all within a short amount of time. This also comes with a number of challenges related to lack of control on research subjects and to data quality.

In this chapter, we first explore a few limitations of conducting experiments in the laboratory and those using crowdsourcing. We then deliberate on the typical requirements for human-centered experiments and the considerations necessary when transitioning from constrained laboratory experiments to the use of crowdsourcing. Previous works have established that crowdsourcing is a suitable means to acquire participants for social and behavioral science experiments [7,26,37,41] and have validated them for use in human-computer interaction and visualization experiments [24]. Several other domains are successfully

---

The original version of this chapter was revised. The affiliation of the third author was corrected. The erratum to this chapter is available at https://doi.org/10.1007/978-3-319-66435-4_8

[1] http://www.wired.com/2006/06/crowds/ last accessed 14 Jun 2017.

© Springer International Publishing AG 2017
D. Archambault et al. (Eds.): Evaluation in the Crowd, LNCS 10264, pp. 6–26, 2017.
DOI: 10.1007/978-3-319-66435-4_2

using crowdsourcing: Quality of Experience (QoE) assessment (see Chap. 7), software testing and software development, and network measurements. In this work, we identify the key factors of an experiment that determine its suitability to benefit from crowdsourcing. By juxtaposing the strengths and weaknesses of controlled laboratory experiments and those using crowdsourcing, determined through the inherent characteristics of the two paradigms, we present the reader with an overall understanding of the kinds of experiments that can benefit from the virtues of crowdsourcing and the cases that are less suitable for the same.

1.1 Limitations of Laboratory Experiments

Before crowdsourcing gained popularity as an alternative means for experimentation, human-centered experiments were traditionally conducted in a controlled laboratory setting. Despite a wealth of experimental findings resulting from such experiments, researchers also face several limitations and difficulties when preparing, running, and analyzing laboratory experiments. Many of the limitations are linked to the possible scale of the experiments. Often the pool of participants is constrained to a rather small and not necessarily representative group of subjects that are easily accessible to an experimenter, e.g., college students enrolled in the same program and required to participate in a number of experiments during their studies. This makes it difficult to generalize the experimental findings to larger and culturally or educationally more heterogeneous groups of the population. Scaling laboratory experiments to larger numbers and more representative groups of participants immediately results in a strong increase in cost for personnel and participant remuneration, as well as in the actual time required to prepare and run the experiment. Both factors may often be prohibitive, especially in an academic setting with limited funds and resources. Moreover, the artificially controlled environment in the laboratory, while advantageous, e.g., for excluding external confounding factors or testing specialized equipment, also leads to a limited ecological validity, as the experimental tasks might be performed differently by the participants in a real-life setting.

1.2 Limitations of Crowdsourcing Experiments

Although crowdsourcing evidently empowers us with an ability to run experiments using a large number of participants at a previously unmatched scale, there are a few concomitant pitfalls. Due to varying motivations of participants in the crowd (in both reward-based and to a lesser extent in altruistic crowdsourcing), quality control is a major challenge. Several prior works have addressed this issue [11, 19]. In cases where the participants are acquired through a crowdsourcing platform, the experimenter has little or no information regarding the background and profile of the crowdworkers. The absolute anonymity of subjects in an experiment is not often desirable. When specialized apparatus, hardware, software, or other equipment is required for a given experiment, leveraging crowdsourcing can be arduous, riddled with inconvenience, or in some cases even nearly impossible. Some ethnographic contexts in which crowdworkers participate in experiments may also be undesirable. These aspects, alongside hidden confounding factors contribute to a lack of complete control over the subjects and the experimental environment.

1.3   Limitations of Existing Crowdsourcing Platforms for Academic Research

When considering using crowdsourcing for academic purposes, we must take into account the platform limitations. In particular, we must remember that these platforms, in general, were not built to support human-centered experiments, but rather for managing microtask units of work. The main purpose of most crowdsourcing systems is to provide a means to distribute the work and provide remuneration for it. As a result, researchers have described and created workarounds to help with these limitations.

A central limitation of using crowdsourcing platforms for human-centered experiments is ensuring that the participant is invested in the experimental tasks. This limitation is related to the absolute anonymity issue described above. Part of this limitation can be alleviated through using the participant reputation scores, but not entirely. As a result, experiments often employ a number of techniques. Consistency checks are conducted as a post process on the experimental results to ensure reasonably consistent answers for the same question or a set of sufficiently diverse answers [4,5,38]. Given drastically different answers for the exact same question (or the exact same answer for all questions even though they differ substantially), one could assume that the participants were not invested in the experimental tasks. Another method to ensure a high level of participant investment is to introduce special tasks in the experiment, or to use these special tasks as a pre-screening method for participants, to determine how much attention the participant is paying to the experiment [19,21]. Any combination of such techniques can be used to help ensure investments of the participants and the collection of high quality experimental data.

The above limitation is just one of many that we must consider when moving our experiments from the laboratory and deploying them in the crowd. Throughout this chapter, we bear in mind that crowdsourcing platforms were made to serve a different purpose and acknowledge the possible threats to validity in our experimental designs and deployments on crowdsourcing platforms.

2   Requirements for Human-Centered Experiments in the Laboratory

Having briefly discussed the limitations of conducting experiments in the laboratory, in this section we will elucidate the characteristics of human-centered experiments which are carried out in the laboratory. We address the goals of possible experiments which have an impact on the experimental structure, the resources needed for the setup, the participant pool, as well as the experimental process. We finish with a SWOT (*strengths, weaknesses, opportunities, threats*) analysis of laboratory experiments regarding these characteristics.

2.1   Goals of the Experiment

Human-centered experiments are no exception when it comes to requiring adequate planning to reach the preset objectives. Validity describes the degree to which the target has been reached, and is a key criterion for assessing the quality of the experiment. Other criteria are the reliability of the results, i.e. whether the results are stable when carrying out the experiment again (in terms of a parallel-test reliability, a re-test reliability, or an internal consistency within an experiment), the objectivity of the experiment, the economy of the process, the standardizability, the usefulness, and the comparability of results between experiments [6].

With respect to validity, generalizing the results of laboratory experiments carries with it the inherent disadvantage that the application of the research findings will normally be outside the laboratory. Thus, if the results themselves are to be applicable, laboratory experiments should be carefully designed to reflect a range of environmental, contextual and task characteristics of the situation in which they are to be applied. As an example, a laboratory experiment designed for finding out how well an object can be identified in an image (surveillance task) should be carried out using the same type of equipment (screen, ambient light situation, timing constraints) which will be used in the later surveillance situation. Otherwise, the experiment might be able to compare different experimental conditions well (relative validity), but not reflect the identification performance in an absolute way (absolute validity). On the other hand, in the case of laboratory experiments, the experimenter is in direct control of the environment. So even if the realistic use case cannot be fully simulated, it can be ensured that all participants in the experiment work with exactly the same hardware, under the same light and sound conditions, without external distractions and so on. Thus, confounding factors can be effectively reduced in a laboratory experiment.

As another example, an experiment might be designed in order to obtain an ordering of audiovisual stimuli which only differ to a very small extent. In such a case, this ordering might be better achieved in a laboratory than in a crowd environment, as the equipment used by the test participants can be controlled to a greater extent. It can be ensured that the test environment is mostly free of impediments (such as ambient noise or visual extractions) which would render the task more difficult, and thereby the test less sensitive for the given purpose.

The experimental situation also needs to be valid with respect to the involvement and potential collaboration of the participants. As an example, an experiment to analyze the communication quality of a Voice-over-IP system needs to be carried out in a conversational rather than a listening-only situation, because the Voice-over-IP system will mostly be used in a conversational mode. This can be reached quite easily in a laboratory situation by inviting test participants in pairs in order to carry out realistic conversations over the system, e.g. following pre-defined scenarios [29]. To do the same in a crowdsourcing environment would be far more difficult, as the scheduling of participants in the crowd is more difficult and might lead to timing and motivational conflicts.

Similarly, experiments designed to analyze usability and participant behavior in collaborative visualizations [32] may depend on direct interactions between participants. While distributed collaboration is often subject to the same kind of scheduling constraints as in the Voice-over-IP example above, experiments on co-located collaborative visualization are even harder to realize outside a laboratory environment. So in collaborative settings, the laboratory appears to have clear advantages.

Finally, some human-centered experiments require repeated participation in multiple phases of the experiment. For such experimental setups, it is crucial to have access to the same participants, maybe even groups of participants, after well-defined time intervals. In a laboratory experiment, participant selection according to these requirements is much easier to achieve than in currently available crowd platforms.

2.2   Resources

A major limitation of laboratory tests is the resources which are required in order to properly conduct an experiment. Formal laboratory tests require a considerable amount of time for the experimental planning, preparation of the environment, acquisition of suitable test participants, execution of the experiment, and finally analysis of the results, typically in the order of weeks or even months. Thus, a trade-off has to be made between the urgency with which the results of an experiment are needed, and the financial investment necessary to facilitate the laboratory experiment. The time which is necessary to carry out a formal laboratory experiment may also limit its applicability in iterative and agile product development cycles, which require iteration times of a week or less for each cycle in order to be efficient; a short timing may render laboratory tests incompatible with such development cycles.

Apart from the time, the test environment and the equipment which needs to be integrated into it are relevant resources. As mentioned above, the test environment is important to guarantee a high validity of the results, either in terms of ecological validity or in terms of sensitivity of the test procedure. Especially the latter requirement may cause high investments in terms of sound-insulated rooms (for sensitive auditory tests), rooms with controlled artificial lighting conditions (for visual tests), combinations of rooms with identical acoustic conditions (for conversation tests), and alike. It should be noted, however, that it is extremely difficult to achieve the same level of controlled and uniform environments in crowdsourced experiments. For highly sensitive experiments, the laboratory seems to be the best choice, despite the considerable investment costs. The investment to make a laboratory environment similar to a real-life usage scenario may be high: acoustic background noise may need to be inserted in a controlled but realistic way, dummy bystanders may need to be hired in order to simulate social presence, or additional furniture and accessories may be necessary to simulate a realistic atmosphere.

Integrated into the environment, the test equipment used by the participants may require further investments. In a laboratory experiment, it is easy to guarantee that all participants use the same type of equipment (e.g. headphones, screens, interactive and connected devices) which has been controlled for its technical characteristics, and is monitored for proper functioning throughout the experiment. Such control is nearly impossible in a crowd-powered setting, where participants are expected to bring their own equipment, and where there is little or no control over the equipment. Having said that, alternate forms of crowdsourcing have been discussed in literature that overcome this issue, for example, by using public displays [22].

Finally, if the test equipment itself is part of the experiment [13], e.g., when testing immersive displays or virtual reality glasses, the required hardware may not even be freely available on the market or too expensive to expect at the disposal of crowdworkers. In many such situations again, there is no real alternative to running the experiments in a controlled laboratory setting or providing carefully selected test participants with the required hardware. Researchers have addressed this challenge by proposing methods to overcome equipment related obstacles in a few different domains [23, 35].

2.3 Participant Pool

As the name suggests, human-centered experiments require human participants who act as "measuring organs". This renders such experiments "subjective", in the sense that human involvement is necessary to achieve the results, but they should be still "objective", such that the outcome is independent of the experimenter. However, the characteristics of the test participants will (and should) largely influence the test results.

According to the purpose of the experiment, participants can be classified according to their traits:

- perceptual and cognitive characteristics (hearing, vision, memory capacity, etc.)
- behavioral characteristics (left-handed vs. right-handed, dialect, sociolect, personality traits, etc.)
- experience and expertise (with the item under investigation, with similar items, with the domain, etc.)
- motivation (intrinsic or extrinsic motivation)
- individual preferences, capabilities or knowledge (sexual orientation, absolute hearing capability, individual background knowledge, language skills, etc.)
- personal characteristics (age, sex, level of education, nationality and cultural background, handicaps)

In a laboratory setting, participants may be selected and screened for all those characteristics which are deemed relevant for the outcome of the experiment. Unfortunately, this screening process is time-consuming, and may significantly limit the time available for the proper experiment. The availability of sufficient numbers of suitable participants with a particular set of characteristics may be very limited. In addition, in many cases the influence factors are not known with respect to their (quantitative) impact, and it may be very difficult to find and access participants who show all relevant characteristics in a way which is representative for the actual use case (target user group). In such cases, one can assess the impact of participant characteristics on the test results only after the experiment. The result of this analysis may then limit the conclusions which can be drawn from the experiment.

The selection of test participants with desired characteristics is possible in a laboratory environment, albeit with a potentially high effort from the experimenter and significant compensation for the participants. For example, it may be possible to recruit computer-illiterate participants in order to test unbiased first-time usage of a computer system. This would be less probable for a crowd environment where participants are necessarily recruited through a computer platform, thus inherently limiting the pool of test participants to those with certain characteristics. To overcome this issue, some platforms offer an API to select workers with certain desired characteristics. For example, CrowdFlower[2] offers three levels of crowdworkers based on their reputation and quality of work.

2.4   Process and Control

In a laboratory setting, the experimental process can be properly designed and closely controlled to achieve an optimum reliability of the results in terms of accuracy and validity. For example, test participants can be properly screened with respect to all their relevant characteristics, and the screening process can be adequately supervised to guarantee that no cheating is possible. In addition, participants can be instructed in a standardized way, giving room for individual questions they might have in order to ascertain their complete understanding of the experimental task at hand. The design and timing of individual tasks and sessions can be closely controlled in order to limit fatigue or mental overload. In addition, the motivation of the test participants can be better controlled, so as to avoid participants "mechanically" resolving the given tasks without making use of the human capabilities which are at the core of the experiment. The simple presence of a human experimenter in the test laboratory, and the social facilitation of talking to him/her and receiving the instructions in a personalized way, may increase the reliability of the results. In addition, participants can easily access the experimenter in case questions or problems arise during the test run.

If the experimental design requires to split tasks across multiple sessions, the experimenter can recruit the same participants again for multiple sessions, thus facilitating a within-subject design. Such designs are more difficult to achieve in a crowd setting, where tasks are usually small and short in duration, and where extrinsic motivation is a big factor that affects participation.

---

[2] http://crowdflower.com/ last accessed 14 Jun 2017.

2.5 SWOT Analysis of Human-Centered Laboratory Experiments

In the following table, we analyze and present the strengths, weaknesses, opportunities and threats that entail the running of human-centered experiments in laboratories.

STRENGTHS	WEAKNESSES
• high level of control over experimental process and environment • reliability of participants • participant screening for special skills and characteristics	• limited participant pool • time-consuming • expensive • artificial, simulated environment

OPPORTUNITIES	THREATS
• collaborative experiments • multi-phase experiments • personal interaction and feedback channels • use of specialized hardware	• limited ecological validity • draw conclusions which may not hold in real life

3 Transition to Using Crowdsourcing for Human-Centered Experiments

In this section we discuss how the different dimensions of a human-centered experiment can be carried out using crowdsourcing. We analyze how characteristic features of crowdsourcing can be exploited in order to run human-centered experiments using the crowd.

3.1 Goals of the Experiment

Crowdsourcing tasks can be executed with a variety of goals, ranging from generating data to building ground truths for evaluation. Previous work has categorized typical crowdsourcing microtasks into an exhaustive taxonomy at the top-level based on the goals of a task requester or experimenter [18]. These categories were determined to be: *information finding, verification and validation, content creation, interpretation and analysis, surveys,* and *content access.* Most commonly crowdsourcing has been used as a tool to solve problems that require human intelligence or input at scale. However over the last few years, researchers have begun considering the paid crowdsourcing paradigm as a potential avenue to run scientific experiments that were previously conducted and constrained in laboratory settings [7, 26, 37, 41]. When it comes to the validity of conducting a human-centered experiment using crowdworkers, the ease with which a diverse and representative population can be acquired is a big advantage. Through the course of this section, we will explore the inherent characteristics of crowdsourcing that need to be further considered to run valid human-centered experiments in the crowd.

3.1.1   Collaboration Between Participants

In a standard microtask crowdsourcing scenario each worker typically contributes independently to the final result. Nevertheless, if an experiment needs the collaboration between subjects, the crowdsourcing scenario can be adapted accordingly. 'Games with a purpose' are a good example of such collaboration, where people collaborate in order to solve different problems, ranging from image tagging [49] to identification of protein structures [33]. Recent work has also shown that team competition designs can be effective in improving the throughput of crowdsourced tasks [46].

On the other hand, none of the primary microtask crowdsourcing platforms (such as Amazon's Mechanical Turk (AMT)[3] or CrowdFlower[4]) facilitate direct collaboration between workers, so the coordination between subjects must be manually implemented and facilitated externally. Furthermore, imposing a schedule and time constraints on the workers may hurt their spirits and increase dropouts. For instance, when proper collaboration means are not employed, a worker may either have to wait for long periods of time before his collaborators are found, or he could be paired with a low quality or undesirable workers.

3.1.2   Multi-phase Experiments with the Same Set of Participants

In case of experiments composed by different repeated phases, where a fundamental requirement is to involve the same set of participants in each phase, the anonymity of the subjects characterizing the crowdsourcing environment makes the execution of such types of experiments very challenging, since the only possibility is to directly contact the worker (typically via email). Hence, if a crowdsourcing platform does not disclose contact information or it does not facilitate reaching particular workers directly, a possible solution is to redirect workers to a customized external platform, where the information needed can be collected in order to contact the same subjects in future. In prior work, authors proposed a two-stage implementation of crowdsourcing for QoE assessment [27].

---

[3] https://www.mturk.com/ last accessed 14 Jun 2017.
[4] http://www.crowdflower.com/ last accessed 14 Jun 2017.

Although freelancing or expert-sourcing platforms such as Upwork[5] facilitate collaboration between participants to complete complex tasks in multiple phases if required, they are less-suitable for human-centered experiments, and beyond the scope of this work.

3.2 Resources

The main characteristic of an experiment performed with the crowd is that each subject uses his own device. As a consequence the time required for environment preparation is curtailed to a large extent; there is no need to prepare the laboratory or to configure the equipment. At the same time, an experimenter has no direct control over the hardware and software configuration with respect to the subjects' environments. This may be particularly detrimental if the experiment requires special hardware, or specific software configurations to ensure validity of the results. It is cumbersome to impose any type of control on the environment with the aim to either create a uniform setting across participants, or to make it more similar to the real-life usage scenario. However, it is still possible to check the reliability of the worker hardware and software using scripts that run on the worker's device reporting its configuration in term of browser version, operative system, hardware configuration and so forth. With this information it is possible to pre-screen the workers who don't satisfy the minimal requirements needed for the experiment.

The cost of setting up the experiment in terms of equipment is virtually zero, but we need to take into the account the costs in terms of effort in designing the crowdsourcing task so as to satisfy the requirements of the experiment. This cost increases exponentially if a specific feature needs to be completely implemented from scratch, due to a lack of support on the crowdsourcing platform of choice. A larger effort is required to implement software compatible to various web browsers, supporting various devices, and so forth. Further, (offline) processing of results requires extra efforts and the monitoring of hidden influence factors needs to be implemented in the test design; all accounting for additional costs. In addition, if the paid crowdsourcing paradigm is employed, then participants need to be monetarily compensated.

3.3 Participant Pool

Some of the key implications of crowdsourcing human-centered experiments with respect to the participant pool, arise from the inherent characteristics of the paradigm, and are presented below.

- *Quantity*: An experimenter can attain access to an extremely large population size via various crowdsourcing platforms. Thus, laboratory experiments which were previously constrained to the order of tens or hundreds of experiment subjects can scale-up to the order of thousands of participants without huge ramifications on the costs entailed.

---

[5] https://www.upwork.com/ last accessed 14 Jun 2017.

- *Availability*: Laboratory experiments are typically constrained by the availability of subjects, as well as open hours of the laboratory itself. The transition of such experiments to using crowdsourcing would mean that participants would be available around the clock, and the experimenter would not necessarily be restricted by the time of the day.
- *Diversity & Reachability*: Crowdworkers that can be reached via crowdsourcing platforms constitute a highly diverse population, covering a wide range of demographic attributes (age, gender, ethnicity, location, and so forth). Thus, a human-centered experiment can benefit from this diversity and consequently arrive at more representative results.
- *Quality & Reliability*: One of the major challenges in exploiting the prowess of crowdsourcing for human-centered experiments is quality control and the reliability of participants. Experiments conducted in a laboratory can benefit from surveillance of the subjects, thereby eliciting adequate behavior and ensuring reliable participation. Over the last few years, researchers have devised a number of quality control mechanisms in crowdsourcing ranging from task design methods, to worker pre-selection, or even post-hoc analysis [11,19,36]. Therefore, although there are additional costs entailed to sustaining the reliability of participants in crowdsourced human-centered experiments, it is certainly possible to achieve.

3.4   Process and Control

A number of aspects need to be considered in order to exercise control over human-centered experiments when using crowdsourcing.

- *Design*: Additional effort is required to design an experiment that is suitable for the participation of crowdworkers. The use of standard microtask crowdsourcing platforms as a source of acquiring subjects for human-centered experiments, means that the experiments may have to be decomposed into micro units of work.
- *Incentives*: A variety of incentives have been used to encourage participation in laboratory experiments previously, such as course credits, monetary compensations, altruistic intent, and so forth. When microtask crowdsourcing platforms are employed for human-centered experiments, the typical mode of participant acquisition is through financial incentives. The entailing costs depend on the complexity of the experiment, the effort required from participants, and amount of time required for task completion.
- *Personal Touch, Social Facilitation, & Feedback Channels*: One of the limiting factors in crowdsourcing human-centered experiments is the lack of personal interaction between the experimenter and the participants. Experimenters benefit in laboratories from facilitating the subjects and providing them with immediate feedback where required. Microtask crowdsourcing platforms typically provide feedback channels with limited flexibility (for example, via chat

rooms or emails). Thus, additional efforts are required from the experimenter to ensure that participants are adequately facilitated and have understood their task objectives sufficiently [27]. Unlike in laboratory environments, subjects cannot be monitored easily and there is lesser control over the experimental protocol.

- *Equipment Configuration*: Human-centered experiments which require specific equipment or special devices (for example, ECG machines), or those that require participants to be embedded in the same environments (screenresolution, distance to the screen, ethnographic contexts, software/hardware configurations, and so forth), are less suitable for the transition to using crowdsourcing. Although there are ways to pre-select crowdworkers in order to satisfy the requirements, this requires additional effort.

- *Optimization*: A big advantage of running human-centered experiments using crowdsourcing is the potential to optimize for given needs (such as accuracy of crowdworkers, or the amount of time within which responses are to be gathered). If the most important criteria of the experiment is to ensure reliable responses from every participant, then one can leverage the in-built filters on the crowdsourcing platform, apart from exercising additional external guidelines [19]. This may lead to longer task completion times. However, if time is of essence then one can assume a more liberal means of allowing participation, and thereafter employ post-hoc analysis to filter out undesirable subjects. The scalability of crowdsourcing allows for such optimization as per the requirements at hand.

3.5 SWOT Analysis for Crowdsourced Human Experiments

Previous works have discussed the role of crowdsourcing in human experiments [44]. Horton et al. showed that experiments using crowdsourcing are valid internally and can be valid externally, just as laboratory experiments [26]. Similarly, Crump et al. evaluated the use of Amazon's Mechanical Turk to conduct behavioral experiments by replicating a variety of tasks from experimental psychology [7]. The authors found that most of the replications were successful, while a few exhibited a disparity with respect to laboratory results. They assert that despite the lack of environmental control while using crowdsourcing, the standardization and control over experiment procedures is an advantage.

We analyze the strengths, weaknesses, opportunities and threats that entail running human-centered experiments using crowdsourcing in the following table.

STRENGTHS	WEAKNESSES
• Ease of access to diverse and representative populations • Large-scale experiments are feasible • Time-efficiency • Flexibility with time of the day, duration of experiments • Relatively inexpensive	• Less control over the experimental environment • Extra effort required for collaborative or multi-phase experiments • Lack of knowledge regarding participants' background
OPPORTUNITIES	THREATS
• Optimization of experiment configuration (time, quality, and reliability) • New possibilities to broaden the research in various domains. For example collaboration and interaction between users, real-life environment (heterogeneous client devices and software, various network access technologies).	• Limited absolute validity of experiment results • Additional technical constraints such as bandwidth, client device compatibility, web-based frameworks, contextual monitoring, etc.

4   Methodological Considerations

As observed through the course of this chapter, using the crowd for performing human-centered experiments provides different opportunities but also raises several challenges. In this section, we discuss existing solutions and propose new approaches to address the concomitant challenges.

4.1   Challenges and Opportunities

Crowdsourcing creates several opportunities for performing human-centered experiments. It provides a fast way to access a wide set of participants, it does not require set up time and it allows to optimize the configuration of an experiment.

4.1.1   Existing Platforms Demand Workarounds – Current Solutions

We note that existing microtask crowdsourcing platforms are not directly meant for human-centered experiments. While platforms for academic research are on the rise (as pointed out in Chap. 4), they are not yet sufficiently established to suit global needs. However, to overcome shortcomings of existing platforms, several workarounds have been proposed over the last decade that address many challenges. We elaborate on the key features of crowdsourcing microtasks that have attracted adequate solutions.

- *Quality Control.* Due to the lack of direct control and supervision over participants in crowdsourced tasks, quality control has been identified as a pivotal aspect that determines the effectiveness of the paradigm. Many mechanisms have been proposed to assert the quality of results produced through crowdsourced tasks. Proposed solutions include the use of gold-standard questions [9,11,40], attention check questions, consistency checks, and psychometric methods [36], worker behavioral metrics and optimal task design [19], feedback and training [10,17], and optimizing task parameters such as task length and monetary compensation [3,20,37]. Qualification tests and pre-screening methods have also been adopted in order to select appropriate workers for a given task. These existing quality control mechanisms can be easily applied when running human-centered experiments using the crowd.

- *Improving Effectiveness.* Several optimization techniques have been introduced in prior works in order to increase the throughput of crowdworkers, maximize the cost-benefit ratio of deploying crowdsourced microtasks [45,46], and improving the overall effectiveness of the microtask crowdsourcing model. Gamification has been shown to improve worker retention and throughput of tasks [12]. Other works have suggested pricing schemes, or achievement priming to retain workers and improve latency in crowdsourced microtasks [8,16]. Similar strategies can be adopted where applicable, while running human-centered experiments using the crowd.

4.1.2   Elegant Solutions – An Outlook for Future Crowdsourcing Platforms

Owing to the great opportunities that crowdsourcing provides for human-centered experiments that were priorly constrained to the laboratory, we envisage a future where crowdsourcing platforms directly support and facilitate greater control to run human-centered experiments in the crowd.

- *Tailored Platforms.* First and foremost, there is a need for tailored platforms that support human-centered experiments. Due to the fact that traditional microtask crowdsourcing platforms have not been built to facilitate human-centered experiments in particular, workarounds are required to execute such experiments using these platforms. Some steps have already been taken towards building such tailored solutions; a good example is that of GraphUnit, a framework for visualization evaluation that leverages crowdsourcing [39].

- *Feedback & Supervision.* Experiment and task administrators currently use implicit feedback channels such as emails or chat rooms to communicate with crowdworkers. Enabling real-time interaction between crowdworkers and the task administrators can go a long way towards the social facilitation of potential experiment subjects in the human-centered experiments.

- *Iterative Design.* Human-centered experiments may require to be carried out in multiple phases using the same set of participants. Thus, platforms need to accommodate such iterative designs of experiments.

- *Worker Profiles.* Elaborate worker profiles that include the skills and interests of crowdworkers (similar to freelancing platforms), and their demographic details need to be made available to the task administrators. Such transparency will enable a seamless match-making process between available experiments and suitable crowdworkers on the platform. See Chap. 3 for a detailed discussion on worker profiles.

4.1.3   Task Complexity

In behavioral research and psychology, the impact of task complexity in various domains has been studied well [2]. Similarly, in the microtask crowdsourcing paradigm, *task complexity* is a complicated aspect that depends on several factors. There has been little research that deliberates on the impact of task complexity on various aspects of crowdsourcing such as worker performance, worker retention rates, and motivation. In order to create crowdsourcing solutions that are generalizable across different types of tasks, we need to consider the aspect of task complexity. Jie et al. recently showed that task complexity is perceived coherently among crowdworkers, and that it is effected by the type of the task [52]. The authors proposed several structural features to model and measure task complexity. We highlight the consideration of task complexity as an important opportunity for future research.

4.2   Guidelines and Ethics: How Do Ethical Values Transfer to Crowdsourced Human Experiments?

The major ethical concerns with microtask crowdsourcing platforms yield from the fact that a considerable number of workers contributing on these platforms earn their livelihood from this work [30,31]. Hence, workers need to be adequately compensated in accordance to the time and effort exerted through their contribution to crowdsourced tasks. A variety of aspects such as task pricing, clarity [15], complexity, and so forth affect crowd work and need to be considered to ensure fair and healthy dynamics between the workers and requesters. The manual labor of crowdworkers was further recognized in recent times by the sentence against CrowdFlower, which undercut the United States minimum wage legislation [50].

We list a few ethical concerns arising from current practice in microtask crowdsourcing platforms. For a more elaborate discourse on ethical values in crowdsourcing human experiments, see Chap. 3.

- Lack of adequate communication channels between workers and task requesters or experimenters. Thus, crowdworkers cannot appeal against declined work or take corrective measures when tasks are misunderstood.
- No guarantee for payments promised as compensation, the task requester has all the power to credit or discredit contributions from crowdworkers.

- Monetary compensation in return for crowd work does not always meet the minimum wage stipulations.
- Often studies on crowdsourcing platforms do not go through ethical review boards of research institutions.

According to [51] it is not sufficient from an ethics point of view to voluntarily increase the rate of payment for Amazon's Mechanical Turk (AMT) tasks as it won't resolve the fundamental inequities of the precarious employment situation of a considerable number of workers. Recent works have addressed the concerns yielding from the power asymmetry in crowdsourcing microtask workflows, with an aim to pave a way towards an ethically balanced paradigm of crowd work [47]. Guidelines to practice ethical crowdsourcing as task requesters from a holistic standpoint have been defined in previous work [28].

5   Future of Crowdsourcing Human Experiments

In this chapter we have discussed and elucidated the opportunities of running human-centered experiments in the crowd. We note that the crowdsourcing paradigm provides a unique means to scale up otherwise constrained laboratory experiments. Although there are a few disadvantages of running human-centered experiments in the crowd as noted earlier, the benefits of using crowdsourcing outweigh the threats in the applicable scenarios.

5.1   Crowdsourcing and Laboratory Experiments - A Complimentary Perspective

In the end it is unlikely that crowdsourcing will replace lab testing altogether. A more likely scenario is that experimenters will learn how best to combine crowd and lab to balance the benefits and drawbacks of each. These mixed-method investigations hold a great deal of promise for creating models that are both highly predictive and generalizable to diverse populations of interest. We will discuss a few examples of ways in which this might be done in the hope that it may inspire new and better approaches to human experimentation.

5.1.1   Lab First, Crowd Second: Evaluation of Theories Generated from Laboratory Studies

While it is tempting for interface designers to directly apply the results of an experiment to an interface design, we must keep in mind that many of these studies were designed to contribute to a natural science of human cognition. Accordingly, the phenomena they describe are not intended to be directly applied to an interface but are instead a means to the end of generating and testing theories of human information processing that are applicable to a broad range of situations. Taking Pylyshyn's FINST theory [43] as an example we can see how studies conducted with a variety of tasks and stimuli including multiple object tracking, subitizing, and visual search were designed specifically to test whether our visual system had a finite number of visuospatial attentional tokens that could facilitate performance of a variety of tasks. These generalizable theories are considered architectural in that they provide specific capabilities that can be assembled in different ways to accomplish different tasks. A key aspect of the research agenda in cognitive science is to identify these capabilities and to assemble them in the form of an overall cognitive architecture, such as Anderson's ACT-R [1]. Indeed, while many in the visualization and HCI communities are aware of Pirolli and Card's Sensemaking theory [42], few are aware that one of the goals of this work was to facilitate application of ACT to sensemaking in Fu and Pirolli's SNIF-ACT model [14].

Because of the need for control of the experimental situation and exploration of the parameter space of these models it is hard to imagine that theory at the level of cognitive architecture could be generated using crowdsourcing methods. Where crowdsourcing might play a role would be in evaluating these models in the context of the more diverse set of participants and situations of use. The research question here would be whether those models can be parameterized in such a way that they can account for a diversity of people and situations.

5.1.2   Crowd First, Lab Second: Identifying Key Individuals and Sub-populations for Future Studies

Many of the more compelling studies in cognitive neuroscience are conducted with the participation of those rare individuals who differ from the general population. Whether it is due to genetics, a neurological accident, or an unusual training experience these extreme cases can give us insight into human limitations and capabilities. One crowdsourcing example comes from Philip Tetlock and Barbara Meller's Good Judgment Project [48]. In this project the researchers crowdsourced predictions about a variety of political developments from over 2000 participants in order to identify a sub-population of individuals who were consistently accurate over time. These individuals were then tested to determine how they differed from the general population. Bringing these individuals into controlled testing situation might well prove effective in establishing more robust cognitive architectures and assessing the range of operating parameters that can be found in the overall population.

5.2   Conclusions

We are only beginning to understand how to best utilize crowdsourcing for human-centered experimentation. The ease with which a large number of participants having desirable traits can be found, the scalability of experiments, the efficiency with respect to time and entailing costs, the flexibility with the time of the day and duration of experiments, makes the crowdsourcing of human-centered experiments very promising. Challenges that pertain to the lack of control over the experimental environment can be overcome to an extent, through prudent experimental design choices and manipulating crowdsourcing task workflows to suit requirements. As we continue to explore the optimum trade-offs between the laboratory and the crowd, we will discover new ways to manage task allocation and delivery, coordination of multiple crowdworkers in collaborative and competitive task performance, and new data analysis methods that can be brought to bear on the rich datasets that can be produced with crowd and mixed method experimentation.

Acknowledgment. We would like to thank Dagstuhl for facilitating the seminar (titled, *'Evaluation in the Crowd: Crowdsourcing and Human-Centred Experiments'*) that brought about this collaboration. Part of this work (Sect. 4) was supported by the German Research Foundation (DFG) within project A05 of SFB/Transregio 161. We also thank Andrea Mauri and Christian Keimel for their valuable contributions and feedback during discussions.

References

1. Anderson, J.R., Matessa, M., Lebiere, C.: ACT-R: a theory of higher level cognition and its relation to visual attention. Hum. Comput. Interact. **12**(4), 439–462 (1997)
2. Campbell, D.J.: Task complexity: a review and analysis. Acad. Manag. Rev. **13**(1), 40–52 (1988)
3. Cheng, J., Teevan, J., Bernstein, M.S.: Measuring crowdsourcing effort with error-time curves. In: Proceedings of the 33rd Annual ACM Conference on Human Factors in Computing Systems, pp. 1365–1374. ACM (2015)
4. Chung, D.H.S., Archambault, D., Borgo, R., Edwards, D.J., Laramee, R.S., Chen, M.: How ordered is it? On the perceptual orderability of visual channels. Comput. Graph. Forum **35**(3), 131–140 (2016). (Proc. of EuroVis 2016)
5. Cole, F., Sanik, K., DeCarlo, D., Finkelstein, A., Funkhouser, T., Rusinkiewicz, S., Singh, M.: How well do line drawings depict shape? ACM Trans. Graph. **28**(3), 1–9 (2009)
6. Cozby, P.: Asking people about themselves: survey research. In: Methods in Behavioral Research, 7th edn., pp. 103–124. Mayfield Publishing Company, Mountain View (2001)
7. Crump, M.J., McDonnell, J.V., Gureckis, T.M.: Evaluating Amazon's Mechanical Turk as a tool for experimental behavioral research. PloS one **8**(3), e57410 (2013)
8. Difallah, D.E., Catasta, M., Demartini, G., Cudré-Mauroux, P.: Scaling-up the crowd: micro-task pricing schemes for worker retention and latency improvement. In: Second AAAI Conference on Human Computation and Crowdsourcing (2014)
9. Difallah, D.E., Demartini, G., Cudré-Mauroux, P.: Mechanical cheat: spamming schemes and adversarial techniques on crowdsourcing platforms. In: CrowdSearch, pp. 26–30. Citeseer (2012)
10. Dow, S., Kulkarni, A., Klemmer, S., Hartmann, B.: Shepherding the crowd yields better work. In: Proceedings of the ACM 2012 conference on Computer Supported Cooperative Work, pp. 1013–1022. ACM (2012)
11. Eickhoff, C., de Vries, A.P.: Increasing cheat robustness of crowdsourcing tasks. Inf. Retr. **16**(2), 121–137 (2013)
12. Feyisetan, O., Luczak-Roesch, M., Simperl, E., Tinati, R., Shadbolt, N.: Towards hybrid NER: a study of content and crowdsourcing-related performance factors. In: Gandon, F., Sabou, M., Sack, H., d'Amato, C., Cudré-Mauroux, P., Zimmermann, A. (eds.) ESWC 2015. LNCS, vol. 9088, pp. 525–540. Springer, Cham (2015). doi:10.1007/978-3-319-18818-8_32

13. Fikkert, W., D'Ambros, M., Bierz, T., Jankun-Kelly, T.J.: Interacting with visualizations. In: Kerren, A., Ebert, A., Meyer, J. (eds.) Human-Centered Visualization Environments. LNCS, vol. 4417, pp. 77–162. Springer, Heidelberg (2007). doi:10.1007/978-3-540-71949-6_3

14. Fu, W.T., Pirolli, P.: SNIF-ACT: a cognitive model of user navigation on the world wide web. Hum. Comput. Interact. **22**(4), 355–412 (2007)

15. Gadiraju, U.: Crystal clear or very vague? Effects of task clarity in the microtask crowdsourcing ecosystem. In: 1st International Workshop on Weaving Relations of Trust in Crowd Work: Transparency and Reputation Across Platforms, Co-located With the 8th International ACM Web Science Conference 2016, Hannover (2016)

16. Gadiraju, U., Dietze, S.: Improving learning through achievement priming in crowdsourced information finding microtasks. In: Proceedings of ACM LAK Conference. ACM (2017, to appear)

17. Gadiraju, U., Fetahu, B., Kawase, R.: Training workers for improving performance in crowdsourcing microtasks. In: Conole, G., Klobučar, T., Rensing, C., Konert, J., Lavoué, É. (eds.) EC-TEL 2015. LNCS, vol. 9307, pp. 100–114. Springer, Cham (2015). doi:10.1007/978-3-319-24258-3_8

18. Gadiraju, U., Kawase, R., Dietze, S.: A taxonomy of microtasks on the web. In: Proceedings of the 25th ACM Conference on Hypertext and Social Media, pp. 218–223. ACM (2014)

19. Gadiraju, U., Kawase, R., Dietze, S., Demartini, G.: Understanding malicious behavior in crowdsourcing platforms: the case of online surveys. In: Proceedings of the 33rd Annual ACM Conference on Human Factors in Computing Systems (CHI 2015), Seoul, 18–23 April 2015, pp. 1631–1640 (2015)

20. Gadiraju, U., Siehndel, P., Fetahu, B., Kawase, R.: Breaking bad: understanding behavior of crowd workers in categorization microtasks. In: Proceedings of the 26th ACM Conference on Hypertext & Social Media, pp. 33–38. ACM (2015)

21. Gardlo, B., Egger, S., Seufert, M., Schatz, R.: Crowdsourcing 2.0: enhancing execution speed and reliability of web-based QoE testing. In: Proceedings of the IEEE International Conference on Communications (ICC), pp. 1070–1075 (2014)

22. Goncalves, J., Ferreira, D., Hosio, S., Liu, Y., Rogstadius, J., Kukka, H., Kostakos, V.: Crowdsourcing on the spot: altruistic use of public displays, feasibility, performance, and behaviours. In: Proceedings of the 2013 ACM International Joint Conference on Pervasive and Ubiquitous Computing, pp. 753–762. ACM (2013)

23. Hanhart, P., Korshunov, P., Ebrahimi, T.: Crowd-based quality assessment of multiview video plus depth coding. In: 2014 IEEE International Conference on Image Processing (ICIP), pp. 743–747. IEEE (2014)

24. Heer, J., Bostock, M.: Crowdsourcing graphical perception: using mechanical turk to assess visualization design. In: Proceedings of the 28th International Conference on Human Factors in Computing Systems (CHI 2010), Atlanta, 10–15 April 2010, pp. 203–212 (2010)

25. Heinzelman, J., Waters, C.: Crowdsourcing crisis information in disaster-affected Haiti. US Institute of Peace (2010)

26. Horton, J.J., Rand, D.G., Zeckhauser, R.J.: The online laboratory: conducting experiments in a real labor market. Exp. Econ. **14**(3), 399–425 (2011)

27. Hoßfeld, T., Keimel, C., Hirth, M., Gardlo, B., Habigt, J., Diepold, K., Tran-Gia, P.: Best practices for QoE crowdtesting: QoE assessment with crowdsourcing. IEEE Trans. Multimed. **16**(2), 541–558 (2014)

28. Hoßfeld, T., Tran-Gia, P., Vucovic, M.: Crowdsourcing: from theory to practice and long-term perspectives (Dagstuhl Seminar 13361). Dagstuhl Rep. **3**(9), 1–33 (2013). http://drops.dagstuhl.de/opus/volltexte/2013/4354

29. ITU-T Rec. P.805: Subjective evaluation of conversational quality. International Telecommunication Union, Geneva (2007)
30. Ipeirotis, P.G.: Analyzing the Amazon Mechanical Turk marketplace. XRDS: Crossroads ACM Mag. Stud. **17**(2), 16–21 (2010)
31. Ipeirotis, P.G.: Demographics of Mechanical Turk (2010)
32. Isenberg, P., Elmqvist, N., Scholtz, J., Cernea, D., Ma, K.L., Hagen, H.: Collaborative visualization: definition, challenges, and research agenda. Inf. Vis. **10**(4), 310–326 (2011)
33. Khatib, F., Cooper, S., Tyka, M.D., Xu, K., Makedon, I., Popović, Z., Baker, D., Players, F.: Algorithm discovery by protein folding game players. Proc. Natl. Acad. Sci. **108**(47), 18949–18953 (2011)
34. Khatib, F., DiMaio, F., Cooper, S., Kazmierczyk, M., Gilski, M., Krzywda, S., Zabranska, H., Pichova, I., Thompson, J., Popović, Z., et al.: Crystal structure of a monomeric retroviral protease solved by protein folding game players. Nat. Struct. Mol. Biol. **18**(10), 1175–1177 (2011)
35. Lebreton, P.R., Mäki, T., Skodras, E., Hupont, I., Hirth, M.: Bridging the gap between eye tracking and crowdsourcing. In: Human Vision and Electronic Imaging XX, San Francisco, 9–12 February 2015, p. 93940W (2015)
36. Marshall, C.C., Shipman, F.M.: Experiences surveying the crowd: reflections on methods, participation, and reliability. In: Proceedings of the 5th Annual ACM Web Science Conference, pp. 234–243. ACM (2013)
37. Mason, W., Suri, S.: Conducting behavioral research on Amazons Mechanical Turk. Behav. Res. Methods **44**(1), 1–23 (2012)
38. McCrae, J., Mitra, N.J., Singh, K.: Surface perception of planar abstractions. ACM Trans. Appl. Percept. **10**(3), 14: 1–14: 20 (2013)
39. Okoe, M., Jianu, R.: GraphUnit: evaluating interactive graph visualizations using crowdsourcing. Comput. Graph. Forum **34**(3), 451–460 (2015)
40. Oleson, D., Sorokin, A., Laughlin, G., Hester, V., Le, J., Biewald, L.: Programmatic gold: targeted and scalable quality assurance in crowdsourcing. In: Workshops at the Twenty-Fifth AAAI Conference on Artificial Intelligence (WS-11-11). AAAI (2011)
41. Paolacci, G., Chandler, J., Ipeirotis, P.G.: Running experiments on Amazon Mechanical Turk. Judgm. Decis. Mak. **5**(5), 411–419 (2010)
42. Pirolli, P., Card, S.: The sensemaking process and leverage points for analyst technology as identified through cognitive task analysis. In: Proceedings of International Conference on Intelligence Analysis, vol. 5, pp. 2–4 (2005)
43. Pylyshyn, Z.W.: Things and Places: How the Mind Connects with the World. MIT Press, Cambridge (2007)
44. Rand, D.G.: The promise of Mechanical Turk: how online labor markets can help theorists run behavioral experiments. J. Theor. Biol. **299**, 172–179 (2012)
45. Rokicki, M., Chelaru, S., Zerr, S., Siersdorfer, S.: Competitive game designs for improving the cost effectiveness of crowdsourcing. In: Proceedings of the 23rd ACM International Conference on Information and Knowledge Management, pp. 1469–1478. ACM (2014)
46. Rokicki, M., Zerr, S., Siersdorfer, S.: Groupsourcing: team competition designs for crowdsourcing. In: Proceedings of the 24th International Conference on World Wide Web, pp. 906–915. International World Wide Web Conferences Steering Committee (2015)

47. Salehi, N., Irani, L.C., Bernstein, M.S., Alkhatib, A., Ogbe, E., Milland, K., et al.: We are dynamo: overcoming stalling and friction in collective action for crowd workers. In: Proceedings of the 33rd Annual ACM Conference on Human Factors in Computing Systems, pp. 1621–1630. ACM (2015)
48. Tetlock, P.E., Mellers, B.A., Rohrbaugh, N., Chen, E.: Forecasting tournaments tools for increasing transparency and improving the quality of debate. Curr. Dir. Psychol. Sci. **23**(4), 290–295 (2014)
49. Von Ahn, L., Dabbish, L.: Labeling images with a computer game. In: Proceedings of the SIGCHI Conference on Human Factors in Computing Systems, pp. 319–326. ACM (2004)
50. Weber, L., Silverman, R.E.: On-demand workers: we are not robots. Wall Str. J. 7 (2015)
51. Williamson, V.: On the ethics of crowdsourced research. PS Political Sci. Politics **49**(01), 77–81 (2016)
52. Yang, J., Redi, J., DeMartini, G., Bozzon, A.: Modeling task complexity in crowdsourcing. In: Proceedings of the Fourth AAAI Conference on Human Computation and Crowdsourcing (HCOMP 2016), pp. 249–258. AAAI (2016)

Understanding the Crowd: Ethical and Practical Matters in the Academic Use of Crowdsourcing

David Martin[1], Sheelagh Carpendale[2], Neha Gupta[3]([⊠]), Tobias Hoßfeld[4],
Babak Naderi[5], Judith Redi[6], Ernestasia Siahaan[6], and Ina Wechsung[5]

[1] Xerox Research Centre Europe, Meylan, France
[2] University of Calgary, Calgary, Canada
[3] University of Nottingham, Nottingham, UK
neha.gupta@nottingham.ac.uk
[4] University of Duisburg-Essen, Duisburg, Germany
[5] TU Berlin, Berlin, Germany
[6] Delft University of Technology, Delft, The Netherlands

1 Introduction

Take the fake novelty of a term like "crowdsourcing" – supposedly one of
the chief attributes of the Internet era ... "Crowdsourcing" is certainly a
very effective term; calling some of the practices it enables as "digitally
distributed sweatshop labor" – for this seems like a much better description
of what's happening on crowdsource-for-money platforms like Amazon's
Mechanical Turk – wouldn't accomplish half as much" [34].

In his recent book "To Save Everything, Click Here" [34] Evgeny Morozov produces a sustained critique of what he calls *technological solutionism*. His key argument is that modern day technology companies, often situated in Silicon Valley, are increasingly touting technological innovation as the quick route to solving complex and thus far relatively intractable social and societal problems. He documents how in many cases the technologies simply do not deliver the wished for result, meaning that this trend ends up as little more than a marketing exercise for new technologies and gadgets. A related phenomenon is one where a technology innovation, that may be of little or ambiguous social merit is presented in a way that it is *value-washed* – given a positive social-spin, and marketed as something inherently virtuous when, once again the situation is far from clear. It is from this perspective that he criticises the use of 'crowdsourcing' to describe the labour situation in relation to Amazon Mechanical Turk (AMT)[1], which in reality often equates to low-paid *piece-work*.

Crowdsourcing refers to accessing a diverse and large workforce via the web and several platforms have emerged to facilitate this, with AMT being the best known. The term crowdsourcing captures ideas like voluntarism, altruism, and community which really do seem relevant in some cases, such as the crowdsourced nature of surveys done as citizen science[2]. However, in other cases it can mask

---

[1] http://mturk.com last accessed 14 Jun 2017.
[2] E.g. http://www.bbc.co.uk/nature/22694347 last accessed 14 Jun 2017.

© Springer International Publishing AG 2017
D. Archambault et al. (Eds.): Evaluation in the Crowd, LNCS 10264, pp. 27–69, 2017.
DOI: 10.1007/978-3-319-66435-4_3

the reality of what the work is really like and why people are doing it. So while it provides an accessible and cheap source of labour for various purposes, does it provide reasonable employment for those workers doing the microtasks? In this chapter, we clarify who these crowdworkers really are and why they do this type of work as it applies to the work through AMT and other similar microtask platforms.

We review studies of the people who work on microtask platforms: who they are; what their motivations are; and how they organise and carry out their work. Our key focus is the AMT platform because within academic literature and in more public and mainstream coverage of crowdsourcing it is the best known, most used and most researched platform. We draw on qualitative and quantitative research in the literature as well as providing some new data and analysis to provide a more up-to-date picture. We also provide some comparative analysis, particularly in terms of demographic information, using data we have gathered from two other crowdsourcing platforms, Microworkers[3] and Crowdee[4]. Our contention is that it is important to understand who the workers are, why they work on these platforms, and what their perspectives on the market and employers, their skills and expertise, and their difficulties are. We use this understanding to outline how academic researchers can use AMT or other similar platforms and work with crowdworkers in a way that is both ethical (in terms of respecting them and their work, through positive and polite communication, decent pay and so forth) and successfully productive (i.e. how things can be best managed to try and ensure good quality, timely work).

While we mainly focus on AMT it is important to understand that there are different platforms available that can have more ethical modes of operation built-into them, although a large part of ethical responsibility within crowdsourcing relationships necessarily lies with the parties involved. Other platforms can also allow access to a different demographic or a more global workforce, people with different types of skills, expertise, and so forth. Crowdsourcing projects and the work they entail vary in terms of their complexity, what the work or activity is about, whether and in what way they are collaborative, whether they are paid (and if so how they are paid) or voluntary. In this way crowdsourcing is best seen as the form and mechanism whereby work projects, campaigns or individual microtasks are handed out to a large distributed workforce. We are interested in digital crowdsourcing, whereby the form is electronic and the mechanism is computers and the Internet. The range of work is essentially all that which is possible in this form and through this mechanism, which will be dependent on the skill and ingenuity of those designing and carrying out the work. The terms, conditions, pay and so forth are primarily determined by the participants.

Crowdsourcing, in the cases we examine (microtask, paid, non-collaborative work), is a form of work and it is remunerated as piece-work. Our key aim is to provide information and advice to current and potential academic requesters who use crowdsourcing for carrying out tests and experimentation with datasets.

---

[3] http://microworkers.com last accessed 14 Jun 2017.

[4] http://crowdee.de last accessed 14 Jun 2017.

Ideally, this advice will make it easier to make better decisions about which platform to use, about how to design and target the right microtasks, and about how to communicate and manage the relationship with workers. Thoughtful use of these labour markets may lead to a more ethical approach while at the same time maximising the chances of receiving good quality, timely work.

A deep understanding of the work that crowdworkers do is important ethically and socio-organisationally, since questions have been raised about the ethics and efficacy of current crowdsourcing practices [2,11,28,38,41,45]. Felsteiner [11] provides a comprehensive summary of research on workers and their legal situation, highlighting the legal ambiguities surrounding AMT, and workers' difficulties in ensuring fair pay, and recompense for bad treatment. Bederson and Quinn [2] outline a series of design and policy guidelines to provide more transparency and fairness for workers, suggesting amongst other things that requesters should be clear about hourly pay, payment procedures and policies, and should offer grievance procedures. Kittur and colleagues [28] consider how crowdwork might be developed technologically and organisationally such that it could be desirable and productive for both workers and employers. They recommend better communication between requesters and workers, and that opportunities should be provided for learning and career progression. Silberman, Irani and colleagues created a 'Turker's Bill of Rights' [44], which illustrated the issues faced by Turkers[5] – primarily, unfair rejection of work, uncertain or slow payment, low wages, and poor communication [44,45]. Recently Salehi et al. have been involved in a project called Dynamo [43] that attempts to support Turkers in an initiative to form a workers guild for organising various campaigns aimed at securing more workers' rights.

The structure of this chapter is as follows: in the opening sections we provide quantitative and qualitative data analysis to show who the Turkers and other crowdworkers on Microworkers and Crowdee are – particularly focusing on their demographic information. We then move onto why and how, looking at why they are working on crowdsourcing platforms as opposed to other sources of work or labour markets, how they got into the work, and what makes or allows them to stay. We can think about this in terms of a set of motivations, reasons or explanations. Then we look at how they organise their work and workplaces, their relationships with employers (requesters) and their participation in communities (both on-line and through their regular social networks). In the closing sections we focus on how this understanding we have provided can be translated into ethical and practical guides for using crowdworking as part of academic research.

2   Who: Understanding Who the People Who Do Crowdwork Are

A number of crowdsourcing platforms exist nowadays, each with its own features, and each populated by a different crowd. Depending on the platform,

---

[5] Crowdworkers in MTurk.

crowds present a different degree of diversity in the country of origin (e.g., AMT poses constraints on the country of residence of both workers and requesters). Thus diversity can vary in gender, socio-economical background, education, and motivation. In addition, research has shown that only a fraction of the workers registered on a platform are highly active: on AMT, it is estimated that 80% of the HITs are carried out by the 20% of the most active Turkers [13]. Furthermore, different parts of the crowd may specialise in certain microtask types and may thus be highly trained [7].

Given the above, the risk of serious sampling issues exists for crowdsourcing-based studies. Highly active workers and highly specialised workers may belong to specific groups exhibiting distinctive characteristics and behaviours, and these characteristics may vary across platforms. In addition, as illustrated by Kazai et al. [27] demographic traits such as gender and location are related to differences in the workers' performance and data quality. Hence, it is important to know who the workers are in order to design microtasks properly (e.g. by setting up pre-qualification questions, adjusting the compensation, balancing the task complexity). Knowing who the workers are will also help in choosing the right platform where to deploy such microtasks, and in taking precautions in analysing results to make them as general as possible.

There is a growing body of research that seeks to understand the operation of the crowdwork market and the people who work within it. Survey-based demographic studies [22,23,41] in 2010 show that the majority of Turkers ($\approx$50–60%) are U.S. based, with Indian workers forming the second largest population ($\approx$30–40%). US Turkers are more likely to be female and are 30+ years old on average. Indian Turkers are more often male and a bit younger, 26–28 years old on average. Both groups are reasonably well educated with the vast majority having at least some college experience. In November 2009 Indian Turkers on average earned \$1.58/hour, as opposed to \$2.30/hour in the US [41]. Over 50% of Indian Turkers reported an annual household income of less than \$10,000, while 45% of US Turkers reported one of less than \$40,000 [22,23].

Although informative, the studies available on crowd (demographic) characterisation have limitations. First, data was collected some years ago and due to the rapidly changing world of crowdworking may not be accurate anymore [46]. Second, the vast majority of studies focus on AMT [22,23,30,33,39,41]. Very little is known about the crowds from other platforms, with the notable exceptions of Berg's study [3] who compared Turkers, both from India and the US, to CrowdFlower workers, Peer's study [40] who compared CrowdFlower workers and Prolific Academic workers with Turkers and a study by Hirth et al. [21], who investigated the locations and home countries of workers and requesters of the Microworkers platform.

2.1   Method

In this work we set out to collect and analyse demographic data of crowds of different platforms, so as to provide the reader with a timely characterisation of crowdworkers, their background, motivation and the ways in which they organise

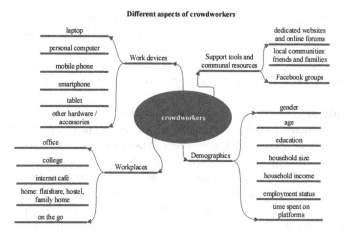

Fig. 1. Summary of these different aspects of the crowdworkers discussed in this article.

their work and personal life. Figure 1 provides a summary of these different aspects of the crowdworkers discussed in this article.

To complement the existing literature on crowd characterisation, we study the demographics of workers on three crowdsourcing platforms, namely AMT, Microworkers and Crowdee. AMT is by far the most popular and the most researched crowdsourcing platform. Thus, the results from AMT may be understood as the reference point to which the other platforms are compared. AMT connects a wide variety of requesters with over 500,000 Turkers (although the analysis of [13] suggests that the real number of active Turkers is between 15,059 and 42.912. Microworkers is an international crowdsourcing platform, active since 2009. With over 600,000 registered workers from over 190 countries, it provides an excellent environment to study workers' demographics and motivation. Contrary to AMT, which imposes restrictions on the geographical location of both workers and requesters, Microworkers gives access to workers and requesters from everywhere across the five continents. In our investigations concerning who is part of the crowd and why s/he is part of it, having access to a diversity of workers, with a wide variety in geographical origin, is core. The third platform, Crowdee, is a German based crowdsourcing platform; in contrast to the other platforms, Crowdee focuses on mobile microtasks with a small but growing worker community from west Europe [35].

Questionnaire. In order to investigate workers' demographics and motivation, we conducted surveys. We posted a questionnaire-based task on AMT, Microworkers and Crowdee; the questionnaire to be filled in contained a similar set of questions for all three platforms, yet customised depending on the specific platform. The questionnaire was created to investigate the following items:

- **Demographics** (gender, age, size of household and education level). As mentioned above, our intention was to demographically characterise the crowds in order to be aware of potential biases in task[6] execution [7], to be accounted for in the platform selection and task result analysis. Here we focused on gender and age, size of household (also related to the economic status characterisation, see below) and education level. The latter was especially of interest to investigate the potential of crowdsourcing platforms for tasks requiring special skills.

- **Economic status** (yearly income, employment status, expenditure purpose of money earned through crowdwork). A second point of interest was related to the economic status of the workers. Martin et al. [31] have shown how the primary motivation of workers is monetary, and how that affects their perception of the marketplace and their preferences in terms of task execution. To this purpose, we focused on gaining knowledge on whether crowdwork was a primary source of income for workers on the different platforms, and on the use they would make of the money earned through it (either primary expenditures such as bills and rent, or secondary expenditures such as hobbies and gadgets).

- **Crowdwork conditions** (time spent on the crowdsourcing platform weekly, number of tasks completed per week, location from which microwork is carried out, equipment and software tools used to support crowdwork, usage of other crowdsourcing platforms). Here, we were interested in characterising working conditions and attitude of crowdworkers, following the findings of Gupta et al. [17]; we were specifically interested in quantifying weekly workload (number of tasks and hours spent), and in investigating working environment conditions, including the physical place from which the crowdwork was carried out (e.g., home, Internet cafe, office), and the devices (mobile or not) from which tasks were executed.

To check the reliability of the answers, at least one gold standard question, also called a trapping question or a honeypot (e.g. [18,36]), was employed in every survey. The question had a straightforward answer which did not require any specific background knowledge (for example, workers had to indicate how many letters were included in the word "crowdsourcing").

Different platforms use different terminologies for crowdwork and the tasks created by the requesters. The work task is called a "Project" or a "HIT" in AMT, "Campaign" in Microworkers and "Job" in Crowdee. Questionnaires were also customised per platform; for example, the AMT questionnaire was adapted to Microworkers by replacing "HIT" by "task" and "AMT" with "Microworkers".

2.2   Data Collection

For AMT, the demographic study was conducted in March 2016 with 100 workers from the US and 100 workers from India. The HITs were created at 9 AM PDT and within 56 min for US workers, and 62 min for Indian workers, all answers

---

[6] The terms 'task' and 'microtask' have been used interchangeably here due to the use of multiple platforms that have different terminology for microtasks on them.

were collected. As a result of the reliability check, 10 responses from US workers and 29 responses from Indian workers were removed. The job was extended for Indian workers to gather more data. Overall, 90 responses from US workers and 87 responses from Indian workers were collected. For every survey, the US workers were rewarded $1 and $0.7 was paid to the Indian workers, following guidance from the Dynamo project[7].

In Microworkers, we set up a number of campaigns to have our questionnaires filled in April 2016. We targeted workers from five continents (North and South America, Africa, Europe, Asia, and Oceania). Previous work has shown that Microworkers' tasks are completed mostly within working hours [21]. As a consequence, launching a single campaign for all continents may have led to collecting responses mostly from workers in time zones for which the campaign started within office hours. To overcome this limitation, we launched independent campaigns in the different continents. In addition, because most continents span a large number of time zones, we took the further precaution to run the campaigns at minimum speed in the beginning. This allowed us to minimise the speed at which the campaign would be completed, and maximise the probability that workers from any time zone in the continent would fill in the questionnaire. Targeting separated continents also allowed us to customise the monetary reward for the questionnaire completion, following the recommendations of the platform.

Table 1 summarises our experimental setup. Note that for some continents, we limited the number of targeted workers, as we knew that the pool of workers in those areas was limited [21]. It is also interesting to note that the recommended monetary rewards vary quite substantially across regions (the suggested payment for US workers is almost three times as high as that suggested for Asian workers), and that in general, they are higher paid than those typically used for AMT HITS. The campaigns were launched simultaneously in the different continents. The fastest was completed within a few hours (Eastern Europe) and the slowest took over a week (South America). We collected data from 474 workers. Again, the reliability of workers' responses was checked using a gold standard question. Eventually, 380 of the original 474 responses were retained.

The third study was conducted using the Crowdee platform. The study took place in March 2016 and was open for 250 participants. The survey was divided into two jobs, which were published one after the other with some hours delay. Overall 242 participants filled in the survey completely. All of them answered the obvious gold standard question correctly; however, inconsistent answers to the repeated birth year question led to the removal of 6 responses. As a result, responses of 236 participants were used for further analyses.

In addition to the studies explained above, we included in our analysis raw data from the MTurk Tracker [10,23], as a reference for the AMT survey. The data covers the time range from April 2015 until January 2016. The data set contains responses to a five-item demographic survey (gender, year of birth,

---

[7] http://wiki.wearedynamo.org/index.php?title=Fair_payment last accessed 14 Jun 2017.

Table 1. Overview of the data collected and analysed in this study. The "Data (acronym)" column reports the origin of the data (survey or MTurk tracker) as well as the acronym used in tables and figures throughout the rest of the chapter.

Platform	Data (acronym)	Continent /country	Date	Valid responses	Payment p. worker ($)	Duration of study
AMT	Survey (AMT US)	US	March 2016	90	1	56 min
	Survey (AMT IN)	India	March 2016	87	0.7	62 min
	MTurk Tracker (AMT US 2016–2016)	US	April 2015–January 2016	23839	0.05	–
	MTurk Tracker (AMT IN 2016–2016)	India	April 2015–January 2016	4627	0.05	–
MW	Survey (MW Western)	Europe	April 2016	122	0.8	5 days
		Oceania		12	1.2	48 h
		North America		64	1.2	3 days
	Survey (MW developing)	South America	April 2016	28	0.48	1 week
		Asia		107	0.46	3 days
		Africa		48	0.48	22 h
Crowdee	Survey (Crowdee)	Western Europe	March 2016	236	€0.8	7 days

household size, household income, and marital status); 23,839 of these responses are from US crowd workers and 4,627 are from Indian crowd workers. The demographic API of the MTurk Tracker creates a survey job in AMT every 15 min to capture time variability. The survey is compensated with 5 cents; participation is restricted, i.e. each worker can participate once a month [24].

2.3   Results

In the following, we report the outcomes of our data collection on crowd characterisation, in order to answer the question "Who are the crowdworkers"? Detailed numbers are presented in the Appendix. To capture the geographical diversity of Microworkers, we differentiate the analysis for two separate groups, roughly identified based on GDP: (1) a group of Western countries, i.e., those included in North America, Europe and Oceania, and (2) a group of developing countries, included in Africa, Asia and Latin America. Although this separation is somewhat artificial, we deemed it sufficiently realistic to provide a good term of comparison to the AMT results, for which US (Western) and India (developing) workers were analysed separately.

Gender. In general, male workers outnumber female workers (see Fig. 2). For AMT, in line with the data reported in recent studies (e.g. [3,5]), we find gender to be more balanced for US Turkers compared to the Indian Turkers. According to our survey results, more than 60% of Indian Turkers are males, as also confirmed by the MTurk tracker data (although in this case more females are observed than in the survey data). On the other hand, for US Turkers, the data obtained from the MTurk Tracker indicates that the majority of Turkers are females, which is in contrast to our survey results, as well as to those of other recent surveys reporting numbers similar to ours [3,5].

The gender distribution of both Crowdee and Microworkers Western countries is close to that found for Indian Turkers: male workers form more than 60% of the population (or at least of the participants in our study). In Microworkers, the prevalence of male workers is more prominent in developing countries as compared to Western countries. In developing countries, our survey captures a ratio of one female to every five male workers.

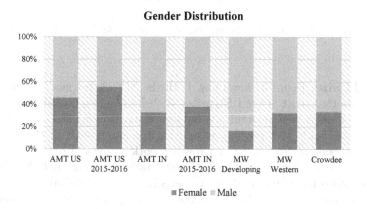

Fig. 2. *Gender* distribution of crowd workers in different platforms observed in survey studies.

Age. As shown in Fig. 3, the age distribution differs considerably across platforms (note that to be a crowdworker, a minimum age of 18 is required in all platforms, hence we set 18 as the starting age for which we analyse data). Within AMT data, there are differences between the outcomes of the survey and the data collected by the MTurk Tracker. Regarding the US Turkers, the group aged between 41–55 years is larger in our survey than in the MTurk tracker data, while the opposite is observed for Turkers in the youngest age group (18–26 years). Discrepancies between the survey and MTurk tracker data are smaller for the Indian population, as was observed for Gender. However, also for the Indian population, we find younger Turkers to be more numerous in the MTurk tracker sample compared to our survey data. These discrepancies make it difficult to properly characterise US and Indian Turkers according to their age.

Crowdee and Microworkers workers seem to be younger than Turkers. For Crowdee this is possibly due to many of workers being students as the platform is developed and maintained by a university team [35]. For Microworkers, independent of the region, the vast majority of workers are 32 or less. Workers in developing countries seem to be younger than their Western counterparts.

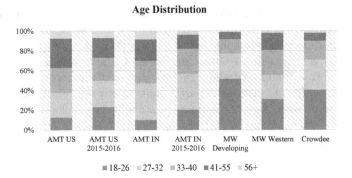

Fig. 3. Distribution of crowd workers' *Age* in different platforms observed in survey studies.

Household Size. Figure 4 shows how both the MTurk tracker and the survey data indicate that most of the US Turkers (>70%) live in a household of utmost two other people. A similar trend is found for Western countries in Microworkers, with big households (>4 people) accounting for about 40% of the total. For Crowdee, the majority (>55%) of Crowdee workers lives either alone or with one other person, which is in line with expectations, being that the Crowdee crowd composed for a large part by students (as will be detailed below).

The data for the Indian Turkers is not as homogeneous across the two data sources as it is for the US Turkers; nevertheless, the data clearly indicates that the household sizes are larger. In contrast to the US Turkers, most of the Indian Turkers (>58%) live together with three persons or more. Even larger sizes are found for Microworkers in developing countries, with only 30% of the total number of workers living with at most two other people. Based on these data, we can see a clear distinction between the composition of the crowd in Western countries (AMT data for US, MW Western and Crowdee) and in developing countries.

Educational Level As reported in previous studies (e.g. [22]), and visible in Fig. 5, the education level of the Turkers is rather high. Only very few Turkers have no high school degree. Most of them have at least some college education with the Indian workers reporting a higher education level compared to the US workers. More than half of the Indian Turkers have a Bachelor's degree[8] and more than 65% report to even have a Master's degree. However, holding a degree[9] is not a good measure of one's foreign language or computer skill in developing countries[10]. Note that for this item, MTurk Tracker data are not available.

[8] http://www.wes.org/educators/pdf/IndiaPolicyPacket.pdf last accessed 14 Jun 2017.
[9] http://www.rediff.com/getahead/report/career-your-skills-not-degree-will-get-you-a-job/20150408.htm last accessed 14 Jun 2017.
[10] http://www.wsj.com/articles/SB10001424052748703515504576142092863219826 last accessed 14 Jun 2017.

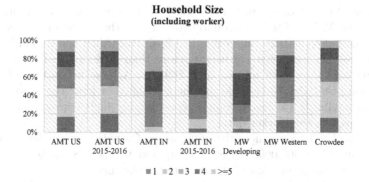

Fig. 4. Distribution of *Household Size* (counted including the worker), for the different platforms considered.

The distribution of the education levels of the Crowdee workers is similar to that reported by the US Turkers. Most of them report to have some college education and about 30% have a Bachelor's degree or higher. Again, it should be noted that Crowdee workers are for a large part students, thus they may still be in the midst of their educational path.

Workers using Microworkers have, in general, achieved higher education levels than Turkers and Crowdee workers. More than half of the workers have a bachelor's degree or higher qualification. This resembles the education level distribution of Indian Turkers. When looking closer at the two regions we are analysing, we find that workers from developing countries have significantly higher education levels than workers in Western countries, in a way that recalls the differences in distribution of education levels between US and Indian Turkers.

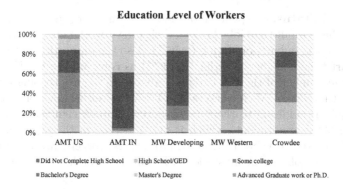

Fig. 5. Distribution of crowd workers' *Education Level* on different platforms, observed on survey studies.

Household Yearly Income. For the US Turkers, survey data are in line with the data from MTurk Tracker. Around two thirds of the Turkers report a household income below $60,000, as visible in Fig. 6. Regarding the Indian Turkers, the data are also somewhat consistent: more than 90% of the Turkers report their household income to be less than $60,000. A large proportion of Indian Turkers state that their household income is $10,000 or less. The proportion of this group having the lowest income is considerably higher in our own survey data compared to the tracker data.

As for the US Turkers, more than 60% of the Crowdee workers have a household income below $60,000; however, compared to the US Turkers, a higher proportion of Crowdee workers belongs to the lowest income group. This may, in combination with the low household size and young age, be explained by the fact that students make a consistent part of the Crowdee crowd; as students, they have no or very low income. Note that 22.18% of participants did not report their household income.

Finally, the Microworkers workers come, in general, from low income households. Almost half of the respondents to the questionnaire earn less than $10,000 per year, and albeit developing countries workers contribute to this number for the most part, still almost 40% of the Western workers claim to have such a low income. This is in contrast with US Turkers, whose average income seems to be much higher (the majority earn $40,000 a year or more), and diverges from the previous similarities observed for US Turkers and Microworkers workers in western countries. In interpreting the data, it should be taken into account that several Eastern European countries were included in the data collection for MW Western countries (15% of the respondents included in the MW Western groups were Serbian, for example); those countries have a significant lower GDP per capita with respect to the US, which may also partially explain these findings. In addition, as illustrated below, about 10% of MW Western workers are students, which may explain the low-size households with low income.

Employment Status. Independent of their location, a large proportion of Turkers (>44%) have a full-time jobs besides their crowd work (Fig. 7). This is more pronounced in the Indian population (≈56%). Also the proportion of the workers working part time is higher in India[11] (≈26%) as compared to the US (≈15%). A fairly large number of the US Turkers – almost 25% – are keeping house.

Also in the case of Microworkers, most workers either have a full-time or part-time job, in addition to their crowdsourcing job. A significant percentage (more than 10%) are students, which is also reflected in the young age of the workers. Compared to (US) Turkers, Microworkers workers, are more likely to have a part time job and being students, less likely to be housekeepers.

---

[11] Note that, *going to school* might have been misunderstood by workers with poor English, as to them education is disseminated in 'colleges' and 'universities', and not in 'schools'. We are replicating our survey based on previous studies here, hence we did not change the terminology in this case.

Yearly Income

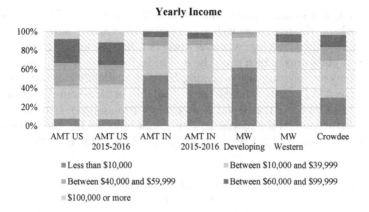

Fig. 6. Distribution of *Household Income* of crowd workers in different platforms observed in survey studies.

As for all other platforms a large proportion of the workers are working full-time additionally to the crowdwork they carry out. Compared to all other platforms, the proportion of Crowdee workers who are students is large.

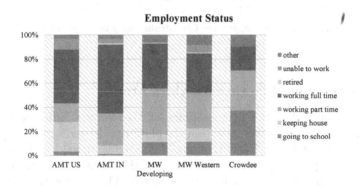

Fig. 7. Distribution of *Employment Status* of crowd workers in different platforms observed in survey studies.

Time Spent on Crowdsourcing Platforms. The majority of Turkers (>60%) stated that they spend more than 15 h per week on AMT; of these, a large number is even working more than 25 h per week (US: >37%; India: >47%, Fig. 8). This is noteworthy as many of the workers reported to have either a full-time or a part-time job in addition to their crowdwork (cf. previous section). Interestingly, whereas most Turkers dedicate a high number of hours to their crowdwork, for Microworkers we find a binomial distribution. A large percentage of workers (≈50%) spend relatively few hours on Microworkers (less than 10) and a lesser but also large percentage spends more than 25 h in crowdwork (≈25%). For Western workers, the distribution is more skewed towards a smaller number of hours spent on crowdsourcing, whereas workers from developing countries spent more time on platforms, which could be due to factors such as geographical time differences between posting and accessing HITs or availability of Batch HITs on platforms like AMT, that although were available in large numbers, paid only modestly[12]. In Crowdee, this trend is even more pronounced. Crowdee workers spend very little time on the platform. This might however be due to the smaller number of jobs available on Crowdee as compared to AMT and Microworkers.

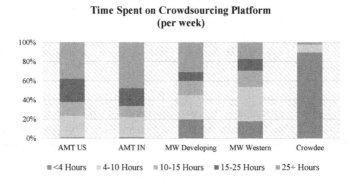

Fig. 8. Distribution of *Time Spent on Crowdsourcing Platforms* observed in survey studies.

2.4 Discussion on Who Crowdworkers Are

The results show that the demographics of the workers differ considerably between the platforms, as well as within the platform, depending on the workers' location. For a number of items (household size, educational level), the Indian Turkers have a profile more similar to that of the Microworkers workers from developing countries, than to their US colleagues. The same is true for the US Turkers, the Crowdee workers and the Microworkers from western countries. In fact, it is interesting to note again that Indian Turkers and Microworkers in developing countries report much higher educational levels than their western counterparts. In developing countries, like India, it is probably linked to the fact that the higher the socio-economic status, the more educated a person is in the Western sense of the word, and the more likely they are to have English and

---

[12] The other explanation is that the workers spent time 'searching' for work in the 'hopes' that they will find something before the end of the day. There isn't data to confirm this from our surveys but the ethnographic studies have. One such exemplar is where an Indian worker searches through HITs on MTurk for as long as 20 min at a stretch 'hoping' to find his or her preferred type of work.

computer literacy and access[13], whereas, in the US, the Internet access has penetrated further down the socio-economic class ladder[14]. This should be taken into account by requesters willing to post tasks which require special skills related to the educational level. Note that high education level, i.e. holding a degree, may not correspond to advanced English language levels in the developing countries as most of education programs are in their mother tongues or local, regional languages, discussed in the 'education level' in Sect. 2.3.

With respect to gender, AMT seems to attract more female workers in the US; requesters seeking gender-specific information, or looking for a diverse pool of workers to carry out a task (e.g., when performing studies related to gendered innovations), should take into account that female workers are more scarce in Microworkers, and especially in developing countries. Conversely, requesters looking for a younger crowd (e.g., requesters investigating new trends among young people), should prefer Microworkers and Crowdee to AMT.

When it comes to working conditions and attitude, we found a high platform-dependency. Our data showed Turkers to be more dedicated to crowdwork, spending longer hours on the platform, which may suggest higher specialisation and possibly efficiency in completing jobs. On the other hand, for the most part, Turkers have a full-time job, and perform crowdwork as a second job. On one hand, tiredness due to excessive workload (and consequent unreliability in task performance) may be a risk in this case. On the other hand it may indicate that crowdworkers have a potential of performing more advance tasks, than the type currently asked of them, as they are qualified enough to have a full-time job.

Finally, it is worth noticing that US Turkers set aside from the other workers and platforms when it comes to income per household: their income is consistently higher than their counterpart of Western workers in Microworkers. This is probably due to comparative living standards: $10,000 per year does not even make minimum wage in the US[15] but is a reasonable income in India[16]. Workers in developing countries have low incomes and large households; in many cases, as also noted by Gupta et al. [17], crowdwork is their primary source of income.

A further finding is related to the methodological validity of crowd-based demographic survey. The discrepancies between our survey data and the data obtained from MTurk Tracker indicate that data from one-shot surveys are not necessarily in line with the results from surveys which collect data repeatedly over a year. Therefore it is not advised to generalise demographic results by

---

[13] http://www.prb.org/Publications/Articles/2012/india-2011-census.aspx last accessed 14 Jun 2017.

[14] http://www.pewinternet.org/2015/10/29/technology-device-ownership-2015/ last accessed 14 Jun 2017, http://www.pewinternet.org/2015/06/26/americans-internet-access-2000-2015/ last accessed 14 Jun 2017.

[15] http://www.citylab.com/work/2015/09/mapping-the-difference-between-minimum-wage-and-cost-of-living/404644/ last accessed 14 Jun 2017.

[16] According to the OECD the net national income in India was $3,718 per year and capita in 2009. https://data.oecd.org/natincome/net-national-income.htm last accessed 14 Jun 2017.

using a survey job: it may be the case that a very specific group of workers will participate in the job. As jobs often have a short time frame, also the participants for the same job type (e.g. surveys vs. annotations) may differ from job to job. This means that participants who are taking part in one specific survey job may not be representative for the crowdworkers who are normally performing this type of job.

Regarding the incomes, it is noteworthy that we do not know how much of these incomes are generated by Turking, and differential costs of living limit the interpretative power of direct dollar comparisons.

3   Why: What Motivates Crowdworkers?

Why do crowdworkers do crowdwork, why do they work on particular platforms and why do they choose particular types of tasks, working for particular requesters? It is rare to find people who would continue happily doing their job if they were no longer paid for it. It is also quite rare to find people who can find no other positive thing about their work than the fact that it pays a wage. Modern crowdwork is a relatively novel type of work if looked at through the prism of technology and the Internet but it is also in many ways simply the modern twist on home-based (or sometimes mobile) *piece-work*. In this section we draw heavily on our previously studied in-depth ethnographic studies of US and Indian crowdworkers on AMT [17,31,32]. When crowdworkers are studied in depth it is obvious that so much of what they talk about and how they talk about it is classic 'shop talk' – i.e. work talk. How to earn best, how to maximise earnings, what jobs pay what amount per hour, how many HITs and how regularly batches are posted, what are the best paid HITs and so forth are the topics that monopolise forums, groups and interviews – money and how to best earn it is the over-riding theme, with workplace relations and topics around managing work, learning and so forth related secondary topics. The obviousness of the work dimension may even lead to crowdworkers to provide other reasons why they do crowdwork in response to why-do-you-do-this questions from researchers while lacing their answers with words like *work, earn, money, job, pay, employer and employee*, as we sometimes saw in our interviews of Indian Turkers.

The problematic other side of this coin is that researchers have often found it hard to believe that people could be possibly doing crowdwork as a job – 'how could anyone accept such a low wage?' This disbelief seemed to be part of a distancing and insulating move – exaggerating the secondary benefits and positive aspects for Turkers – and making academic researchers feel better, since Turkers could be conceived of as doing things for fun, passing time, enjoying helping out in academic research. This trend reached its apotheosis with the publishing of a couple of papers [1,26] that employed rather dubious techniques in order to re-interpret their own questionnaire-based results on reasons and motivations. Both these studies had indicated that money was the primary factor but sought to minimise this result by employing 'social desirability bias' detection to essentially suggest that respondents had answered in this way because they thought they should. We can see no technical or analytic justification for their decisions – and given the overwhelming evidence to the contrary across the media and other academic work, and in the forums, web-resources and so forth – we feel their work can be discounted.

3.1   US Turkers

In our in-depth study of the Turker Nation forum [31] we gathered many materials to demonstrate as strongly as we could just how clear it was that participations in doing HITs on AMT was for the vast majority of Turkers a form of paid work, where the pay was of key importance. As evidence we produced a variety of material from a number of threads, beginning with a thread titled "Turkers Turking for Fun" where the opening post questioned whether money was the primary motive in all cases of Turking or whether sometimes Turkers chose work according to other criteria. The replies to this essentially took two forms. The first form was reactions with opprobrium:

> **danturker**: "This attitude would be requesters dream come true. The workers come here to have fun and play and the lousy pay for work is not an issue. This attitude helps create low pay for the MTurk work force that does care about fair pay."

In these cases the Turkers made it clear that they believed that even discussing such issues promoted the discourse that pay was not important, and that people worked for fun or charity, and undermined the fight for respectable wages. In the second form of response the reaction was milder, simply stating that pay was clearly the most important factor, secondary factors like interest or fun could figure in the decision if there was no pay difference:

> **larak56**: "I agree with most everyone here. While I do find some of the HITS fun and actually learn an incredible amount by doing HITS, I do it for the cash."

The idea that this perspective is not shared by the overwhelming majority of Turkers does not seem credible. One of the clearest features of all of the forums and resources dedicated to serving Turkers, and the tools and scripts they use is that the massive preoccupation is on how to find and do the best paid HITs, which good HITs come at the biggest frequency in the biggest volume, how to maximise earnings and who can be trusted to pay, quickly. As soon as new HITs come on the market people try them out and post their projections on what their pay rate is, whether their work has been accepted and how long it took them to be paid. They talk about how often requesters post tasks in what volume, and how they arrange their work around the periods where there will be high availability of good tasks. They are concerned about their ratings and HIT count as these are passports to more work. They worry about being suspended or banned as AMT is such a valuable source of income. They talk about how much they make in a day or in a year. Their targets are either purely financial or when they talk about ratings or HIT targets it is as the means to improve earning. The weight of evidence on this matter is massive. These are people who identify as workers working in a low paid labour market where it seems that some of the best workers can earn around $15,000 per year, which represents around the minimum wage income for US workers in a 40 h per week job. It is quite likely that many earn less than this for doing longer hours.

When we consider whether US Turkers work full-time, part-time, alongside another job and more generally how many hours of work per day or week, it is important to separate what they would ideally be doing from what they are actually doing. In fact Turking is not often a job of preference even though they like the fact that they can work from home, be pseudonymous and can choose when and where they work. The problems of the general precariousness of the work, the fact that income can fluctuate by large amounts, low pay and lack of rights (their right to participate can be taken away at any point and there are no specific procedures for dealing with worker grievances) all mean that most Turkers would rather have a secure job in a more conventional labour market. In terms of wages, we can see it is hard to attain more than the US minimum wage and for many it is considerably less. The fact is that many earn what they can, but for many that is not enough to live on; they need to have other income. It is clear, however that some people do carry out the work as supplementary income, which may allow them to buy non-essential luxuries from time to time, but that is a function of their needs rather than indicating it is not a serious job.

3.2 Indian Turkers

Indian Turkers do crowdsourced tasks for the money too. They can earn comparatively more given lower living costs in India – you could support a family to a reasonable standard of living in a reasonably-sized town on $10,000 a year. But once again their level of earnings (or earning potential) is a function of (1) available volume of HITs they are able to do and the earnings paid on those HITs, (2) how crowdwork lines up alongside their other responsibilities, e.g. other work they may do, and (3) how much they need the money, i.e. do they (or their family) have other sources of income? One can think of these as adjustable sliders whereby greater consistent availability of good paying HITs may mean they put in more hours or even go full time. If they really need money to survive they will put in time crowdsourcing even after working a full day in another job. If they have other reasonable sources of income they are more likely to pick and choose the crowdsourcing work they do, and are less likely to do long hours and are more likely to spend their money on treats. In many cases the Indian Turkers (as with all Turkers) are limited in the amount they can earn due to lack of availability of work they can do, and also the pay level of that work. For example, if they can only do relatively simple tasks where the English language is particularly clear in the instructions, and these tasks are limited in number, pay approximately $0.01, and take 5 min to complete, they will not be able to fully support themselves in their living costs with this.

While US Turkers in general are realists or even cynical about the other benefits of Turking – over and above the money earned (see above) – they do prefer tasks that pay well and are interesting, provide learning opportunities, are engaging, funny, creative and so forth. They do feel that they can learn some things. The contrast with the Indian Turkers is that for the Indians the opportunities for learning are more strongly stressed and they place a strong emphasis on 'timepass' which in our study was not just 'passing the time' but rather passing the time doing something of value as opposed to wasting time. There was a moral component focused on using your spare time in a good way; earning money, self-improvement, and developing skills. While it was clear that US Turkers also indicated in various ways that it was seen as a more productive way to spend spare time they tended to view this through the lenses of *necessity* far more than *moral improvement*.

3.3   Complementary Survey Findings

In addition to the qualitative studies reported above, Naderi et al. [37] developed the Crowdsourcing Work Motivation Scale (CWMS) for measuring motivation of crowdworkers. This scale is based on the Self-Determination Theory (SDT) of motivation [9,42]. The SDT not only differentiates between intrinsic and extrinsic motivation but also considers a spectrum of different types of extrinsic motivation. These different types of extrinsic motivation vary depending on the level of internalisation of the goal, i.e. how much a person can identify with the activity and its outcomes, and therefore how much personal investment or enthusiasm they have for the task.

Internalised extrinsic motivations share similar consequences with intrinsic motivation, i.e. the more people believe a task to be of value, whether in a purely personal way or to have, for example, societal worth, the more effective performance is in complex tasks, the higher participation rates are, and this also leads to higher well-being and satisfaction scores amongst the workers [14]. Results from the study by Naderi et al. [37], show that US Turkers have very high external motivation (i.e. earning money). However, it was also shown that their levels of intrinsic and internalised extrinsic motivation are positively correlated with their participation rate and the reliability of their responses. These results back up the position argued above. Money is the highest motivator but both features of the work and what it is for and features of the task are also important in recruitment and quality, as well as making crowdworkers feel more positive and satisfied. In citizen science projects people gladly give their time for free due to personal interest and an idea of giving something positive to nature and society. In micro-task markets workers often talk more positively if they feel they are contributing to research and the task itself is interesting and engaging, and they may learn something themselves. These are ways to get more people interested and get higher quality output but the bottom line is still work for pay.

3.4 What Does Identifying Motivations Tell Us About Task Design?

The most important thing to take away from this discussion is that there is a strict hierarchy of importance in motivations – pay comes first, and all other motivations are secondary. Really interesting badly paid tasks will not be as attractive as boring well paid tasks. This does not mean that a really interesting but badly paid task will not get done but there will be less of the Turker population who will be attracted to it, and so it may well take longer to, for example, have the batch completed, the quality may be lower, and it may attract more bad behaviour. However, it must also be noted that it is very clear that simply paying more and more does not guarantee more success, better quality work, or faster batch completion times. Crowdsourcing platforms are markets and being as such there are norms and standards of market rates (as well as other things like *behaviour* and *etiquette*). If prices outlie the norms by too great a margin people will be suspicious of the task (occasionally 'earn 100s of dollars quickly' scam tasks are posted). You should, however, pay at the upper level of market rates – and certainly have an eye to paying an amount that given reasonable/average completion times would pay roundabout minimum wage per hour. This is not necessarily a calculation that is easy to do precisely but that is not really necessary. If you try to do this honestly it will be transparent to the Turkers.

There are another series of features of tasks that are not really Turker motivations – so to speak – but they are elements that motivate them – or attract them – to do your tasks, and they are: how well your task is designed (does it work well, is it clear, are the instructions good); how quickly do you pay, and overall how do you conduct yourself in your dealings and interactions with Turkers (are you fair, polite etc.?). In short, your reputation will impact how easy it is to get good quality work, quickly. A good reputation, earned over time, makes your tasks very attractive and they will be looked out for, picked up quickly and generally done to a high standard. If you have all of these components and can add interest, engagement, creativity – these will serve like the icing on the cake but good pay, good design and good conduct are the most important aspects.

In the survey (see Sect. 2.1), workers were asked about expenditure purposes of the money that they earned through crowdwork. Although similarities in patterns based on countries of crowdworkers (Western vs. developing) was expected, differences based on platforms are observed (see Fig. 9). Crowdee and Microworkers workers mostly use their earnings for 'secondary' expenses (>65%) or as pocket change (for hobbies, gadgets, going out etc.). The majority of Indian Turkers (59%) and half of US Turkers (51%) use their earnings for 'primary' expenses (like paying bills, gas, groceries etc.). As a result, Turkers rely on their crowdwork income for everyday living expenses which can be indicator of crowdwork being taken more seriously, and used to support workers and even their families, on the income from AMT.

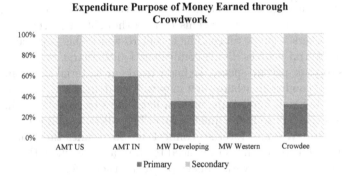

Fig. 9. Distribution of *Expenditure Purposes of Income* through crowdwork observed in survey studies.

4   How: Social and Organisational Aspects of Doing Crowdwork

In this section we want to review the data and findings we have available on how crowdworkers organise and manage their work. For the most part this section will deal with qualitative insights about how crowdworkers organise their working lives, their worksites and their actual crowdworking. To do this we will draw again most specifically on the ethnographic studies of Indian and US Turkers [17,31,32]. The study by Gupta et al. [17] of Indian Turkers is our richest source of observational data as the lead author actually visited a number of Turkers, saw their worksites and observed them Turking. In the work by Martin and colleagues [31,32] we draw on forum discussion of these matters to provide insights into the ways in which people work, the circumstances of their work, how they manage work and life and what other resources and technologies they use in organising their work. We cannot make statements with absolute certainty about the correlation between our findings of crowdworkers with that of workers using other platforms that we have not directly studied, but given that a number of these crowdworkers do crowdwork on other platforms with a similar social and organisational set up, and given other studies (e.g. [29]) indicating similar circumstances, we believe that our findings have general wider application than just for AMT, Microworkers or Crowdee.

4.1   Workplaces

In order to do crowdsourcing work, workers require an account, a computing device and an Internet connection. Therefore technically crowdwork can be done in a wide range of places, on the move, in public or private, and it is. In our qualitative studies of Turkers we have examples of a wide variety of workplaces, varying at an individual level too. More generally there is a preference towards having a dedicated place, often in the home with some degree of privacy; quite simply to allow a degree of concentration for the worker and to not disturb other members of the household. This can be thought of as the aspiration of most crowdworkers: a home office. The extent to which this is possible depends to a large degree on peoples' living conditions. Quite a large amount of Turkers have access to some private space. We know from our material that some Turkers live in crowded conditions where they may well be doing their work in a shared space – living in small family apartments, flat shares or co-habiting in a hostel. In these cases they try to find a quiet corner. This also assumes they have access to a computing device and Internet connection. Sometimes they can work on a shared device while other times they need to go to a place where they can access a device; and this may be work, college or an Internet cafe.

We have examples from our US study where some people are specifically allowed by their work to do Turking during periods of work down time. We have an example in India where employees in a small business process outsourcing company do Turking as a part of their work. Turking in Internet cafes appears more common in India, and this is likely a feature of the depth of penetration of computing technology there. That is, it is more common to have to go to an Internet cafe in order to access more traditional personal computing (PC) technology and the Internet. In some of our examples from India, turking is much more fluid and social in Internet cafes, where people work cooperatively on HITs and may share accounts or do HITs on one another's behalf. Although mobile phone penetration in India is massive with over a billion mobile phone subscriptions for a population of $\approx$1.2 billion[17], the same is not true for PC penetration and the number of people with smartphone, while impressive at 220 million[18] only represents $\approx$22% of mobile phones, and it is clear that smartphones are only suitable for a proportion of microtasks.

A final point to note is that people may prefer certain types of microtasks according to their current workplace (and device and Internet connection). Certain microtasks may be easily done on the move, and using a smartphone (simple tagging and clicking tasks) while others may require a set up with a better connection, keyboard and bigger screen (requiring research, writing, sustained concentration). As such, places and technologies can dictate what microtasks are doable and desirable. Finally it should be noted that sometimes places and devices are used for different sub-tasks in Turking – we have a number of examples of people using their smartphones to search for and book out work (to be done later) or to check up on job status, payment etc. while on the move and then to do the saved work later when they get to their workplace.

Results from our survey studies (see Sect. 2.1) show that crowdworkers work on microtasks from their homes most of the time (>80%) and secondly, from

---

[17] http://www.forbes.com/sites/saritharai/2016/01/06/india-just-crossed-1-billion-mobile-subscribers-milestone-and-the-excitements-just-beginning/#786ee6915ac2 last accessed 14 Jun 2017.

[18] http://www.thehindu.com/news/cities/mumbai/business/with-220mn-users-india-is-now-worlds-secondbiggest-smartphone-market/article8186543.ece last accessed 14 Jun 2017.

their offices (see Fig. 10). On the other hand, Crowdee workers also work on the move (31%). This is easily explained by the fact that the platform takes the form of a mobile application (as of June 2016). As shown in Fig. 11, crowdworkers mostly used their desktop computer or laptop for crowdwork except Crowdee where workers had to use their mobile phones to do crowdwork. Microworkers workers from developing countries worked more (>15%) using their phones than their colleagues from Western countries. Similar patterns were observed between Indian and US Turkers, which could be due to high mobile phone (see Footnote 17) use in developing countries.

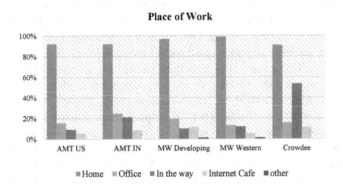

Fig. 10. Distribution of crowdworkers' *Place of Work* observed in survey studies.

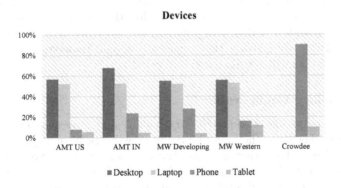

Fig. 11. Distribution of *Type of Devices* used for crowd working observed in survey studies.

4.2   Informational and Communal Resources

When you study Turkers, one thing that quickly becomes clear is that a *lack of information* is their biggest problem and that knowledge is a key component in earning power. Crowdsourcing platforms and markets, particularly as exemplified in AMT, are information poor and rather opaque, by design, even if we do not know if this was a thought-through design decision. An individual crowdworker, through trial and error, can clearly learn a certain amount about different types of jobs, what suits them, what pays better and more reliably, who is a good requester for them and so forth, but limited to personal experience their view will be narrow and their learning experiences will be limited to their imagination and abilities.

It may be striking but should not be surprising that they depend upon a number of on-line resources and social and familial networks in order to ameliorate this information deficit and access community support. These sources allow them to acquire much useful knowledge and information, find out what the good resources and technologies are, get tips on how to learn and acquire new skills, and learn what the best strategies and techniques are for finding and completing particular HITs. These resources also help them to understand what to avoid, how best to comport themselves in their dealings with platform owners and requesters and other practical and emotional support. These sites are crucial for many Turkers and other crowdworkers in helping them reach a stage where they can earn a reasonable amount and sustain those earnings. There are a number of websites, forums and Facebook groups that provide a number of informational and supporting services for Turkers, such as Turker Nation (the forum studied by the authors), mTurk Forum, mTurk Grind and Reddit groups[19]. Crowdsourcing can and could be a form of synchronous or asynchronous cooperative work but it is not supported on platforms like AMT, but one thing that requesters should understand is that there is a very strong community outside the platform – online and even offline. They work together on 'the work to make the turking work' [31] – i.e. the work that they do in order to manage their crowdsourcing work and career, like searching, configuring their system and practices for particular jobs, understanding and judging jobs and requesters, learning and so forth. One of the key features that requesters should understand is that both they and their jobs will get discussed and rated.

4.3   Technology Configurations

Technology set-ups like workplaces vary widely, and may even do so for the same crowdworker since they may be doing crowdwork in multiple places with multiple device and Internet configurations. When we talk about technology configurations this takes in hardware, software and Internet connections. Again, as with workplaces (with the private, dedicated space), there is an ideal set-up that involves high performance, ergonomically comfortable hardware technology, a sophisticated (but often cumbersome) bricolage of apps and browser plug-ins and a reliable high-speed Internet connection.

---

[19] Last accessed (the following) 14 Jun 2017, https://www.reddit.com/r/HITsWorthTurkingFor/wiki/index, http://www.cloudmebaby.com/forums/portal.php, http://www.mturkforum.com/, http://turkernation.com/, http://www.mturkgrind.com/.

In some of the forum threads on Turker Nation (or other forums and lists) there are dedicated discussions about the best hardware and technology set-up, including discussions of the fastest most durable keyboards, best screens, set-ups and so forth. Speed is of the essence, but durability for repetitive HITs involving speed of key strokes means some may use special keyboards or configure their set-up with better ergonomic properties to avoid repetitive strain injury. A powerful computer with a reliable high-speed Internet connection is obviously desirable to enable faster downloads, searching, better handling of images, sound files and videos. This set-up also should be more dependable meaning that fewer jobs will be lost half-way through with slow Internet speeds or crashing. Large screens, multiple screens, good headphones, and peripherals like transcription pedals all are ways in which equipment can make a difference to how easy HITs are to do. In general better hardware and network connections extend the variety of HITs that can be done and the speed at which they can be completed, i.e. it increases earning power.

In the US there is a wider spread of Turkers who have good quality device set ups, although there is clearly diversity in quality depending on peoples' material circumstances. In India, however, the general trend was that there was more variability and often poorer quality device and Internet configurations. We observed people working on older computers, smartphones for HITs not ideally suited to such devices, poor or intermittent Internet connections, and even problems with their electricity supply. These problems were common to the extent that Indian Turkers had worked out various back-up electricity sources and Internet access possibilities [16].

Through our studies it also became clear that software, scripts, apps and plug-ins are crucial to carrying out the work and optimising it. When Turkers can access more, better quality information through their networks and on-line resources this allows them to be more effective in learning and operating in the market. In participating in the forums and so forth they can gain a lot of information, but then another problem is posed; how do they marshal that information to their best advantage? One answer is through the development of tools. A well-known tool in the Turker and academic community is TurkOpticon[20] [25]. This is a simple to use qualitative, community-based rating tool, where Turkers provide their ratings out of five on four categories relating to each HIT; *communication, generosity, fairness, promptness*. The tool comes as a browser extension such that when looking at specific HITs they can view the ratings and be assisted in their decision making. TurkOpticon therefore is a conduit for the type of information on HITs that is informally shared on forums every day. It is also implemented in an embedded fashion in the Turker workflow, i.e. they can see the rating during the search rather than having to look at the HIT then search on a forum for information on that HIT. The tool therefore helps both *decision making* and *productivity*.

There are a wide range of tools and these generally come in two forms – (1) tools that help you to navigate to and grab the HITs that you want quickly, and

---

[20] https://turkopticon.ucsd.edu/ last accessed 14 Jun 2017.

(2) tools that help you to optimise the speed with which you can do HITs. In the case of TurkOpticon they may help with both. A few academic researchers have developed tools – and they are mainly centred around how Turkers can find good paying, reliable jobs, more quickly. Of note is Crowd-Workers [6] that cooperatively collects and aggregates ratings and information on pay. A small application called TurkBench, was also designed to automatically create dynamic work schedules based around the best paying work [19] – the concept was well received but the technology unfortunately ran into technically insoluble issues.

However, the vast majority of tools are designed and produced by Turkers themselves. Whole suites of tools that, for example, notify them when certain HITs become available (e.g. Turk Alert[21]), automatically grab those HITs, enable better search, enable shortcuts for quick navigation and form-filling, and other browser enhancements as well as tools that help assess pay rates and keep track of earnings etc. These can help change the value of HITs (i.e. make them more worthwhile because they can be done quicker) but also help Turkers to operate in the market, they can filter the good from the bad and spend less time searching and more time working on good HITs. Detailed discussions and links can be found on forum pages[22]. A few important points come out of understanding the role of tools. Firstly, the amount and ingenuity of tools and scripts underlines the fact that Turkers are knowledgeable and inventive people. Secondly, it shows that pretty much anywhere in the workflow where time can be saved through tool use and where technical development is possible it seems to have been done – once again demonstrating that saving time increases earnings power. Thirdly, however, AMT does not have a Turker API and is not configured to support these tools. And these tools form a fragile ecosystem (i.e. they are not fully integrated nor fully compatible with browsers, AMT etc.) and they are liable to cause application or system crashes from time to time. And finally, and importantly, it should be noted that Turking experts using these tools have a market advantage in being first in the market to take the good jobs, and some HIT batches consequently disappear in a matter of seconds. Novice Turkers stand little chance of accessing those HITs.

4.4 Managing Work and Life

As should be becoming clear, one of the elements we wish to emphasise in regard to crowdsourced work is that the motivations, concerns and problems of crowdworkers are very similar to those of any group of workers, but particularly those of more precarious[23] workers. It is however, important to look at what is different to other forms and sectors of work and what the implications of these differences are. Some of the key differences between crowdworking and many

---

[21] http://www.turkalert.com/ last accessed 14 Jun 2017.

[22] http://turkernation.com/forumdisplay.php?167-mTurk-Scripts-Programs-amp-Tools last accessed 14 Jun 2017.

[23] For information on 'precarious work': http://www.laborrights.org/issues/precarious-work last accessed 14 Jun 2017.

other sectors are the fact that it is often anonymous work, with little direct communication between employer and employee, it is a form of radical freelancing in that crowdworkers can work for various different employers in a day and may have no stable relationships, and finally, the market is open all hours, and crowdworkers can choose whatever hours they like. The lack of rights, protections and grievance processes separate crowdwork from many other forms and sectors of work, although things are different in different markets, once again with AMT being an example of a market with little legal coverage [32].

When it comes to managing work and life Turkers are very similar to many other workers. They have a life outside of work with desires, needs, responsibilities and relationships just like everyone else. Their personal life and their work life have to be juggled, but how does that organisation work, and what are the effects of having an always-on market? In theory an always-on market would provide a positive flexibility, i.e. work could be accommodated to life. When you were available, on your terms, you could pick and choose the work to do. This would allow you to accommodate a complex personal life (e.g. with uneven demands on time), you could go on holiday when you wanted, sickness would not have to be reported. In reality things are a little more complicated.

First of all, you can choose your schedule, but if it is not possible to earn a decent wage without putting in long, monotonous hours, suddenly you do not have the same flexibility. Secondly, while you do not need to get approval for holidays or sick leave, you are not paid for them, and you have no long term benefits like pension rights or healthcare. Finally, if you work in a market where there is in general an over-supply of labour and an under supply of good (well-paying regularly available) jobs you are in stiff competition and need to take the good work if and when it is available, thus finding the flexibility in your personal and family life to accommodate doing the work when it is good. Flexibility, as others have pointed out (e.g. [4]), while touted as good for all often leads to a situation where workers compromise their personal lives to accommodate the variable needs and fluctuations of their work. The testimony across all of the Turkers we studied was that very often they organised their hours based on when better work was available, or they hoped would be available (guessing market dynamics is not always an easy task), and when good jobs in large batches came along they were willing to drop everything to make the most of this work.

Another interesting set of observations that come from our studies is some similarities to gambling. In the forums and amongst Turkers there are various stories about $100 HITs or ones where the hourly rate turned out to be $50 or something similar. When this is added to the uncertainty over whether HITs are genuine, whether you will be paid or not, and the slightly addictive desire to keep looking, checking out whether you have been paid or not, or whether a great job has just been posted, one can appreciate the draw on attention it has, that promotes a certain set of compulsions. This does not make it much different from so much of the World Wide Web these days in the attention economy (see [8] for a sustained discussion and critique of this), where much is designed and delivered to keep grabbing your attention, encouraging you to click on links and keep you returning to particular sites but it is nevertheless an interesting feature of the work. However, much more importantly, it should be understood that the casino aspects of the work and the market are not what the majority of workers seek. They instead seek stability and predictability; regular, dependable, decent paid work for people they can trust and who will communicate with them politely and productively when required. One of the biggest secrets of the AMT market is the amount of stable working relationships going on under the hood, managed either informally as certain Turkers always try to work for certain requesters or more formally through the qualification system or through direct contacts. This really should be no surprise because it makes the work and earnings less unpredictable and more trustable for all involved.

4.5   So What Does This Knowledge About Turking Tell Us?

The knowledge about how Turkers organise their work brings forth issues about task design and relationship management. Firstly it suggests that requesters should be tolerant and understanding. There are a set of reasons why jobs may be poorly done, terminated without being finished and so forth that may be due to technical difficulties or an inappropriate set-up for the microtask. Also, and this relates to other aspects of Turker profiles and demographics, it can be helpful to make HITs as intuitive as possible and include visual instructions, to make it easier for people with lower levels of English comprehension and even computer skills complete your tasks properly. There is a notable degree of variability in physical infrastructure and resources required to carry out crowdwork, not just globally, but within the same country. Where possible and sensible requesters could try to design tasks that are 'light-weight' and more 'accessible' in terms of technology, which would make crowdwork more 'inclusive' – for people of different quality of resources and different abilities; and reduce the time and effort spent 'managing' work that was not completed due to infrastructure failure issues [16]. Microtasks can also be designed specifically for mobile devices or with workflows that would mean that the HIT would not be failed if there was a loss in Internet connection or similar problem.

Secondly, be aware that in the vast majority of HITs, for the vast majority of Turkers (and this may well apply to crowdworkers in general) speed-to-HIT completion (and often HIT-to-HIT speed) are crucial to their earning power. They will do HITs as quickly as possible to acceptable quality. This is testified in their use of tools, shortcuts and scripts that buy them small amounts of time, and it is also clear from their many discussions on how to optimise for particular tasks. The nature of the work is that unless it is somehow required and enforced (e.g. if you want a crowdworker to reflect before answering, you might best not allow them to answer straightaway) you cannot expect the worker to take any more time than the minimum. This is a key feature of the work that requesters need to think seriously about in the design of their experiments, questionnaires and so forth.

Thirdly, try to build up a good reputation but be aware of who is doing your HITs, how quickly. If you have a good reputation in general you will attract the more expert workers with the tool set-ups that allow them to grab your jobs almost instantaneously. This will be more pronounced if your pay is at the high end and your jobs come in large batches. The effect will be less pronounced if each worker can only do the job once, as in the case of a questionnaire, and/or your pay is lower. It is important that you understand as to whether your research is compromised in terms of sampling if you have too much of your work done by a smaller or more stable returning group of workers. Whether these aspects of the market create issues for you will depend on your research and your experimental design.

Finally, it is worth considering that you may want to develop professional working relationships with a corpus of crowdworkers, particularly if you want to do repeated work over a period of time. You could establish a group of workers through a system of qualifications for accreditation and post jobs directly to them through the qualification system. You could even collect enough workers that you could sub-sample within them. Another feature of this is that you could notify them in advance of upcoming work and use them in the beta and usability testing of your experimental design. If you have large projects that you intend to crowdsource over time this type of model, that involves some organisation without it being too laborious, would have a number of key benefits in terms of much less uncertainty over their work products while also being an ethical approach that was generally welcomed by the crowdworkers.

5   Leveraging Our Understanding of the Crowd for Research

As has been stated on a number of occasions, crowdsourcing currently operates in a legal grey area – i.e. pre-existing laws do not clearly map onto the territory it occupies, and therefore, which legal principles should apply and how they should be applied are still open questions [11,12,32]. The producers and owners of platforms are keen to remove and excuse themselves from the labour relations of those employers and employees, or requesters and providers (as independent contractors). The discussions over how these entities should be named and known is also a reflection of a desire to carve out a new legal territory in a number of ways. The ambiguity about how to categorise this work legally – while providing platform owners and requesters with opportunities to take advantage of lower standards regarding pay and conditions – is also reflected in the way in which crowdsourcing has been treated by the academic research community. Was crowdsourcing simply a cheap data service, was experimentation with the crowd somehow different, and in which cases, which ethical policies procedures should apply, what about codes of conduct, pay and so forth?

Initially much of crowdsourcing use – most often AMT use – by the academic community basically fell under the radar in terms of ethics and legal considerations, most likely because it was new and unknown, it was anonymous and lacking a human face, academics generally followed market rates, and it was mostly used for data services (rather than testing or experimentally manipulating the workers themselves). Now, the legal discourse – if not yet fully the law itself – is catching up (e.g. [11,12,32]) and so are institutional and national ethics committees. This work seems to be trending in particular directions but it is not unanimous in position. In this section we will try to provide navigation through the key features of the ethics and legal aspects of crowdsourced piece-work.

Crowdsourcing platforms clearly have their own sets of rules – or *policies*[24], although these are both wide-ranging and vague, and it is not clear just how stringently or fairly they are enforced. More importantly, however, Turkers themselves have very few rights and no clear and transparent means of complaint and restitution if they think they have been mistreated. If they are understood as being independent contractors entering into a series of singular HIT-based contracts with essentially anonymous requesters they can only really appeal to Amazon at the moment about bad behaviour on the part of requesters. However, Amazon does not have a transparent and binding grievance process and the evidence from Turkers suggests that Amazon is not particularly responsive to complaints. It would not make sense practically for a Turker to pursue a requester legally over a single non-payment given the small amounts of money involved. As has been stated on a number of occasions (e.g [1,35,45]) in order to deal with this issue Turkers essentially follow a social policy of 'name and shame' through their forums, groups or technologies like TurkOpticon. This does not recover the money unpaid but it helps them avoid losing more.

In light of this current situation we would suggest that researchers navigate the situation as follows. (1) as we wait for the law to fully catch up with crowdsourcing it seems like we should heed the argumentation of legal experts already writing about the topic and should follow their suggested classification of the situation. This can set standards for how this work should be viewed and managed, what sorts of principles might apply and so forth. (2) Professional bodies and academic institutions are now beginning to subject research applications involving the use of crowdsourcing to ethics committees and are writing about it in their ethics guidelines – for many in e.g. universities this is becoming an institutional 'fact of life' – they will need to submit their work for prior approval, and so this will impact the way they do research. We want to discuss the key features coming out of both of these domains without offering an exhaustive or precise position, but rather mapping out the general territory and pointing out the key issues at stake. (3) As a pragmatic counterpoint to these professional, technical, and official responses and guides we would also like to offer some comments on best practice and ethical conduct from a mundane perspective, i.e. what should the everyday, human, interpersonal ethics be that operate in this situation? There are now a number of on-line resources that offer best practice guidelines from this perspective, the most detailed of which is provided by the Dynamo project[25], in their guidelines for academic requesters. Their site pro-

---

[24] https://www.mturk.com/mturk/help?helpPage=policies last accessed 14 Jun 2017.
[25] http://wiki.wearedynamo.org/index.php/Guidelines_for_Academic_Requesters last accessed 14 Jun 2017.

vides detail on such matters as pay and conduct and links to external resources on ethics and other guides as well as having a considerable amount of academic and Turker signatories to their guidelines. We believe that by following ordinary practical ethical approaches like these researchers' actions will be compatible with legal and ethical requirements and that these ordinary ethical principles should be followed simply as a demonstration of good faith and courtesy.

When we explore what is good or best practice in relation to crowdsourcing one important strand of discussion is about labour rights, working conditions and employment ethics, the second strand concerns academic ethics, treatment of participants and 'subjects', and national ethics documentation and review boards. The first strand should apply in *all cases* of crowdsourcing use while the second strand should apply as additional principles and practices to a subset of crowdsourcing use; for academic or professional use where the situation is covered by institutional or professional rules regarding research. We would argue strongly that within academic/professional research there are clear differences between cases of crowdsourcing use for data services (e.g. image tagging) and use for, for example, psychological experiments, and thus some differentiation is most likely needed in terms of required principles and practices. However, there will always be marginal cases – and indeed ruling on these cases is a key aspect of ethics committees' work – but there is a general difference in situations in academic or professional research where someone is being employed in a job as opposed to someone being employed as what used to be termed a 'subject' (but now more often as a participant) in an experiment. As stated there is also a third strand – and that is the one of ordinary ethics – which we will discuss as well. Firstly, we think it is a set of foundational principles that should apply in these situations, and therefore it underpins both the legal and formal ethical strands. Secondly, we think it is important to have guidelines that can be used in the current absence of a rigorous legal framework and for situations where ethical scrutiny and approval is not in play, even for research. In these cases we will provide a set of straightforward values and principles to apply to how the work and the relationships are managed, as well as pointing researchers towards relevant detailed resources.

6   The Legal Position

Crowdsourcing companies such as Amazon, with their AMT platform generally have sought to define the situation where they remove themselves from the labour relationship, simply acting as the market facilitator in enabling employers (requesters) to connect with independent contractors (providers). However – the lack of responsibility in this relationship seems a bit more tenuous when you consider that they extract a fee of between 20 and 40% per HIT. Configured (or viewed) in this fashion Amazon basically carries little legal responsibility apart policing the market for illegal use. It does not accept any legal responsibility over the functioning of the labour relationship.

In the US independent contractors are not covered for the following laws: *minimum wage, compensation for overtime, antidiscrimination, family and medical leave, social security, unemployment compensation, protection for unionisation and collective bargaining,* and more [12]. The anomaly, here though, as pointed out by Felsteiner [11], Finkin [12] and others, is that the only reason for these exemptions being applied to independent contractors is that it was aimed at highly qualified and paid professional people mainly doing consultancy work, with the thinking being that they would be more than enough compensated for their work and this would ease any bureaucratic burden on either side that would serve as a barrier to their doing business. The law was never intended to further penalise those in precarious badly-paid work.

The alternative analysis of the legal situation offered by both Felsteiner and Finkin is that crowdwork should be viewed as home-based piece-work in the same way that filling envelopes, craft industries and routine administrative work was 'put-out' to a mass distributed workforce, mainly working from home. While this work has always been a welcome source of income for part of the workforce, with various benefits (working at home and not incurring travel and other expenses, diminished supervision and control, some flexibility on working hours and so forth) it has historically also been favoured by employers due less legal protection combined with the ability to scale production up-and-down easily according to demand without extra cost – both of which can save them a considerable amount of money. Finkin (*ibid.*) points out that digital crowdsourcing also offers (to the employer) a few advantages over traditional home-based piece-work: there is no need to provide any equipment, surveillance can be much greater, and there is less opportunity for sharp practice.

In consideration of home-based piece-work it took a lengthy legal battle until the right to minimum wage and other protections were established, so while the precedent seems sound overall it may take some time for the legal situation to be clarified. As Felsteiner (*ibid.*) points out, one of the main sticking points may be the fact that crowdworkers work for multiple employers on a HIT per HIT basis, rather than a single employer, who would assume legal contractual responsibility as sole employer. However, in the case of Crowdflower, a company that contracts workers to do crowdsourcing work on different platforms (including previously AMT), there has been a definitive ruling that minimum wage should apply[26]. In Europe there are already much stricter labour laws which is one of the reasons why AMT does not operate there, and on balance the evidence suggests that at some point minimum wage will apply to crowdsourcing in the US. All of this suggests that crowdsourcing employers should pre-emptively look to price work at *at least* minimum wage level of the most developed country targeted – in this case that would be $7.25/hour.

7   Professional Ethics

Most nations have developed ethical principles for conducting research basically derived from the following documents: the UN Declaration of

---

[26] http://www.overtimepaylaws.org/federal-court-approves-settlement-in-crowdsourc ing-labor-company-wage-suit/ last accessed 14 Jun 2017.

Human Rights[27], the Nuremberg Code[28], the Declaration of Helsinki [29], and the Belmont Report[30]. In fact, often the terms used in documents about research ethics relate to the key terms in the Belmont report (1979) [20]:

- *Respect*: which covers that people must be treated as their own agents and that people who have diminished capacity in some manner (are very young, do not speak the language, are coping with some other challenges, etc.) have the right to some protection. The notion of respect in research studies is usually implemented through informed consent.
- *Beneficence*: that treating people in an ethical manner goes beyond not just doing no harm but includes the importance of some effort into ensuring their well-being. This concept requires the thorough assessment of the type and extent of the associated risks.
- *Justice*: builds on the idea that injustice can occur from over-burdening a person or a group of people or from denying access to a person or a group of people. The idea of justice is usually reflected in the use of fair distribution and selection of participants.

One can see how these concepts are reflected in most ethics guidelines. Through the 1980s and 1990s most nations have developed ethics boards and associated procedures to ensure that research involving humans is conducted ethically.

To look slightly more closely at one particular national example, in Canada there are three primary federal research funding bodies – one each for health, natural sciences and social sciences. For ensuring that research is conducted ethically they have joined forces forming a tri-council. In August 2010 they released the 2nd version of what they term a living document: *Tri-Council Policy Statement: Ethical Conduct for Research Involving Humans (TCPS)*. They call it a living document because the intention is that it continues to be a work in progress that can be adjusted. The formulation of this document deeply involved the active research community including over 2,000 interviews and 370 briefs. The basic premise is to preserve human dignity through adhering to principles of respect, concern for welfare and justice. In Canada adherence to TCPS is strictly enforced. One cannot get research funding if one does not follow these ethical guidelines. Respect includes factors like making sure that all participants give consent prior to the study starting and that this is open and informed consent. Concern for welfare of participants covers not increasing the risks beyond the risks of everyday life. Justice includes concerns about treating all people equally – so that no one group is either unfairly receiving either more possible harms or

---

[27] http://www.un.org/en/universal-declaration-human-rights/ last accessed 14 Jun 2017.

[28] http://www.cirp.org/library/ethics/nuremberg/ last accessed 14 Jun 2017.

[29] https://www.wma.net/policies-post/wma-declaration-of-helsinki-ethical-principles-for-medical-research-involving-human-subjects/ last accessed 14 Jun 2017.

[30] http://www.hhs.gov/ohrp/humansubjects/guidance/belmont.html last accessed 14 Jun 2017.

more rewards by being involved with the research. This very brief summary does not get into the innumerable subtle details such as the possibility of obtaining ethics board consent to run a study where *deception* is part of the study design but the board authorises the research if it feels that the long term benefit to humans outweighs the short term effects of the deception. For any research to be conducted a detailed ethics proposal must be approved by an ethics board. In Canada running a study with crowdworkers falls under TCPS and experimenters are required to get TCPS approval before commencing. In many countries there will be similar guidelines and procedures to follow, particularly in academic or professional work.

However, if one steps through the normal ethical experimental process, the process for a crowdworker, of necessity, differs.

1. *Informed consent*: the process of informed consent could be thought of as comparable in that similar information can be provided on-line as in person. However, on-line one does not really know that the participant has read the information but one can know that they had the opportunity to do so.
2. *Task or activities*: when the experimenter is there in person they can ensure that the conditions are reasonable with respect to such factors as adequate lighting, reasonable temperature, comfortable situation, etc. For a crowdworker, the experimenter does not really know under what conditions they are completing the activity.
3. *Voluntary activity*: it is important for ethical experiments that the participant knows that they can stop any time. This probably does hold up for on line experiments.
4. *Risk*: since the actual situations are not known, associated risk is not known either.
5. *Debriefing*: while ethical experiments always include the possibility of debriefing where the participant can ask the experimenter for more information or explanations, this is often not a part of the crowdworker experience.

However, there is a fundamental difference in that the crowdworkers are doing the HIT as a job. Their motivation is the pay. In a lab, while there might be some reward, it could be juice and cookies or a gift certificate or possibly some money but is not often thought of as pay and people do not usually make a living being participants. This puts quite a different colouring on the Turkers' activities. Different rights emerge such as the right for a minimum wage (see legal section above). This is further complicated by the fact it is piece-work, and further complicated by the fact it is 'perfect' piece-work. That is a Turker is quite likely to not get paid if the requester does not like the work they have done. The important point to note – is that employment law and minimum wage considerations apply in the vast majority of crowdsourcing situations (especially in microtask based crowdsourcing) just as much as the ethical guidelines and procedures of any given national or professional jurisdiction.

8   Practical Relationship Ethics

Human interaction and relationships are morally ordered and organised all the way down. This is not to say that interaction and relationships continually involve elevated moral questions, seen in the local micro-organisation of talk up to the topics of everyday conversation, although serious moral and ethical questions can and do arise. The key point we want to make here is that participants orient to the organisation of interaction and therefore the management of relationships at the lowest level as having a moral order to do with norms, convention, expectations and trust. When these are broken without apparent due clear reason, people react with moral indignation. Garfinkel [15] brought this into clear view through getting his students to conduct a series of 'breaching experiments' in which they were to break the often unarticulated 'rules' of forms of interaction and relationships. For example, by asking for continual clarification of open but accepted norms of interacting such as responding to 'how are you feeling?' by asking 'mentally or physically?', then when answered 'physically' to again ask for clarification 'muscle ache or in your bones?' and so forth until the interlocutor became often rather annoyed. Or in another case the student was to behave as if they were a 'boarder' in their own (family) home – again causing real consternation to their family. The purpose of these 'breaches' was to demonstrate what normally was simply taken for granted in the ways in which interaction and relationships were managed – what was the trusted context and set of norms that people we expected to adhere to.

The reason for introducing this material in relation to crowdsourcing is that one of its strongest selling-points was the idea that the need for human interaction and relationships could be removed from the work situation – everything could be handled, anonymously and digitally, in cold 'mechanical' transactions. Looking beneath the surface, away from the sparse, emotion-free interface we find that even in these stripped-down interactions and relationships which may be simply comprised of pseudonyms, the microtasks themselves, the speed and form of acceptance or rejection and the pay (or not), there is a whole moral order of interactions and relationships. We see this most clearly in the forum and group discussions concerning how good or bad behaviour, respect or the lack of and so on are inferred often from very small details. Trust in crowdsourcing comes through human relationships even though they are diminished by the distance and the technology: the qualities of the exchanges determine the level of trust from the most basic ways in which impersonal transactions are handled, up to direct communication (it is important and even necessary to communicate at times), and even on to regular employer-employee relationships[31]. The other key point to note is that in general a lot of what we need and expect in terms of relationships and interaction in more conventional work carries over in principle, although sometimes differently in detail, to crowdsourced work: people still want

---

[31] One of the interesting features is that are a number of situations – relatively hidden – where a relatively stable workforce of Turkers work for a given requester over a reasonable period of time.

to be valued, have their work appreciated and to be treated with politeness and respect – although they do generally like the fact that there is a degree of privacy. This really should not surprise us since it is integral to healthy well-functioning human relationships.

9   Conclusions

As a grassroots campaign, two popular initiatives have emerged from a practical approach to ethics: the Dynamo project (see Footnote 26) [43] and the Code of Conduct[32]. The Dynamo project provides a set of guidelines and links to further resources detailing best practices and professional ethics for research, with the added bonus of Turker and requester signatories. The Code of Conduct is an example of a more concise set of principles and guidelines developed in Germany as a joint production between crowdsourcing platforms – Testbirds, clickworker and Streetspotr[33]. For researchers planning to use crowdsourcing, following the guidelines offered in these two campaigns would be a good place to start. Researchers should make themselves aware of the rules and policies of the platform that they are aiming to use, and the rights for different parties involved before they set out to get the crowd to do any crowdwork. Conducting research or supporting a business through crowdwork should serve by promoting respect and trust in the marketplace. For the requesters this has a straightforward practice advantage: it would attract more of the better workers to their microtasks, as well as enhance their reputation as a requester.

We believe developing an understanding of the broader context of ethics in research is important. It is of practical value for researchers and academics using or wanting to use crowdsourcing platforms for their research, or simply to get work done. The information given in this chapter should help them make choices about platforms, microtask design and how they interact with and treat crowdworkers. In this chapter we have discussed in detail who the crowdworkers are, why they do this form of work and how they organise it. We have then set this in context of legal, research and labour ethics. We finished the chapter with an in-depth discussion of legal and ethical issues that are relevant to both the use of crowdworking platforms and the way relationships are managed. We want to conclude this chapter by providing six clear take-away points for people interested in using crowdsourcing:

1. The people completing microtasks on crowdsourcing platforms are overwhelmingly workers providing labour, rather than people volunteering for a good cause or doings microtasks for leisure. Accordingly, they should be paid a decent wage/fee for their services and should be treated with respect and communicated with politely.

---

[32] http://crowdsourcing-code.com/documents/5/Code_of_Conduct_Crowdworking_English_072015 last accessed 14 Jun 2017.

[33] It should be noted that Germany has a strong trade union tradition – and a culture of cooperation between companies and workers that persists to this day, and that it has been progressive in its approach to crowdsourcing labour rights.

2. Building a good reputation as a requester will make microtasks attractive to skilled, trustworthy crowdworkers. A good reputation comprises of a selection of the following attributes: good pay, prompt pay, is fair, polite, good at communicating, has well designed tasks (nice interfaces, function well, clear instructions), posts batch tasks regularly.
3. Following ethical guidelines and engaging in productive communication and relationships with crowdworkers should help maximise the effectiveness in using these platforms and gaining high quality results for tests, experiments and any microtasks in general. In this chapter we have described some ways in which this can be put into practice.
4. Different platforms have different orientations towards governance, care of those using the sites, worker rights and pay. You may wish to choose a platform on an ethical basis, however, you may also use a platform like AMT – which has a laissez-faire approach to governance – in an ethical manner.
5. You can choose between platforms as a means of accessing workforces with different demographic constitutions and different skills sets or different task capacities. You may want to look further than simple cost in choosing a platform such as technological support and expertise offered by platforms. This is crucial as this can help you avoid hidden costs associated with design problems as well as avoiding frustrating the workers.
6. Academic work making use of crowdsourcing often requires ethics approval, and even when this is not the case researchers should still follow professional ethics and use the ideas from ethical research to interact with their participants in an ethical manner. A number of sets of codes and guidelines on ethical use of platforms are readily accessible and are referenced in this chapter.

Acknowledgment. This book chapter is dedicated to David Martin who was a fantastic, motivating and inspiring researcher, who unexpectedly passed away in the summer of 2016. This book chapter was one of his final projects, on a subject that he cared about deeply – the people who are behind the scenes, the life and blood of online platforms like AMT: the crowdworkers. Through his ethnomethodological work, he brought forward the working conditions faced by the workers, advocating to bring fairness and humanness to crowdsourcing through technology design and conscious implementation of professional ethics. The authors are glad to have met him at the Dagstuhl Seminar and to have worked with him together on this book chapter. We have lost a valuable member of the academic community, and a good friend.

Appendix: Survey Data

See Tables 2, 3, 4, 5, 6, 7, 8, 9, 10, 11, 12 and 13.

Table 2. Distribution of *Gender* observed for AMT workers (survey studies and on MTurk Tracker).

Gender	AMT US	AMT US 2015–2016	AMT IN	AMT IN 2015–2016
Female	45.56%	55.25%	32.56%	37.74%
Male	54.44%	44.75%	67.44%	62.26%

Table 3. Distribution of *Gender* observed for Microworkers and Crowdee workers using survey studies.

Gender	MW developing	MW Western	MW total	Crowdee
Female	16.39%	32.49%	24.74%	33.47%
Male	83.61%	67.51%	75.26%	66.53%

Table 4. Distribution of *Age* observed for AMT workers (survey studies and on MTurk Tracker).

Age	AMT US	AMT US 2015–2016	AMT IN	AMT IN 2015–2016
18–26	12.61%	23.07%	9.97%	20.45%
27–32	24.98%	26.67%	37.23%	36.18%
33–40	25.26%	23.32%	22.92%	25.68%
41–55	29.57%	19.97%	21.48%	13.98%
56+	7.58%	6.98%	8.40%	3.72%

Table 5. Distribution of *Age* observed for Microworkers and Crowdee workers using survey studies.

Age	MW developing	MW Western	MW total	Crowdee
18–26	51.37%	30.96%	40.79%	40.25%
27–32	25.68%	24.37%	25.00%	30.51%
33–40	14.75%	25.38%	20.26%	19.07%
41–55	7.10%	17.26%	12.37%	8.05%
56+	1.09%	2.03%	1.58%	2.12%

Table 6. Distribution of *Household Income* observed for AMT workers (survey studies and on MTurk Tracker). Please note that for the MTurk tracker data, the data is not available for all income classes (rows) and is therefore aggregated over two classes.

Household income	AMT US	AMT US 2015–2016	AMT IN	AMT IN 2015–2016
Less than $10,000	7.78%	7.10%	53.49%	44.78%
Between $10,000 and $19,999	14.44%	36.69%	18.60%	41.00%
Between $20,000 and $39,999	20.00%		12.79%	
Between $40,000 and $59,999	24.44%	20.82%	9.30%	6.76%
Between $60,000 and $79,999	12.22%	23.80%	5.81%	6.44%
Between $80,000 and $99,999	13.33%		0.00%	
$100,000 or more	7.78%	11.59%	0.00%	1.02%

Table 7. Distribution of *Household Income* observed for Microworkers and Crowdee workers using survey studies. 22.18% of Crowdee participants did not report their household income.

Gender	MW developing	MW Western	MW total	Crowdee
Less than $10,000	61.75%	37.95%	49.47%	23.43%
Between $10,000 and $19,999	21.86%	22.56%	22.22%	12.13%
Between $20,000 and $39,999	9.84%	17.95%	14.02%	18.41%
Between $40,000 and $59,999	4.92%	10.26%	7.67%	11.30%
Between $60,000 and $79,999	0.55%	6.67%	3.70%	7.53%
Between $80,000 and $99,999	0.00%	2.05%	1.06%	2.51%
$100,000 or more	1.09%	2.56%	1.85%	2.51%

Table 8. Distribution of *Household Size* (including the worker) observed for AMT workers (survey studies and on MTurk Tracker).

Household size	AMT US	AMT US 2015–2016	AMT IN	AMT IN 2015–2016
1	16.67%	20.09%	0.00%	4.21%
2	31.11%	30.35%	5.81%	10.27%
3	23.33%	20.57%	38.37%	26.58%
4	16.67%	17.24%	22.09%	34.45%
5+	12.22%	11.74%	33.72%	24.49%

Table 9. Distribution of *Household Size* (including the worker) observed for Microworkers and Crowdee workers using survey studies.

Household size	MW developing	MW Western	MW total	Crowdee
1	3.85%	13.71%	8.97%	16.10%
2	8.24%	18.27%	13.46%	39.41%
3	18.13%	27.92%	23.22%	24.15%
4	34.07%	24.37%	29.02%	12.71%
5+	35.71%	15.74%	25.33%	7.63%

Table 10. Distribution of highest *Education Level* achieved observed for all platforms using survey studies.

Education level	AMT US	AMT IN	MW Western	MW developing	MW total	Crowdee
Not complete high school	1.11%	0.00%	3.06%	1.10%	2.12%	2.93%
High school/GED	23.33%	2.33%	20.92%	11.60%	16.45%	28.45%
Some college	36.67%	2.33%	23.98%	14.92%	19.63%	35.56%
Bachelor's degree	23.33%	56.98%	38.78%	55.80%	46.95%	15.90%
Master's degree	11.11%	37.21%	11.73%	14.36%	13.00%	16.74%
Adv. graduate work or Ph.D.	4.44%	1.16%	1.53%	2.21%	1.86%	0.41%

Table 11. Distribution of *Employment Status* of crowd workers from all platforms using survey studies.

Employment status	AMT US	AMT IN	MW Western	MW developing	MW total	Crowdee
Going to school	3.33%	1.16%	11.34%	10.99%	11.17%	37.29%
Keeping house	24.44%	6.98%	11.34%	6.59%	9.04%	–
Working part time	15.56%	26.74%	29.38%	37.91%	33.51%	33.05%
Working full time	44.44%	56.98%	32.47%	37.36%	34.84%	19.92%
Retired	0.00%	1.16%	1.03%	0.55%	0.80%	–
Unable to work	8.89%	3.49%	6.19%	0.55%	3.46%	–
Other	3.33%	3.49%	8.25%	6.04%	7.18%	9.75%

Table 12. Distribution of *Times Crowd Workers Spent on All Platforms* (per week).

Time	AMT US	AMT IN	MW Western	MW developing	MW total	Crowdee
<4 h	1.11%	1.16%	17.77%	19.67%	22.11%	89.50%
4–10 h	22.22%	20.93%	36.04%	25.14%	31.32%	7.76%
10–15 h	14.44%	11.63%	16.75%	14.75%	12.11%	1.83%
15–25 h	24.44%	18.60%	12.18%	9.29%	10.79%	0.46%
25+ h	37.78%	47.67%	17.26%	30.60%	23.68%	0.46%

Table 13. Distribution of *Stated Task Approval Rate* of crowd workers on all platforms. For the Crowdee platform, no data is available for the stated task approval rate.

Approval rate	AMT US	AMT IN	MW Western	MW developing	MW total	Crowdee
[0, 85]	0.00%	3.49%	44.16%	63.39%	53.42%	n/a
(85, 90]	0.00%	1.16%	23.35%	14.21%	18.95%	
(90, 95]	1.11%	11.63%	17.77%	4.37%	11.32%	
(95, 98]	2.22%	19.77%	6.60%	8.74%	7.63%	
(98, 100]	96.67%	63.95%	8.12%	8.74%	8.42%	

References

1. Antin, J., Shaw, A.: Social desirability bias and self-reports of motivation: a study of Amazon mechanical turk in the US and India. In: Proceedings of the SIGCHI Conference on Human Factors in Computing Systems (CHI 2012), pp. 2925–2934 (2012)
2. Bederson, B.B., Quinn, A.J.: Web workers unite! Addressing challenges of online laborers. In: CHI 2011 Extended Abstracts on Human Factors in Computing Systems, pp. 97–106. ACM (2011)
3. Berg, J.: Income security in the on-demand economy: findings and policy lessons from a survey of crowdworkers. Comp. Labor Law Policy J. **37**(3) (2016)
4. Bourne, K.A., Forman, P.J.: Living in a culture of overwork an ethnographic study of flexibility. J. Manag. Inquiry **23**(1), 68–79 (2014)
5. Brawley, A.M., Pury, C.L.: Work experiences on MTurk: job satisfaction, turnover, and information sharing. Comput. Hum. Behav. **54**, 531–546 (2016)
6. Callison-Burch, C.: Crowd-workers: aggregating information across turkers to help them find higher paying work. In: Second AAAI Conference on Human Computation and Crowdsourcing (2014)
7. Chandler, J., Mueller, P., Paolacci, G.: Nonnavet among Amazon mechanical turk workers: consequences and solutions for behavioral researchers. Behav. Res. Methods **46**(1), 112–130 (2014)
8. Crary, J.: 24/7: Late Capitalism and the Ends of Sleep. Verso Books, New York (2013)
9. Deci, E., Ryan, R.: Intrinsic Motivation and Self-determination in Human Behavior. Plenum Press, New York (1985)
10. Difallah, D.E., Catasta, M., Demartini, G., Ipeirotis, P.G., Cudr-Mauroux, P.: The dynamics of micro-task crowdsourcing: the case of Amazon MTurk. In: Proceedings of the 24th International Conference on World Wide Web (WWW 2015), pp. 238–247. ACM (2015)
11. Felstiner, A.: Working the crowd: employment and labor law in the crowdsourcing industry. Berkeley J. Employ. Labor Law **32**, 143–203 (2011)
12. Finkin, M.: Beclouded work in historical perspective. Comp. Labor Law Policy J. **37**(3) (2016)
13. Fort, K., Adda, G., Cohen, K.B.: Amazon mechanical turk: gold mine or coal mine? Comput. Linguist. **37**(2), 413–420 (2011)
14. Gagné, M., Deci, E.L.: Self-determination theory and work motivation. J. Organ. Behav. **26**(4), 331–362 (2005)

15. Garfinkel, H.: A conception of and experiments with "trust" as a condition of concerted stable actions. In: The Production of Reality: Essays and Readings on Social Interaction, pp. 381–392 (1963)

16. Gupta, N.: An ethnographic study of crowdwork via Amazon mechanical turk in India. Unpublished manuscript (2017). http://eprints.nottingham.ac.uk/41062/

17. Gupta, N., Martin, D., Hanrahan, B.V., O'Neill, J.: Turk-life in India. In: Proceedings of the 18th International Conference on Supporting Group Work, pp. 1–11. ACM (2014)

18. Hanhart, P., Korshunov, P., Ebrahimi, T.: Crowdsourcing evaluation of high dynamic range image compression. In: SPIE Optical Engineering + Applications, p. 92170D. International Society for Optics and Photonics (2014)

19. Hanrahan, B.V., Willamowski, J.K., Swaminathan, S., Martin, D.B.: TurkBench: rendering the market for turkers. In: Proceedings of the 33rd Annual ACM Conference on Human Factors in Computing Systems, pp. 1613–1616. ACM (2015)

20. Health UDo, Services H et al.: The Belmont report. Office for Human Research Protections (OHRP) (1979). Accessed 19 Nov 2008

21. Hirth, M., Hofeld, T., Tran-Gia, P.: Anatomy of a crowdsourcing platform-using the example of microworkers.com. In: 2011 Fifth International Conference on Innovative Mobile and Internet Services in Ubiquitous Computing (IMIS), pp. 322–329. IEEE (2011)

22. Ipeirotis, P.G.: Demographics of mechanical turk (2010)

23. Ipeirotis, P.G.: Analyzing the Amazon mechanical turk marketplace. XRDS **17**(2), 16–21 (2010)

24. Ipeirotis, P.: Demographics of mechanical turk: now live! April 2015. http://www.behind-the-enemy-lines.com/2015/04/demographics-of-mechanical-turk-now.html

25. Irani, L.C., Silberman, M.S.: Turkopticon: interrupting worker invisibility in Amazon mechanical turk. In: Proceedings of CHI 2013 (CHI 2013), pp. 611–620. ACM (2013)

26. Kaufmann, N., Schulze, T., Veit, D.: More than fun and money. Worker motivation in crowdsourcing: a study on mechanical turk. In: Proceedings of the Seventeenth Americas Conference on Information Systems, pp. 1–11 (2011)

27. Kazai, G., Kamps, J., Milic-Frayling, N.: The face of quality in crowdsourcing relevance labels: demographics, personality and labeling accuracy. In: Proceedings of the 21st ACM International Conference on Information and Knowledge Management, pp. 2583–2586. ACM (2012)

28. Kittur, A., Nickerson, J.V., Bernstein, M., Gerber, E., Shaw, A., Zimmerman, J., Lease, M., Horton, J.: The future of crowd work. In: Proceedings of the 2013 Conference on Computer Supported Cooperative Work, p. 1301. ACM Press (2013)

29. Kuek, S.C., Paradi-Guilford, C., Fayomi, T., Imaizumi, S., Ipeirotis, P., Pina, P., Singh, M.: The global opportunity in online outsourcing. Technical report, The World Bank (2015)

30. Marshall, C.C., Shipman, F.M.: Experiences surveying the crowd: reflections on methods, participation, and reliability. In: Proceedings of the 5th Annual ACM Web Science Conference, pp. 234–243. ACM (2013)

31. Martin, D., Hanrahan, B.V., O'Neill, J., Gupta, N.: Being a turker. In: Proceedings of the 17th ACM Conference on Computer Supported Cooperative Work & Social Computing, pp. 224–235. ACM (2014)

32. Martin, D., O'Neill, J., Gupta, N., Hanrahan, B.V.: Turking in a global labour market. Comput. Support. Coop. Work (CSCW) **25**(1), 39–77 (2016)

33. Mason, W., Suri, S.: Conducting behavioral research on Amazons mechanical turk. Behav. Res. Methods **44**(1), 1–23 (2012)
34. Morozov, E.: To Save Everything, Click Here: The Folly of Technological Solutionism. PublicAffairs (2013)
35. Naderi, B., Polzehl, T., Beyer, A., Pilz, t., Möller, S.: Crowdee: mobile crowdsourcing micro-task platform - for celebrating the diversity of languages. In: Proceedings of the 15th Annual Conference of the International Speech Communication Association (Interspeech 2014). IEEE, September 2014
36. Naderi, B., Wechsung, I., Möller, S.: Effect of being observed on the reliability of responses in crowdsourcing micro-task platforms. In: 2015 Seventh International Workshop on Quality of Multimedia Experience (QoMEX), pp. 1–2. IEEE (2015)
37. Naderi, B., Wechsung, I., Möller, S.: Crowdsourcing work motivation scale: development and validation for crowdsourcing micro-task platforms. In prepration (2016)
38. O'Neill, J., Martin, D.: Relationship-based business process crowdsourcing? In: Kotzé, P., Marsden, G., Lindgaard, G., Wesson, J., Winckler, M. (eds.) INTERACT 2013. LNCS, vol. 8120, pp. 429–446. Springer, Heidelberg (2013). doi:10.1007/978-3-642-40498-6_33
39. Paolacci, G., Chandler, J.: Inside the Turk understanding mechanical turk as a participant pool. Curr. Dir. Psychol. Sci. **23**(3), 184–188 (2014)
40. Peer, E., Samat, S., Brandimarte, L., Acquisti, A.: Beyond the turk: an empirical comparison of alternative platforms for crowdsourcing online behavioral research (2015). http://dx.doi.org/10.2139/ssrn.2594183
41. Ross, J., Irani, L., Silberman, M., Zaldivar, A., Tomlinson, B.: Who are the crowdworkers? Shifting demographics in mechanical turk. In: CHI 2010 Extended Abstracts on Human Factors in Computing Systems, pp. 2863–2872. ACM (2010)
42. Ryan, R.M., Deci, E.L.: Self-determination theory and the facilitation of intrinsic motivation, social development, and well-being. Am. Psychol. **55**(1), 68 (2000)
43. Salehi, N., Irani, L.C., Bernstein, M.S., Alkhatib, A., Ogbe, E., Milland, K., et al.: We are dynamo: overcoming stalling and friction in collective action for crowd workers. In: Proceedings of the 33rd Annual ACM Conference on Human Factors in Computing Systems, pp. 1621–1630. ACM (2015)
44. Silberman, M., Irani, L., Ross, J.: Ethics and tactics of professional crowdwork. XRDS Crossroads ACM Mag. Stud. **17**(2), 39–43 (2010)
45. Silberman, M.S.: What's fair? Rational action and its residuals in an electronic market. Unpublished manuscript (2010). http://www.scribd.com/doc/86592724/Whats-Fair
46. Silberman, S., Milland, K., LaPlante, R., Ross, J., Irani, L.: Stop citing Ross et al. 2010, Who are the crowdworkers? (2015). https://medium.com/@silberman/stop-citing-ross-et-al-2010-who-are-the-crowdworkers-b3b9b1e8d300

Crowdsourcing Technology to Support Academic Research

Matthias Hirth[1](✉), Jason Jacques[2](✉), Peter Rodgers[3](✉),
Ognjen Scekic[4](✉), and Michael Wybrow[5](✉)

[1] University of Würzburg, Würzburg, Germany
matthias.hirth@informatik.uni-wuerzburg.de
[2] University of Cambridge, Cambridge, UK
jtj21@cam.ac.uk
[3] University of Kent, Canterbury, UK
P.J.Rodgers@kent.ac.uk
[4] TU Wien, Vienna, Austria
oscekic@gmail.com
[5] Monash University, Melbourne, Australia
michael.wybrow@monash.edu

1 Introduction

Many academic research studies have small numbers of participants. One reason for this is the difficulty of finding participants to take part in research, especially when people with certain characteristics are required. Most researchers would welcome additional participants. As such, there is growing interest from researchers in the use of crowdsourcing platforms due to the large populations of workers. We use the term "worker", sometimes called crowdworker, to mean the remote user who performs the tasks.

Despite the diversity of current commercial crowdsourcing platforms, most of them lack of support for academic research and its special needs. In this chapter we discuss the possibilities for practical improvement of crowdsourced studies through adaption of technological solutions.

As of April 2016 Crowdsourcing.org[1] lists over 130 web sites focusing on crowd labour. Noticeably absent from this list are large platforms like Witmart (formerly Zhubajie)[2] which itself has about 13 million users. Most of these commercial platform providers focus mainly on large scale requesters with repetitive types of microtasks. We use the term "requester" to mean the person or organisation that places tasks on the platform for workers to complete. The special needs and the comparatively low number of tasks submitted by researchers make them unattractive as main business customers for most providers.

Current crowdsourcing systems do not fully support scientific research as the requirements are often very different from common commercial use cases. While

---

[1] Crowdsourcing LLC. "List of Crowdsourcing Providers". http://www.crowdsour
cing.org last accessed Apr 2016.
[2] ZBJ Network Inc. "Witmart". http://www.witmart.com last accessed 14 Jun 2017.

© Springer International Publishing AG 2017
D. Archambault et al. (Eds.): Evaluation in the Crowd, LNCS 10264, pp. 70–95, 2017.
DOI: 10.1007/978-3-319-66435-4_4

platforms like Prolific Academic[3] aim to fill this niche, they still fall short of providing many of the necessary features. Researchers will often try to overcome the limitations of a platform by designing specialised software tools, e.g., for crowdsourced Quality of Experience tests (see Chap. 7). However, as these software tools are only loosely coupled to the actual crowdsourcing provider they cannot compete with the full potential of a commercial crowdsourcing platform with integrated support for academic research.

This chapter is focused on the needs of research studies performed on commercial crowdsourcing systems. We do not include internal enterprise crowd systems, or other closed work allocation systems such as EasyChair, as these typically lack the flexibility necessary to be used for such research. We discuss existing platforms and propose enhanced features, many of which would be relatively easy to implement, that would greatly assist the adoption of crowdsourcing as a basis for performing research studies.

This chapter is organised into two main sections: Sect. 2 provides an overview of the current state-of-the-art in crowdsourcing technology, whilst Sect. 3 has a detailed discussion of possible new technology and features. This second section includes Subsect. 3.1 on possible improvements to the user management of crowdsourcing platforms; Subsect. 3.2 on technological solutions to payment issues; Subsect. 3.3 on the ethical aspect of technology for crowdsourcing; Subsect. 3.4 on further hardware and instrumentation that might be adopted for crowdsourced studies; Subsect. 3.5 on the potential for advanced study designs provided for by technological improvements. Finally Sect. 4 gives our conclusions.

2 Existing Crowdsourcing Platforms

Crowdsourcing aims to leverage a huge and diverse set of people to efficiently solve tasks that cannot easily be solved computationally. This is made possible by online platforms providing tools for requester users to create microtasks and make these available to worker users. In the following section we give a brief overview of the basic functionality currently available in commercial crowdsourcing platforms, where workers are financially rewarded for completed microtasks. Non-commercial crowdsourcing approaches, like posting microtask on social networks or online communities, or platforms focusing on voluntary participation, e.g., *Galaxy Zoo* or *Zooniverse* [40,41], are not considered as the implementation effort required to develop such platforms means they are only applicable to large scale projects. Thereafter given this brief overview of the basic functionality, we present a coarse-grained categorisation scheme for those platforms that helps to identify a suitable platform type for specific use cases. Finally, we discuss the suitability of current commercial systems for use in academic research.

2.1 Functions of a Crowdsourcing Platform

Crowdsourcing platforms act as mediator between workers and requesters. However, most platform operators focus more on providing features that benefit

---

[3] Prolific Academic. "Prolific". http://prolific.ac/ last accessed 14 Jun 2017.

requesters, since they are the customers of the service. In general, crowdsourcing platforms aim to support requesters in three main aspects: (1) managing the crowdsourcing workforce, (2) creation of the microtasks, and (3) processing of the microtasks.

Maintaining a large and diverse workforce is one of the key aspects in crowdsourcing but also one of the most challenging ones. One reason is that an equilibrium between requesters and workers is required. That is, enough microtasks need to be submitted to keep the workers active, and enough workers need to be available to complete the available microtasks within the time constraints of the requesters. Another reason is the complexity of the remuneration for international workers, due to the different banking systems and legal constraints. Both aspects are completely abstracted for a requester on a commercial crowdsourcing platform. Moreover, some crowdsourcing platforms also offer more advanced features for requesters to maintain specialised groups of worker, e.g., based on demographic properties, worker skills, or requester-specific criteria.

The creation of microtasks can be supported by crowdsourcing platform providers both on a technical and conceptional level. On the technical level, a crowdsourcing platform can provide the infrastructure required to run a microtask. This can include resources like online storage for image upload, or software tools that can be used to generate surveys. On the conceptional level, crowdsourcing providers may provide best practices for microtask design, may recheck the requester's microtask design and correct common pitfalls, or may even create the microtask design for the requester.

Finally, crowdsourcing platforms provide means to process the microtasks submitted by the requesters. Here, the tasks might again be preprocessed by the platform, e.g., tasks may be replicated in order to enable quality control via majority voting. Then the microtasks are distributed to the workers. This can be either in an open call, i.e., the microtasks are publicly posted and any workers can decide to work on them, or a sophisticated worker selection can be performed, e.g., based on the workers' skills. After the workers complete the microtask, an optional post-processing of the results can be applied. This may include quality control or the aggregation of multiple submissions.

While all crowdsourcing platforms generally implement these three building blocks, different commercial providers put different emphases on each of them. In order to find an appropriate crowdsourcing platform for a specific research task, it needs to be clear which functions are required to successfully crowdsource the task. Consider a psychological study. Here, detailed knowledge about the demographic data of the participants can be of interest, i.e., detailed user profiles are required. In contrast, an image tagging task which is intended to create training data for a machine learning algorithm requires high quality results and consequently quality assurance mechanisms within the platform would be desirable.

2.2   Types of Crowdsourcing Platforms

As an intermediate step of identifying an appropriate platform for research tasks we will discuss three different types of crowdsourcing platforms: *Mediator crowd-*

sourcing platforms, *specialised crowdsourcing platforms*, and *platforms focusing on crowd provision* [22]. This coarse-grained categorisation can easily be applied to most existing crowdsourcing platforms and can be used for a first filtering of possible platforms. Figure 1 illustrates the types of crowdsourcing platforms and their interactions. In the following we briefly summarise the main aspects of the platform types and illustrate them with some commercial providers as described in [22].

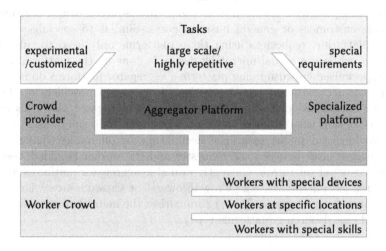

Fig. 1. Classification of crowdsourcing platforms.

Crowd providers are the most generic type of platform and mainly focus on building large-scale worker crowds. They provide means for accessing and managing the available workforce, e.g., filtering mechanisms, demographic information about the workers, and support for worker remuneration. Due to the direct access to the workers, these platforms allow for easily creating experimental tasks or building specialised enterprise solutions. However, due to this flexibility it is generally not possible for the platform operator to provide general purpose quality control mechanisms suitable for every use case. Platforms like AMT,[4] Microworkers,[5] RapidWorkers,[6] or ShortTask[7] are typical crowd providers. In a broader sense online Social Networks can be considered crowd providers. They can provide access to a large workforce but do not implement task routing or worker management systems.

Specialised crowdsourcing platforms maintain their own worker crowd and only focus either on a limited subset of workers (Crowdee[8] or Streetspotr[9]) or

---

[4] "Amazon Mechanical Turk". http://www.mturk.com last accessed 14 Jun 2017.
[5] "Microworkers". https://microworkers.com last accessed 14 Jun 2017.
[6] "RapidWorkers". http://rapidworkers.com/ last accessed 14 Jun 2017.
[7] "ShortTask". http://www.shorttask.com/ last accessed 14 Jun 2017.
[8] "Crowdee". https://www.crowdee.de last accessed 14 Jun 2017.
[9] "Streetspotr". https://streetspotr.com/ last accessed 14 Jun 2017.

a specific type of microtask, e.g., Microtask[10] that mainly focuses on text digitalisation. Specialised crowdsourcing platforms like Microtask provide elaborate workflows for certain use cases. In this case, the users of the platform have no influence on the actual microtask design, and only contribute to the data that will be processed. Platforms focusing on specialised workers, for example, with specific devices or skills, allow a more flexible microtask design that can be customised by the requester. However, there are often more restrictions on the microtask design than on crowd provider platforms.

Aggregator platforms focus on developing crowdsourcing-based solutions for large scale customers or general business cases. Similar to specialised crowdsourcing platforms, requesters using these platforms only need to submit the input data, while the actual microtask design is done by the platform. In contrast to specialised crowdsourcing platforms, aggregator platforms do not maintain their own crowd, but use the workers from crowd providers or the services from specialised platforms. Moreover, some aggregator platforms offer a self-service option where requesters can freely design their microtasks. As with crowd providers, no quality assurance mechanisms are offered here but the additional business layer between the requester and the worker is added, resulting in higher costs per microtask. Currently available aggregator platforms focus on business related microtasks, e.g., CrowdFlower[11] or CrowdSource[12] for content moderation or image tagging. Table 1 summarises the main characteristics of the introduced crowdsourcing platforms types.

Table 1. Crowdsourcing platform categories

	Crowd provider	Aggregator platform	Specialised crowdsourcing platform
Own worker pool	Yes	Yes	No
Costs per microtask	Low	High	Medium
Focus on specific microtask set	No	Yes	Yes
Predefined quality assurance mechanisms for specific microtasks	No	Yes	Yes
Unfiltered access to workers	Yes	No	No
Suitable for research tasks	Yes	Sometimes	Sometimes
Exemplary platform providers	AMT, Microworkers	CrowdFlower, CrowdSource	Microtask, TaskRabbit, Streetspotr

---

[10] "Microtask". http://www.microtask.com/ last accessed 14 Jun 2017.

[11] "CrowdFlower". http://www.crowdflower.com last accessed 14 Jun 2017.

[12] "CrowdSource". http://www.crowdsource.com last accessed 14 Jun 2017.

2.3 Applicability of Crowdsourcing Platform Types for Research

For most scientific use-cases *crowd providers* are the platform of choice. They allow direct, unfiltered access to the workers, enabling researchers to conduct tests on, for example, novel quality assurance mechanisms or incentive schemes, or conduct sociological or demographic studies. Moreover, the platforms usually allow requesters to create individual microtask interfaces on external servers that are required for research tasks or research on task design principles. However, running research tasks on *crowd provider* platforms usually requires higher conceptual efforts, for example, because no quality assurance mechanisms are applied by the platform. Also the higher technical requirements cannot be neglected, as the microtask interface has to be provided by the requester, possibly along with the infrastructure for the workers to work on.

Sometimes there is a need to run studies exclusively on specific user groups, for example, crowd-sensing tasks or studies about perceptual quality on smart devices. In this case, *specialised platforms* can be helpful, as some of them provide easy access to those groups. However, *specialised platforms* often offer predefined interfaces for the workers, thus it might be difficult to run studies on these platforms. Moreover, *specialised platforms* focusing on a specific task, such as transcription of handwriting, are only of value for the research community if exactly that task is required.

Aggregator platforms are most suitable for research tasks that are closely related to the main business focus of the platform, for example, tagging of different image content. In this case *aggregator platforms* can support the scientists with means of quality control, interface design guidelines, or even provide the required infrastructure. If the task is not related to the platform's main business cases, *aggregator platforms* provide as little help as *crowd providers*. However, *aggregator platforms* sometimes apply filtering mechanisms to their user base that are not transparent to the requester. Thus, the crowdsourcing participants might be biased due to these mechanisms, while the researchers are not aware of this fact. Further, *aggregator platforms* are often more expensive then *crowd provider* as they represent an additional commercial layer between the requester and the workers.

2.4 Use of Existing Crowdsourcing Platforms for Research

Most existing crowdsourcing platforms can be assigned to one of the previously mentioned categories, which can serve as a first step towards finding the right platform for a scientific task. However, even if platforms belong to the same category, they can still differ in the supported types of tasks, demographics of their users [20], and their features for requesters and workers [48]. In particular, the platform access, the diversity of participants, the costs per microtask and for qualification tests, payment features, the procedure to acquire testers, and the integration of the measurement software into the platform must be considered while selecting a platform for crowdsourcing scientific tasks.

AMT initially became popular for collecting research data, especially for US researchers. However, access to AMT is restricted both for requesters and workers in most countries, resulting in biased platform demographics. Due to the platform's payout policy,[13] the vast majority of workers are from India and the USA.[14] Requesters needed to provide a U.S. billing address,[15] which also significantly limits access for non-US users. Even, this restriction was loosened in 2016, mid of 2017 it is only possible to register as requester from 27 different countries. To overcome these restrictions, Vakhara et al. [48] and Peer et al. [39]) tried to find and evaluate alternative platforms for crowdsourcing research, but finding an appropriate platform is difficult due to the high diversity of the platforms, their sheer number, and newly emerging enterprises.

One commercial crowdsourcing platform aimed at scientific tasks is Prolific Academic.[16] They provide extensive demographic information and support the usage of well-known external survey tools like SurveyMonkey.[17] Prolific Academic is a young platform, so the sustainability of their business model is still unproven. Additionally, it needs to be determined if crowds exclusively working on scientific tasks, like surveys and subjective evaluations, will become highly biased. It has already been shown that even workers on AMT exhibit a growing non-naivety to typical research tasks [6].

The remainder of this chapter will shed light on some of the technical aspects that would significantly improve the usability of crowdsourcing platforms for use in research.

3   Proposed Features to Support Academic Research

The previous section outlined the capabilities of existing crowdsourcing platforms. This section examines the technological possibilities for enhancing such platforms to support their use in academic research.

3.1   User Management

In this subsection we look at desirable features aimed at improving the crowdsourcing experience for both academic requesters and their workers. Problems with population sampling have been identified by various studies [7,15],

---

[13] Amazon.com, Inc. "Worker Web Site FAQs". https://www.mturk.com/mturk/help?helpPage=worker#how_paid last accessed 14 Jun 2017.

[14] Panos Ipeirotis. "mTurk Tracker". http://demographics.mturk-tracker.com/#/countries/all last accessed 14 Jun 2017.

[15] Amazon, Inc. "Support for Requesters outside US on MTurk". https://requester.mturk.com/help/faq#do_support_outside_us last accessed 14 Jun 2017.

[16] Prolific Academic. "Prolific". http://prolific.ac/ last accessed 14 Jun 2017.

[17] SurveyMonkey Inc. "SurveyMonkey". https://surveymonkey.com last accessed 14 Jun 2017.

hence greater access to reliable user profiles is likely to reduce these issues. In many cases existing crowdsourcing platforms or third party add-ons have provided basic functionality, but more advanced and integrated features may allow requesters to target the most appropriate worker and so get better data. For the worker this leads to lower rejection rates for their work and makes it easier for them to find the best paying microtasks.

3.1.1 Worker Profiling

Current crowdsourcing platforms do include the ability to find limited user profile information, usually about the abilities of the workers in relation to microtasks performed. However, information about basic demographics such as age, sex, location or education level is typically not accessible. Either this information is not stored by the platform or is hidden from view. Researchers often need access to this information, either to restrict a study to a particular subset of the population, or to examine differences in results from various demographics. For instance, a study might look into the differences in understanding of computer security by different age groups. However, it should be noted that providing increased information about workers is not without risk to their privacy. As the number of data points about a worker increases, the potential for requesters to be able to successfully use de-anonymisation techniques to find their identity also increases [37].

As a result, demographics should be released to requesters with caution. Perhaps a more in-depth relationship between requester and platform might allow access to such information. One could imagine the requirement for evidence of ethics approval, plus a demonstrated commitment to data and worker confidentiality as a subset of the requirements for such certification. Similarly, those workers who could verify their profile and were happy for it to be released to certified requesters could access more interesting and well paid work. Characteristics such as physical attributes or medical conditions may be also be included in such demographics, but this sensitive data introduces further legal and moral issues.

Abilities and characteristics can be measured by computerised tests. There are numerous tests for English comprehension, colour blindness and other features of vision [16]. There are batteries of tests for various cognitive abilities including spatial, intelligence and memory [3], including the well known, but controversial IQ tests. Personality may also be measured, for instance, using Big Five Inventory tests [2]. Workers declaring background knowledge and domain expertise in a particular area may also be of interest, and can be verified online. For example, a requester may be interested in examining the abilities of computer programmers when presented with particular problems. However, testing online leads to concerns about cheating and also tuning to perceived biases from requesters. The latter is particularly an issue in personality tests. Cheating, where the worker gains help from others, can be mitigated to some extent by the platform initiating the tests randomly, rather than the worker starting the test at their convenience when they are prepared and have resources to hand. The issues with tuning test results are more difficult to counter. A major impact on avoiding problems of this sort is to increase the trust within the worker, requester and platform relationship. One factor here is the number of microtasks that have an upper bound in tests, rather than a lower bound. For instance, researchers may be interested in evaluating computer interfaces for those with low cognitive ability. When there are sufficient microtasks that have an upper bound on test results, cheating on such tests is less of a problem as there is no obvious advantage to having a better performance.

3.1.2   Worker Hardware Details

Another dimension of user management that is subtly different from worker profiling involves understanding the technology that the worker is using to perform any particular microtask on. Gaining access to detailed information about screen size and resolution, input mechanism, operating system, internet connection speed—even whether the participant is having to scroll within the page to answer the question—would be useful information in many studies. This sort of information could allow a requester to restrict studies to those with a minimum screen size, or only to those accessing the study via a mobile device.

3.1.3   Reputation Management

The reputation workers have on crowdsourcing systems is a powerful driver of behaviour as it encourages workers to be more accurate and reliable. Workers concerned about maintaining their reputation are more likely to accurately state their abilities and skills. The main motivation for workers to maintain a good reputation is that they can get better paid jobs (see Sect. 3.2 on payments and motivation). At present worker reputation is restricted to single sites and revolves around measuring job performance accuracy and acceptance/rejection rates from requesters. Requesters also have a reputation and those with good standing attract more and better workers. Requester reputation is typically measured by workers, and can be across a number of factors, such as promptness of payment and generosity. Worker reputation is managed by the crowdsourcing site, however, access to requester reputation is via third-party sites, such as Turkopticon [23].

Current tools for reviewing completed microtasks on crowdsourcing systems are seriously limited. AMT restricts reviewing of microtasks (HITs) to only acceptance or rejection of work. Microworkers allows the requester to ask workers to revise a microtask instead of just rejecting it. However, a more fine-grained approach would allow the requester to give feedback on performance without resorting to the 'binary' option of refusing payment. The quality of feedback from requesters could then be part of the profile required for particular jobs.

There is a strong case to be made for crowdsourcing platforms to directly manage information about the reputation of requesters. This is typically not a feature of current platforms. As noted above, requester reputation information is usually only available via third party sources. The current situation might be considered problematic for requesters as it has the danger of incomplete information and lack of redress and so there is the potential for malicious and inaccurate information about requesters to be circulated. Adding requester reputation information onto current platforms would mitigate against these issues, making this information more reliable. The consequence for workers is that they are provided with more accurate information about the requester when choosing jobs.

The impact of reputation might be even stronger if it could be transferred across different platforms. This would avoid platform lock-in and foster more open and flexible digital labour markets. Technically this would be feasible through a server-client approach, where reputation is managed centrally, and crowdsourcing platforms communicate with a reputation server. An alternative solution would be to maintain a peer-to-peer architecture, allowing a more flexible approach to platforms leaving and entering the network. In either case, defined web service standards for distributing encrypted reputation information are needed. However, since most crowdsourcing platforms are commercial entities, they would prefer to keep requesters and workers on their system, and there is very little motivation for them to provide this sort of functionality.

3.1.4 Requester-Worker Communication

As noted elsewhere the requester-worker relationship is unbalanced, with workers having little recourse when payment is refused. The main communication channel is typically email, which removes anonymity and usually does not allow communication before or during a microtask. Channels to enable more immediate, confidential and anonymous communication between workers and requesters are easily within technical grasp: chat systems and message boards are now familiar through prevalence in social media sites. These could integrated into crowdsourcing platforms. Workers would get a mechanism for getting clearer, interactive instruction and a more controlled system for raising concerns about payment. The advantage for requesters is better communication about complex and time-consuming microtasks. Research studies are often some of the more sophisticated microtasks, and thus stand to benefit from improved communication. There is however a challenge of requester availability for communication, particularly across time zones.

3.2 Payments and Motivation

In many contexts workers expect some kind of reward for their participation in collaborative activities and studies. For some microtasks this can be intrinsic, such as collaboratively building an encyclopaedia, for others this is direct financial reward.

3.2.1   International Payments

Most commercial crowdsourcing platforms have a primary currency. For Germany-based Crowdee it is the Euro; for British platform Prolific, it is Pounds Sterling; and for AMT, the U.S. dollar. This means that for a proportion of the user-base payments must cross financial borders. Exactly how this is processed depends on the chosen platform, the currencies available to the requester, and the supported deposit facilities of the worker. AMT, for example, supports direct deposit payments to U.S. bank accounts in U.S. dollars and Indian bank accounts in Indian Rupees only. All other workers are issued payment only as Amazon.com gift cards.[18]

3.2.2   Alternative Payments

Going forward, new payment options may help sustain and grow the crowd-sourcing labour market. It may already be possible to make payments outside of existing frameworks. For example, international payment processors like PayPal offer an alternative when the platform does not directly support payments or where payments are difficult and payment costs are prohibitive. More novel payment methods, such as Bitcoin may also be used to support more anonymous payments to workers. These alternative payments may raise additional issues with regard to circumventing commission charged by platforms, obligations for transaction traceability within the requesting organisation, or with local laws.

3.2.3   Legal Concerns

A particular concern for platforms is their legal liability for tax and money laundering. Crowd providers may try to minimise any potential involvement in an employer-employee relationship and any potential tax liability or labour responsibilities arising from it. Some platforms, like AMT, have strict sign up requirements for workers and requesters alike. AMT requests personal information, including tax reference numbers for requesters who deposit money for the platform as well as those receiving payments.[19] AMT gathers this information to support their legal reporting obligations with regard to both the U.S. Patriot Act and Internal Revenue Service (IRS) regulations.[20]

Another consideration for requesters is the employment status of workers. In many cases workers are considered independent contractors, hired by the

---

[18] Amazon.com, Inc. "Worker Web Site FAQs". https://www.mturk.com/mturk/help?helpPage=worker#how_paid last accessed 14 Jun 2017.

[19] Amazon.com, Inc. "Requirements for Purchasing Prepaid HITs". https://requester.mturk.com/mturk/amazonpaymentsacctreqmts last accessed 14 Jun 2017.

[20] Amazon.com, Inc. "IRS Reporting Regulations on Third-Party Payment Transactions For Personal or Business Account Holders". https://payments.amazon.com/help/200831230 last accessed 14 Jun 2017.

requester. While this approach may limit legal liability for the platform provider and requester alike some jurisdictions may consider regular, repeat workers of a given requester to be eligible for additional rights and benefits [12] such as healthcare or pension contributions. In these cases it may be important to restrict repeat patronage of a given worker to limit unintentional additional liabilities. Many platforms provide a consistent worker ID and it can be recorded, along with microtask durations, to allow zealous workers to be excluded from future microtasks if needed.

While platforms may supply some documentation and support for requesters and workers, it is important to consider any local implications for cross-border payments and any inferred employment relationship that payment may create. Exact liabilities may not be immediately obvious and should be thoroughly investigated before carrying out crowdwork, especially on an ongoing basis.

3.2.4   Non-monetary Rewards

Workers may also be encouraged to participate by offering non-financial incentives. In the case of tasks such as the usability evaluation of a software product, workers may consider early access to unreleased software as a sufficient incentive to participate. Large collaborative projects like Wikipedia provide a product directly to the user base and encourage a collective ownership [9]. Similarly the popular "citizen science" project *Galaxy Zoo* and later the *Zooniverse*, depends on a variety of intrinsic motivations among their participants to support the categorisation process. Here, participants are engaged by appealing to their enjoyment of astronomy, learning and discovery, and their willingness to contribute to scientific research [40, 41].

Participants can also be rewarded by providing them with their own processed data. Seeing how they compare to other workers is a core concept of "gamification". By improving the enjoyment and competitiveness, workers can be encouraged to better engage with the microtask. This approach gives workers a target or goal that they wish to meet to highlight their own competence and can lead to a higher efficiency and improved quality [10]. Also, workers may become engaged with the scientific process and be motivated by seeing their contribution, for example in extreme cases workers have become so engaged in the research outcome as to warrant authorship of published work [43].

3.3   Ethics

Here we summarise issues connecting ethics with technology when using crowdsourcing tools (Chap. 3 has a more detailed and general discussion on ethics in crowdsourcing). When such technology is used to support academic research one needs to consider ethical questions from different perspectives, related to the two roles of the participating humans (workers):

- Objective – Workers are active, conscious participants of the research effort, providing their expertise to help obtain, process or interpret scientific data. Examples include protein folding,[21] space exploration [41].
- Subjective – Workers are subjects of the research, where the crowdsourcing platform acts as the environment for study execution, during which the workers are observed interacting with the platform, microtasks and other workers. Examples include evaluation of working patterns [30], evaluation of monetary incentives [33].

3.3.1 Objective Participation

Workers participating in crowdsourced studies need to be clearly informed about the conditions of their participation. Usually this implies explicitly stating the participation conditions beforehand (description of requested contribution, time constrains, rewards), presenting ethics approval for the study from a trusted organisation and requesting the participant read and accept this, and stipulating how sensitive data will be handled.

Apart from legal reasons, being informed about the precise participation conditions and the effects the participant's contribution may have on the overall outcome is important because many crowdsourced research efforts are based on volunteering, and it has been shown [14,19,31] that the expectation of the positive contribution to the science is the principal motivational factor in this case. At the same time, not being clear on the participating conditions demotivates many participants who fear that providing subpar contributions will harm the overall effort, which often leads to high attrition rates. Regardless of the fact that many workers are willing to contribute voluntarily to various scientific efforts, the study organiser needs to be aware that the study they run still represents an exploitation of otherwise expensive cognitive labour. This is why it is important to compensate for the missing or symbolic monetary rewards by introducing a set of psychological incentives acting on the intrinsic motivation of the participants and helping them achieve a sense of self-fulfilment. An informative case study can be found as part of the Smart Society project.[22]

Storage of sensitive data must be considered from both legal and technical perspectives. Both can have direct ethical implications. The information contained in the stored data should be reduced to the minimum needed for successful functioning of the platform and execution of the study. Techniques such as data anonymisation and semantic obfuscation [11,17] can be used to reduce the exploitability potential of the stored data. The simplest examples include storing age range instead of concrete age (birth date), and storing geographical area instead of concrete address. Even when appropriate care is taken to assure the protection of sensitive user data, one should consider third-party services as

---

[21] FoldIt. "Solve puzzles for science". https://fold.it/ last accessed 14 Jun 2017.
[22] SmartSociety Consortium. "Deliverable 5.3 - Specification of advanced incentive design and decision-assisting algorithms for CAS" http://www.smart-society-project.eu/publications/deliverables/D_5_3 last accessed 14 Jun 2017.

well. Consider, for example, a crowdsourced study where participants are asked to provide personal anonymised health data and are rewarded with monetary rewards. Even when the requesters act in best faith and follow all precautions for keeping the health data anonymised, poor management of payment data can allow matching the two datasets and ultimately breaching the promised data policy. It is therefore advisable to choose a crowdsourcing platform which can guarantee a safe and separate handling of payments, or delegate the payment management to a trusted third party (cf. Sect. 3.2). The choice of the payment processor and the payment data retention policy should also be clearly stated in the consent form, together with the country-specific conditions which may apply.

3.3.2   Subjective Participation

Crowdsourced studies where the workers are subjects of the study are typical in social sciences and experimental economics. They generally involve use of general-purpose crowdsourcing platforms where the study setup is obtained through a combination of a specific microtask design, worker selection procedure and the set of incentives (rewards). Selected workers are commonly divided into experimental and control groups, and are usually not aware that they are taking part in an study, as this might otherwise yield skewed results. During such studies, the microtasks given to the workers may (purposefully or not) exhibit properties that will cause certain behavioural responses to be more accentuated than for an average microtask, e.g., fatigue, drop of concentration, sense of insecurity, frustration, competitiveness. Since many people working as crowdworkers receive a significant amount of income [32] this aspect becomes increasingly important with the potential to affect daily lives.[23] If an study is expected to cause the described effects, the setup should include distraction and leisure tasks or incentives. For example, a common strategy for image tagging microtasks is to occasionally offer interesting and funny pictures to the crowd. Similarly, in Galaxy Zoo project, participants are occasionally shown easy pictures to boost their self-confidence, or even sent personalised motivational messages.[24]

The aforementioned issues are just a part of a wider debate on worker rights that is currently raising much interest in the research and the worker community (see the Fair Crowd Work website[25] for a compilation of relevant topics). Currently, the working conditions are determined solely by the crowdsourcing platforms and the requesters. This means that crowdworkers are often treated as isolated individuals and harnessed as 'human subroutines'. This has in turn lead

---

[23] Harris, Mark. "Amazon's Mechanical Turk workers protest: 'I am a human being, not an algorithm'". http://www.theguardian.com/technology/2014/dec/03/amazon-mechanical-turk-workers-protest-jeff-bezos last accessed 14 Jun 2017.

[24] SmartSociety Consortium. "Deliverable 5.3 - Specification of advanced incentive design and decision-assisting algorithms for CAS" http://www.smart-society-project.eu/publications/deliverables/D_5_3 last accessed 14 Jun 2017.

[25] Fair Crowd Work. "Fair Crowd Work". http://prolific.ac/ last accessed 14 Jun 2017.

to self-organisation of crowdworkers using alternative, independent forums or platforms, such as Turkopticon [23]. This has direct implications for requesters as well, since the requester's reputation among the worker population can determine which workers will accept the microtask and under which conditions, potentially affecting the outcomes of the study. Therefore, fair microtask rewards and execution conditions become important factors to consider when designing a crowdsourced study.

At the same time, these worker self-organisation platforms are also allowing the workers to share hints and advice on gaming a particular requester to maximise their rewards for the smallest amount of effort. While data quality control is necessary in most crowdsourcing efforts since part of the worker population will always be producing subpar results [9], integrating robust mechanisms for quality control and incentive mechanisms becomes even more important for crowdsourced studies as they usually offer microtask compensations that are higher than the average, thus attracting attention of malicious users and prompting their exploitative actions.

Apart from providing a means to collectively defend worker rights, the self-organisation platforms are also a tool for today's crowdworkers to socialise and establish informal communities. While native support for socialisation is an expected [27] property of future crowdsourcing platforms, for a study designer this will pose yet another important trade-off to consider, particularly during longitudinal studies. It has been shown [30,45] that socialisation and communication among workers can significantly affect task outcomes and thus the study itself, for example, by possibly 'contaminating' the control group. The key thing to consider here is finding a fair way to maintain the experimental setup, while not isolating the workers. We are not aware of any standards or widely agreed-upon conventions regulating the worker organisation and socialisation; each crowdsourcing platform is free to decide if and how to implement support for such functionalities. Therefore, the study designer must consider this on a case-by-case basis.

3.4 Additional Instrumentation

Basic reporting of results is a staple of crowdsourcing platforms but is often limited to a simple key-value store for each question. Additional instrumentation can be beneficial to better understand user engagement with microtasks, especially in research settings.

Platforms vary in their ability to support monitoring of worker behaviour and their devices. For example, web-based platforms such as AMT will not be able to provide direct access to hardware sensors [42]. For web-based platforms the availability of technologies and abstractions supported by the browser including JavaScript and HTML5 will impact study design and collected data. Device-focused studies can offer much more comprehensive data collection opportunities and provide richer context awareness [13]. However, app-based platforms may require more extensive programming and may narrow the diversity of workers for a microtask or result in an unintentional selection bias.

3.4.1 Behaviour Monitoring

Additional behavioural data can contextualise existing findings and offer new avenues for research into user behaviour in crowdsourced environments. By capitalising on existing inputs in new ways, a richer understanding of worker behaviour can be discerned. Recording additional user information can also provide validation and verification of the primary data. As workers may employ techniques to minimise the time spent working on microtasks—such as automation or more complex group activities—additional understanding of user activity is vital to gathering high quality data [8].

Keyboard and mouse
As the primary input devices for non-touchscreen devices, the keyboard and mouse can provide significant insights into user interactions [38]. Recording keyboard and mouse events is possible, even in web-based platforms such as AMT. For basic interactions—such as to identify the order in which questions were attempted or whether the user left the microtask—timestamped actions, such as `focus` and `blur` (unfocus) events, can be recorded.[26] This allows for detection of which items are selected and deselected and can also be used to track when the web page showing the microtask is in the foreground. This indicates whether a user is fully engaged with a microtask and can aid in identifying multitasking or the use of external resources. For more complete analysis of user activity full keyboard and mouse interactions can be recorded. Events including `keypress`, `mousemove`, and `click` are fired when users engage with the microtask. By recording these interactions a comprehensive picture of user activity can be built and analysed, or even played back [4] for example in evaluating the evolution of a user's design [26]. Additionally, these user interactions can be correlated with accuracy and, going forward, be used as a potential indicator of the quality of a worker's efforts [21,25,36].

Audio and video
Another commonly available input is audio and video. Audio recording can be used to capture user thoughts and support think-aloud protocol studies, while video offers a variety of user engagement opportunities such as eye-tracking [28], emotion detection [34], and augmented reality [46]. For web-based studies the Adobe Flash plugin provides a widely deployed platform that can be used to allow audio and video inputs to be captured [35]. Similarly, the emerging HTML5 WebRTC API provides plugin-free support for capturing audio and video [28]. This data can be uploaded to a server either in real-time or after microtask completion depending on the study needs. However, this type of monitoring of user interactions in an otherwise uncontrolled environment may raise privacy concerns for workers and requesters alike [1].

Combining techniques
Where techniques such as audio recording are problematic for otherwise anonymous remote interaction, surveying may provide an alternative. Surveying the

---

[26] World Wide Web Consortium (W3C). "UI Events Specification". https://www.w3.org/TR/uievents/ last accessed 14 Jun 2017.

user on their thoughts both about the microtask and how they chose to carry it out can provide richer qualitative information that may otherwise be missed in these interactions. Simply asking the user to indicate how long they have spent on a task, noting their absences or engagement can provide an increased insight over a purely technological approach to measuring engagement.

Some services such as *Upwork* (previously known as *oDesk*) use a combination of monitoring and surveys. Their software client both asks users to record time worked (which is used for billing purposes) and allows requesters to inspect details of key presses, mouse movements, and periodic screen shots [5]. While the Upwork model more closely mirrors a typical employer-employee relationship, the pseudo-anonymised nature of many crowdsourcing platforms limits the acceptance for this type of monitoring. However, as the prevalence of both technological support and user acceptance for audio-visual recording grows, it may become practical to reintegrate these methods into crowdsourced-based research.

3.4.2 Emerging Opportunities

Combining existing sensor technology, emerging browser and device support, and new algorithms, further advances in user monitoring can be achieved. Once seemingly limited to keyboard-based desktop-bound tasks, crowdsourcing has become far more mobile, and with a much broader input modality [44].

Mobile devices
Consumer mobile devices commonly include a multitude of sensors including location sensors and movement sensors. In web-based environments, these sensors are abstracted and supported by the Geolocation API[27] and `devicemotion` events.[28] Geolocation can support "in the wild" crowdsourcing of data, such as generating location-based datasets. Additionally, device motion offers opportunities for unique device interaction techniques and can aid in recognising user activity [18]. Newer devices offer additional dedicated sensors such as pedometers and heart rate monitors. As these devices become more common and their interfaces are standardised, additional data collection opportunities will emerge.

Eye tracking and biometrics
Understanding what engages users can provide important pointers for improving microtask design and research outcomes [24]. Eye tracking offers an improved measure of what parts of a microtask attract the most attention compared to mouse tracking [29]. By tapping into the nearly ubiquitous webcam, identifying salient features of on-screen images can already be achieved [50]. Video can also lend itself to biometric monitoring—offline video processing to highlight seemingly imperceptible changes such as breathing and heart rate has been

---

[27] World Wide Web Consortium (W3C). "Geolocation API Specification". https://www.w3.org/TR/geolocation-API/ last accessed 14 Jun 2017.
[28] World Wide Web Consortium (W3C). "DeviceOrientation Event Specification". https://www.w3.org/TR/orientation-event/ last accessed 14 Jun 2017.

demonstrated [49]. Using such processing in real time has the potential to offer biometric data from already deployed sensors.

3.5 Supporting Different Study Designs

In considering the question of whether crowdsourcing technology can support academic research, it is necessary to discuss the needs of academic research studies beyond traditional surveys offered as microtasks through crowdsourcing services like AMT. Research studies can vary greatly in their design, however there are some common considerations that affect many of these study designs.

Most researchers are not computer programmers, but they follow certain processes in order to conduct rigorous academic research. This means if they are to utilise crowdsourcing platforms for conducting studies, these platforms will need to provide out-of-the-box support for some common types of studies. This section talks about the requirements for different study designs as they regard to potentially conducting academic research through crowdsourcing platforms.

While most of the existing crowdsourcing platforms discussed earlier do not directly support academic research, there are several that cover a subset of the desired features. Qualtrics[29] provides online software specifically for running customer experience surveys. As mentioned earlier, Prolific[30] is a crowdsourcing platform specifically designed for conducting academic studies. Some of Prolific's features are: high-quality participants, flexible prescreening, support for longitudinal research, bonus payments based on quality.

3.5.1 Focus

One of the issues with current crowdsourcing platforms is the potential lack of focus of the workers during data collection. Traditional studies often compare times taken to achieve a task, or gauge reaction to one stimuli after viewing another. In-person studies can carefully control for variables such as external stimulus, distractions and time between stimuli. For example, many studies will put a participant in a quiet, empty room free of distractions. However these factors are almost impossible to control when using crowdsourcing approaches where people are completing projects in a variety of locations surrounded by potential distractions. It is possible to work around this problem by designing studies around the constraints of the platform, but in general this is a major hurdle to academic research being conducted on crowdsourcing platforms.

3.5.2 Interactivity

Many Human-Computer Interaction (HCI) studies involve participants interacting with software. Crowdsourcing platforms are appealing for such research from

---

[29] Qualtrics LLC. "Qualtrics". http://qualtrics.com/ last accessed 14 Jun 2017.
[30] Prolific Academic. "Prolific". http://prolific.ac/ last accessed 14 Jun 2017.

the perspective of attracting and managing participants, and for the number of participants they potentially provide. However this sort of usability research often tests software with novel user interfaces. Earlier in the chapter we discussed how crowdsourcing platforms are predominantly web-based, and are limited in the customisability of web pages presented as microtasks for workers. The diverse background, locations and computer capabilities of crowdsourcing workers means that any software being studied is almost certainly required to be web-based. Luckily, increasing numbers of software applications (especially research applications) are being built using web technologies. This increases the prospect that these applications could be presented and studied via crowdsourcing platforms. However some of these web applications can still be quite demanding in their resource needs (e.g., processor speed, bandwidth, persistent connection to a remote server) which could be a problem for workers without fast computers or reliable connections. This information about worker's hardware capabilities could be evaluated by the crowdsourcing platform and used for participant selection.

HCI researchers often use specific study designs in order to collect data they want. For example, in some studies all participant interaction with the software will be recorded. Historically this has been done with a video camera pointed at a screen, with screen recording software, or with the application recording the individual interaction events. The purpose of this data collection is to see what the participant did. In the case of crowdsourced workers, only the last of these options is really feasible. It is definitely possible to instrument a web application in this way, but it is not trivial and requires a large amount of additional work on the part of the developer or researcher.

Another approach used for in-person usability studies is to have a researcher observe the actions made by participants, and for the researcher to take notes of interesting events and discuss these with the participant once the tasks are complete. Remote workers in different time zones mean such observation and discussion—if possible at all—would need to involve the researcher viewing the tasks after the fact and contacting the worker to obtain feedback. This requires the cooperation of the worker to provide this follow-up feedback at a time when they may no longer recall their actions or the motivation behind them.

Ultimately such studies aim to determine places where participants do or do not understand the intentions of the interface, and therefore where they can or cannot use it effectively. This requires a significant understanding of the participants' reasoning while performing actions. Another approach for this is to use a think-aloud protocol and get the participant to (try to) verbalise their thinking behind the actions they are performing. This is a very effective tool for usability evaluations but generally some amount of questioning and prompting from a study facilitator is required to get the necessary data (i.e., keep them thinking aloud). Even assuming that crowd workers are set up to record and transmit back audio, this prompting is not something that can be easily duplicated if studies are being conducted in a crowdsourced setting.

3.5.3 Collaboration

An issue with existing crowdsourcing platforms potentially being used in research is the lack of support for collaboration. Many research studies involve two or more participants working on a task simultaneously, or collaborating to reach a shared goal. To support this kind of research, crowdsourcing platforms would need to provide better support for collaboration. This is not a technological impossibility—an internet-connected software environment for running studies could obviously be extended to support the communication required to support collaboration. However this would likely require crowdsourcing platforms to move to a model where the requester (researcher) can be more directly involved in the data collection, i.e., they can interact with the workers in some way while the study is in progress in order to facilitate collaboration or discussion. This is in contrast to the current model where completion of microtasks produces data which is then processed by the requester at a later date. This has also further implications for the quality control mechanisms, as currently most mechanisms use the assumption that the submissions of the workers are independent of each other.

A common qualitative data collection technique is to conduct *focus groups*. Focus groups involve a group of participants being shown or told about something, and then providing their opinions and thoughts on the thing in question via a group discussion. Focus groups require the researcher to facilitate the discussion with prompting questions. It is a very effective technique, but one that is hard to translate to the crowdsourced environment, both because of requiring worker-to-worker communication but also the involvement of a facilitator.

In both these case we see that a research-oriented crowdsourcing platform would almost certainly require come capability for researchers to communicate or interact with workers while they are completing microtasks.

3.5.4 Randomisation, Group Assignment

Some common study designs are *between-groups* or *within-groups*. Between-groups studies get similar groups of participants to do the same task while keeping all but one variable the same. The groups can then be compared to determine the effect of the variable on the task. It is obviously important to control the number of differences between groups that could be a confounding variable. Such studies also require participants to be randomised between groups and for groups to be balanced. These last two needs would be easy to address in a crowdsourcing-based study, but controlling for confounding variables is difficult to do when there is no direct control over the environment in which the worker does the study, and whether they have access to external resources.

Within-group studies use the same participants and get them to do all tasks under the different sets of conditions. In this case it is important to get participants to perform tasks in a randomised other. Possible confounding factors could be introduced by participants conducting the study over a longer period in multiple sittings, or due to the researcher being unable to control the environment in which the participant completes the task.

3.5.5 Longer Studies

Many research studies repeatedly collect data over long periods of time from the same participants. Such studies are known as longitudinal studies. The longest longitudinal studies are over 75 years (e.g., [47]). These kinds of studies are difficult to conduct and tend to lose many participants over time.

Such studies should not be any harder to conduct using online crowdsourcing platforms. In fact it might be easier in this environment since researchers could begin with a larger pool of participants, an online system can more easily remind or prompt people to participate, and it may be easier to keep track of people via email accounts than postal addresses (which are likely to be more transient).

Crowdsourcing platforms that were to support longitudinal research would need capabilities for repeating studies with the same participants, a targeted notification system, and support for incremental payments with a possible bonus for completing entire term of the study.

3.5.6 Participant Selection

Scientific studies typically have some requirements in terms of selecting participants. Even if they do not select participants based on specific criteria it is usually necessary to report on the characteristics of the participants – i.e., their ages, gender, background, or any other attributes that could seen to affect the results. One such characteristic is familiarity – there might be a requirement that participants have not participated in a similar study before, or that they do not have any familiarity with the thing being tested. Current crowdsourcing platforms provide only minimal details of workers to the requester. It would be easy for crowdsourcing platforms to store additional details of their workers. This is also useful information for the platforms to have, since it is effectively information on the demographics of their workers.

Additionally, many research studies need the ability to automatically assign participants to different conditions (i.e., different participant groups who are given different tools or stimuli during the study). For example, a study might require different groups of participants to do different tasks. The work of handling this assignment to conditions and of randomising the study itself would usually be done by the researcher, but would require automation in crowdsourcing platform setting. For this, the platform would be required to understand details of the study, such as how participants are assigned to conditions, and how the study is structured for these groups, so that this information could be automatically applied when workers undertake the study microtasks.

While research studies may sometimes utilise a very small number of participants, it is common for these people to have specialised skills, that is, for them to be subject experts in a particular domain. For example, a study may seek the opinion of people familiar with perception, visual algorithms, or interaction techniques. As noted in Subsect. 3.1, a crowdsourcing platform could allow a worker to specify such expertise, but it may be necessary to have a mechanism for verifying such information. Also, subject matter experts may want to provide qualitative feedback on designs. Such feedback would traditionally be free-form, comprising of verbal feedback, written notes, annotation of paper designs, or gesturing. An online form can certainly be used to collect textual comments, but in order to get useful feedback of the same quality as in-person studies it might be necessary for research crowdsourcing platforms to provide a richer means of providing feedback. Some possibilities would be allowing video responses or web-based annotation of diagrams.

3.5.7   Activity-Tracking Studies

Many health, fitness, or product related studies get participants to record information about their daily activities, such as food intake, exercise activity, or purchasing decisions. The traditional method for conducting these studies involves participants keeping a journal of activities and submitting this to the researchers at regular intervals.

Such manual journalling is not ideal since participants may forget to enter some data, they may enter incorrect data (accidentally or by choice), or may make errors during data entry. Online systems, including a web-based crowdsourcing approach, have the benefit of being able to prompt or remind the participant to enter their data (especially when they are using a mobile browser). They can also validate data to check that, for instance, specified data is within a particular range or is close to expected values. Additionally, many classes of errors can be avoided because sensors on computers or mobile devices can be used to check values that a participant would otherwise have to check and enter manually. As discussed in Subsect. 3.4 the rise in mobile computing means that information from a wide variety sensors could considered when designing studies. Some examples of such information are date, time, physical location and heart rate. Another benefit is that such a system can provide immediate feedback or advice to the participant, in additional to tradition participation payments discussed in Subsect. 3.2. The requirements here are for research crowdsourcing platforms to be able to use device capabilities to check some values and to be able to validate other data that is entered and provide the participant with immediate feedback when it is not valid.

A recent example of collection of study data via mobile devices is Apple's ResearchKit. Introduced in mid 2015, ResearchKit is an iOS framework that developers can use to build apps for conducting scientific research via mobile apps. It allows participants to use their device for collection of study data, e.g., using the "accelerometer, microphone, gyroscope and GPS sensors in iPhone to gain insight into a patient's gait, motor impairment, fitness, speech and memory".[31] ResearchKit allows access to this data in a controlled manner that is clear to the participant. Collection of data via a sensor-rich mobile app has further benefits such as the fact that participants always have the device (and therefore the app) with them and that such apps can communicate with connected devices to collect data via additional sensors, such as a heart-rate monitor on a watch or fitness band.

4   Conclusions

In this chapter we examined how various platforms, technologies, and techniques can support crowdsourcing in an academic context. We first discussed the capabilities of existing public crowdsourcing platforms and outlined the types of features they provide to requesters. We then discussed possible feature additions or enhancements that would benefit research studies conducted via these platforms. The proposed features fall into the broad categories of user management, payments and motivation, ethics, additional instrumentation, and supporting different study designs.

Finally, we considered the advantages and disadvantages of crowdsourcing some broad classes of study design, including between-groups, within-groups and longitudinal studies. We discussed the particular needs of research-related microtasks and how some of these could also enhance or benefit existing (non-research) microtasks conducted on these platforms. Some of features we proposed included, richer demographic information for workers, better reputation tracking or certification to gauge worker quality, support for varied forms of payment, better microtask monitoring and communication channels between workers and requesters, and platforms support for study designs and enforcement of study procedures.

We suggest there are many relevant features that could be easily added to crowdsourcing platforms that would greatly increase their appeal to researchers. Many of these features are straightforward to implement and would benefit existing workers and requesters in additional to potential research users. While we recognise there are still significant hurdles to the wide adoption of crowdsourcing within academia, there are many easy steps that crowdsourcing platforms can take to increase their usefulness to such domains.

Acknowledgment. The genesis and planning of this chapter took place at the Dagstuhl Seminar #15481, "Evaluation in the Crowd: Crowdsourcing and Human-Centred Experiments" held in November 2015. Jason Jacques was supported by a studentship from the Engineering and Physical Sciences Research Council. Ognjen Scekic was supported by the EU FP7 SmartSociety project under grant #600854. Michael Wybrow was supported by the Australian Research Council Discovery Project grant DP140100077. This work was partially funded by the Deutsche Forschungsgemeinschaft (DFG) under Grants HO4770/2-2 and TR257/38-2. The authors alone are responsible for the content.

---

[31] Apple Inc. "ResearchKit". http://www.apple.com/researchkit/ last accessed 14 Jun 2017.

References

1. Adams, A.A., Ferryman, J.M.: The future of video analytics for surveillance and its ethical implications. Secur. J. **28**(3), 272–289 (2015)
2. Barrick, M.R., Mount, M.K.: The big five personality dimensions and job performance: a meta-analysis. Person. Psychol. **44**(1), 1–26 (1991)
3. Bertua, C., Anderson, N., Salgado, J.F.: The predictive validity of cognitive ability tests: a UK meta-analysis. J. Occup. Organ. Psychol. **78**(3), 387–409 (2005)
4. Breslav, S., Khan, A., Hornbæk, K.: Mimic: visual analytics of online micro-interactions. In: Proceedings of the 2014 International Working Conference on Advanced Visual Interfaces (AVI 2014), pp. 245–252, NY, USA. ACM, New York (2014)
5. Caraway, B.: Online labour markets: an inquiry into oDesk providers. Work Organ. Labour Globalisation **4**(2), 111–125 (2010)
6. Chandler, J., Mueller, P., Paolacci, G.: Nonnaïveté among amazon mechanical turk workers: consequences and solutions for behavioral researchers. Behav. Res. Methods **46**(1), 112–130 (2014)
7. Crump, M.J., McDonnell, J.V., Gureckis, T.M.: Evaluating amazon's mechanical turk as a tool for experimental behavioral research. PloS one **8**(3), e57410 (2013)
8. Difallah, D.E., Demartini, G., Cudré-Mauroux, P.: Mechanical cheat: spamming schemes and adversarial techniques on crowdsourcing platforms. In: CrowdSearch, pp. 26–30 (2012)
9. Doan, A., Ramakrishnan, R., Halevy, A.Y.: Crowdsourcing systems on the World-Wide Web. Commun. ACM **54**(4), 86–96 (2011)
10. Eickhoff, C., Harris, C.G., de Vries, A.P., Srinivasan, P.: Quality through flow and immersion: gamifying crowdsourced relevance assessments. In: Proceedings of the 35th International ACM SIGIR Conference on Research and Development in Information Retrieval (SIGIR 2012), pp. 871–880, NY, USA. ACM, New York (2012)
11. Elkhodr, M., Shahrestani, S., Cheung, H.: A semantic obfuscation technique for the internet of things. In: 2014 IEEE International Conference on Communications Workshops (ICC), pp. 448–453, June 2014
12. Felstiner, A.: Working the crowd: employment and labor law in the crowdsourcing industry. Berkeley J. Employ. Labor Law **32**(1), 143 (2011)
13. Ferreira, D., Kostakos, V., Dey, A.K.: AWARE: mobile context instrumentation framework. Front. ICT **2** (2015). http://journal.frontiersin.org/article/10.3389/fict.2015.00006/full
14. Glazer, A.: Motivating devoted workers. Int. J. Ind. Organ. **22**(3), 427–440 (2004)
15. Goodman, J.K., Cryder, C.E., Cheema, A.: Data collection in a flat world: the strengths and weaknesses of mechanical turk samples. J. Behav. Decis. Making **26**(3), 213–224 (2013)
16. Gualtieri, C.T., Johnson, L.G.: Reliability and validity of a computerized neurocognitive test battery, CNS vital signs. Arch. Clin. Neuropsychol. **21**(7), 623–643 (2006)
17. Hartswood, M., Jirotka, M., Chenu-Abente, R., Hume, A., Giunchiglia, F., Martucci, L.A., Fischer-Hübner, S.: Privacy for peer profiling in collective adaptive systems. In: Camenisch, J., Fischer-Hübner, S., Hansen, M. (eds.) Privacy and Identity 2014. IAICT, vol. 457, pp. 237–252. Springer, Cham (2015). doi:10.1007/978-3-319-18621-4_16

18. Hauber, M., Bachmann, A., Budde, M., Beigl, M.: jActivity: supporting mobile web developers with HTML5/JavaScript based human activity recognition. In: Proceedings of the 12th International Conference on Mobile and Ubiquitous Multimedia (MUM 2013), pp. 45:1–45:2, NY, USA. ACM, New York (2013)

19. Heckman, J.J., Smith, J.A., Taber, C.: What do bureaucrats do? The effects of performance standards and bureaucratic preferences on acceptance into the JTPA program. In: Advances in the Study of Entrepreneurship Innovation and Economic Growth, vol. 7, pp. 191–217 (1996)

20. Hirth, M., Hoßfeld, T., Tran-Gia, P.: Anatomy of a crowdsourcing platform – using the example of Microworkers.com. In: Workshop on Future Internet and Next Generation Networks (FINGNet), Seoul, Korea, June 2011

21. Hirth, M., Scheuring, S., Hoßfeld, T., Schwartz, C., Tran-Gia, P.: Predicting result quality in crowdsourcing using application layer monitoring. In: 2014 Fifth International Conference on Communications and Electronics (ICCE). IEEE (2014)

22. Hossfeld, T., Keimel, C., Hirth, M., Gardlo, B., Habigt, J., Diepold, K., Tran-Gia, P.: Best practices for QoE crowdtesting: QoE assessment with crowdsourcing. Trans. Multimed. **16**(2), 541–558 (2014)

23. Irani, L.C., Silberman, M.S.: Turkopticon: interrupting worker invisibility in amazon mechanical turk. In: Proceedings of the SIGCHI Conference on Human Factors in Computing Systems (CHI 2013), pp. 611–620, NY, USA. ACM, New York (2013)

24. Jacques, J.T., Kristensson, P.O.: Crowdsourcing a HIT: measuring workers' pre-task interactions on microtask markets. In: First AAAI Conference on Human Computation and Crowdsourcing, November 2013

25. Kazai, G., Zitouni, I.: Quality management in crowdsourcing using gold judges behavior. In: Proceedings of the Ninth ACM International Conference on Web Search and Data Mining, pp. 267–276. ACM (2016)

26. Kieffer, S., Dwyer, T., Marriott, K., Wybrow, M.: Hola: human-like orthogonal network layout. IEEE Trans. Vis. Comput. Graph. **22**(1), 349–358 (2016)

27. Kittur, A., Nickerson, J.V., Bernstein, M., Gerber, E., Shaw, A., Zimmerman, J., Lease, M., Horton, J.: The future of crowd work. In: Proceedings of the 2013 Conference on Computer Supported Cooperative Work (CSCW 2013), pp. 1301–1318. ACM (2013)

28. Lebreton, P., Hupont, I., Mäki, T., Skodras, E., Hirth, M.: Eye tracker in the wild: studying the delta between what is said and measured in a crowdsourcing experiment. In: Proceedings of the Fourth International Workshop on Crowdsourcing for Multimedia, pp. 3–8. ACM (2015)

29. Lebreton, P., Mäki, T., Skodras, E., Hupont, I., Hirth, M.: Bridging the gap between eye tracking and crowdsourcing, vol. 9394, pp. 93940W–93940W-14 (2015)

30. Little, G.: Exploring iterative and parallel human computation processes. In: Proceedings of the 28th International Conference on Human Factors in Computing Systems, CHI 2010, Extended Abstracts Volume, Atlanta, Georgia, USA, 10–15 April 2010, pp. 4309–4314 (2010)

31. Mao, A., Kamar, E., Chen, Y., Horvitz, E., Schwamb, M.E., Lintott, C.J., Smith, A.M.: Volunteering versus work for pay: incentives and tradeoffs in crowdsourcing. In: Hartman, B., Horvitz, E. (eds.) HCOMP. AAAI (2013)

32. Martin, D.B., Hanrahan, B.V., O'Neill, J., Gupta, N.: Being a turker. In: Computer Supported Cooperative Work (CSCW 2014), Baltimore, MD, USA, 15–19 February 2014, pp. 224–235 (2014)

33. Mason, W., Watts, D.J.: Financial incentives and the "performance of crowds". In: Proceedings of the ACM SIGKDD Workshop on Human Computation (HCOMP 2009), NY, USA, pp. 77–85. ACM, New York (2009)

34. McDuff, D., el Kaliouby, R., Picard, R.W.: Crowdsourcing facial responses to online videos: extended abstract. In: 2015 International Conference on Affective Computing and Intelligent Interaction (ACII), pp. 512–518, September 2015
35. McDuff, D., el Kaliouby, R., Picard, R.: Crowdsourced data collection of facial responses. In: Proceedings of the 13th International Conference on Multimodal Interfaces (ICMI 2011), NY, USA pp. 11–18. ACM, New York (2011)
36. Mok, R.K., Li, W., Chang, R.K.: Detecting low-quality crowdtesting workers. In: 2015 IEEE 23rd International Symposium on Quality of Service (IWQoS), pp. 201–206. IEEE (2015)
37. Narayanan, A., Shmatikov, V.: Robust de-anonymization of large sparse datasets. In: IEEE Symposium on Security and Privacy (SP 2008), pp. 111–125. IEEE (2008)
38. Navalpakkam, V., Churchill, E.: Mouse tracking: measuring and predicting users' experience of web-based content. In: Proceedings of the SIGCHI Conference on Human Factors in Computing Systems (CHI 2012), NY, USA, pp. 2963–2972. ACM, New York (2012)
39. Peer, E., Samat, S., Brandimarte, L., Acquisti, A.: Beyond the turk: an empirical comparison of alternative platforms for online behavioral research. Available at SSRN 2594183, April 2015
40. Raddick, M.J., Bracey, G., Gay, P.L., Lintott, C.J., Murray, P., Schawinski, K., Szalay, A.S., Vandenberg, J.: Galaxy zoo: exploring the motivations of citizen science volunteers. Astron. Educ. Rev. 9(1) (2010). http://portico.org/Portico/#!journalAUSimpleView/tab=HTML?cs=ISSN_15391515?ct=E-Journal%20Content?auId=ark:/27927/pgg3ztfdp8z
41. Reed, J., Raddick, M.J., Lardner, A., Carney, K.: An exploratory factor analysis of motivations for participating in Zooniverse, a collection of virtual citizen science projects. In: 2013 46th Hawaii International Conference on System Sciences (HICSS), pp. 610–619, January 2013
42. Richardson, D.W., Gribble, S.D.: Maverick: providing web applications with safe and flexible access to local devices. In: Proceedings of the 2011 USENIX Conference on Web Application Development (2011)
43. Salehi, N., Irani, L.C., Bernstein, M.S., Alkhatib, A., Ogbe, E., Milland, K.: Clickhappier: we are dynamo: overcoming stalling and friction in collective action for crowd workers. In: Proceedings of the 33rd Annual ACM Conference on Human Factors in Computing Systems (CHI 2015), pp. 1621–1630. ACM, New York (2015)
44. Shen, X.: Mobile crowdsourcing [Editor's note]. IEEE Netw. 29(3), 2–3 (2015)
45. Thuan, N.H., Antunes, P., Johnstone, D.: Factors influencing the decision to crowdsource: a systematic literature review. Inf. Syst. Front. 18(1), 47–68 (2016)
46. Väätäjä, H.K., Ahvenainen, M.J., Jaakola, M.S., Olsson, T.D.: Exploring augmented reality for user-generated hyperlocal news content. In: CHI 2013 Extended Abstracts on Human Factors in Computing Systems (CHI EA 2013), NY, USA, pp. 967–972. ACM, New York (2013)
47. Vaillant, G.: Triumphs of Experience. Harvard University Press, Boston (2012)
48. Vakharia, D., Lease, M.: Beyond AMT: an analysis of crowd work platforms. In: iConference 2015 Proceedings. iSchools, March 2015
49. Wu, H.Y., Rubinstein, M., Shih, E., Guttag, J., Durand, F., Freeman, W.: Eulerian video magnification for revealing subtle changes in the world. ACM Trans. Graph. 31(4), 65:1–65:8 (2012)
50. Xu, P., Ehinger, K.A., Zhang, Y., Finkelstein, A., Kulkarni, S.R., Xiao, J.: TurkerGaze: crowdsourcing saliency with webcam based eye tracking, April 2015. arXiv:1504.06755 [cs]

Crowdsourcing for Information Visualization: Promises and Pitfalls

Rita Borgo[1]($\boxtimes$), Bongshin Lee[2], Benjamin Bach[3], Sara Fabrikant[4],
Radu Jianu[5], Andreas Kerren[6], Stephen Kobourov[7], Fintan McGee[8],
Luana Micallef[9], Tatiana von Landesberger[10], Katrin Ballweg[10],
Stephan Diehl[11], Paolo Simonetto[13], and Michelle Zhou[12]

[1] King's College London, London, UK
rita.borgo@kcl.ac.uk
[2] Microsoft Research, Redmond, USA
[3] Microsoft Research - Inria, Paris, France
[4] University of Zurich, Zurich, Switzerland
[5] City University London, London, UK
[6] Linnaeus University, Växjö, Sweden
[7] University of Arizona, Tucson, USA
[8] Luxembourg Institute of Science and Technology,
Esch-sur-Alzette, Luxembourg
[9] Helsinki Institute for Information Technology, Aalto, Finland
[10] Darmstadt University, Darmstadt, Germany
[11] University Trier, Trier, Germany
[12] Juji, Saratoga, USA
[13] Swansea University, Swansea, UK

1   Introduction

The term *crowdsourcing*, coined in 2006[1], describes a new labor market phenomenon where simple, often monotonous labor tasks are replaced by open self-managed recruitment of large groups of people from the general public. Online platforms such as Amazon Mechanical Turk and CrowdFlower have stimulated this trend, and made crowdsourcing attractive for user studies in visualization and human-computer interaction. The visualization community increasingly employs crowdsourcing mechanisms for conducting empirical visualization research with the goal to increase access to and take advantage of large and diverse participant groups for evaluation.

Crowdsourcing has the potential to overcome the limitations of controlled lab studies, such as small participant sample sizes and participant pools with narrow demographic backgrounds. These limitations can lead to empirical results that might be difficult to generalize or have low ecological validity. Through crowdsourcing, a large number of participants with a broad background can be recruited more easily and quickly, often at a much lower cost compared to traditional lab studies. Within the visualization community, van Ham and Rogowitz [42] first set the scene for the use of online evaluations in the context

---

[1] http://www.wired.com/2006/06/crowds last accessed 14 Jun 2017.

© Springer International Publishing AG 2017
D. Archambault et al. (Eds.): Evaluation in the Crowd, LNCS 10264, pp. 96–138, 2017.
DOI: 10.1007/978-3-319-66435-4_5

of graph-layout aesthetics, clearly separating their game-inspired online study from a traditional laboratory setup.

However, the studies employing crowdsourcing pose additional conceptual and methodological challenges for rigorous empirical visualization research. Known challenges to crowdsourcing-based studies relate to, but are not limited to: reduced control in the assessment of participants' background and training, use of evaluation criteria that go beyond classic performance measures (e.g., task completion time and accuracy), and need of additional testing mechanisms for complex evaluation tasks that require increased cognitive efforts over a prolonged period of time. The benefit of larger numbers of participants is contrasted by limited participant sampling and selection mechanisms, based on demographics or backgrounds of the participants required for the study. A large, potentially diverse but anonymous, and remote pool of participants can have undesired impacts on the internal validity of the empirical study, and thus can limit the quality of study results. Moreover, crowdsourcing-based experiments typically do not allow for direct interactions between experimenters and participants, and do not permit systematic control of the testing environment.

In this chapter, we review research that has attempted to take advantage of crowdsourcing for empirical evaluations of visualizations. With an aim to identifying best practices and potential pitfalls to guide future designs of crowdsourcing-based studies for visualization, we discuss core aspects for successful employment of crowdsourcing in empirical studies for visualization; participants (Sect. 2), study design (Sect. 3), study procedure (Sect. 4), data (Sect. 5), tasks (Sect. 6), and metrics & measures (Sect. 7). We also present case studies, discussing potential mechanisms to overcome the common pitfalls (Sect. 8). This chapter will help the visualization community understand how to effectively and efficiently take advantage of the exciting potential crowdsourcing might offer to empirical visualization research.

2 Participants

Scaling to a large number of participants and increasing their diversity (e.g., age, cultural background, or expertise), is the main objective in using crowdsourcing techniques. Typical lab studies in information visualization (InfoVis) involve a small number of participants. A larger and more diverse pool of participants can potentially provide the following advantages:

- **Large samples:** In most cases, participant sample sizes can be increased by simply running more Human Intelligence Tasks (HITs)[2]. A larger number of participants, first of all, result in larger samples (e.g., 480 participants in [67], 550 in [30]). Having more samples makes the data analysis more robust to outliers, since outliers can be removed while maintaining a large number of "good" samples. Larger samples can also provide more evidence with respect to distribution and significance between conditions.

---

[2] We adopt this terminology, which means a single self-contained task, from Amazon Mechanical Turk.

- **Easier and faster data collection:** The time and effort that are dedicated to participant supervision in traditional studies are virtually eliminated in crowdsourcing studies. Crowdsourcing platforms make it convenient to recruit people automatically, while tasks are solved without direct interaction with the study experimenter. Moreover, multiple participants can perform their tasks in parallel, further speeding up the data collection process [45].
- **Diverse samples:** Accessing a larger pool of potential participants allows to search for participants with specific characteristics such as age, gender, educational background, familiarity with the visualization methods, visual abilities, profession, etc. These diverse criteria can be used to provide valuable insight which would be nearly impossible to find with typical lab studies.

To make the best use of these advantages, the experimenter needs to take into account a number of factors when including participants through crowdsourcing:

- **Anonymity:** The true identity and motivation of participants is unknown to the study experimenter. Thus, the experimenter should assess the level of expertise with explicit tests, and cannot entirely trust the demographic data entered by the participant into the online system.
- **Reliability:** Participants in lab studies are typically in a more direct connection with the study experimenter, leading to a reasonable expectation of dedication of the participants and truthfulness of the answers. On the other hand, crowdworkers engage with the tasks without supervision, and there is no direct communication between the experimenter and the crowdworker. The experimenter cannot check if they are working on multiple tasks at the same time [38], and needs to put extra efforts to check if a crowdworker is paying attention to the task.
- **Confidentiality:** In having participants executing the study on a remote machine (in most cases their own machine), the study experimenter implicitly makes the study code and data available. Some studies might rely on confidential data or code that should not be made widely available.

The remainder of this section discusses visualization-related issues about how potential participants can vary (Sect. 2.1), how to find participants with a desired skill set (Sect. 2.2), and how to train the remote crowdworker (Sect. 2.3).

2.1 Demographics and Expertise

There have been efforts to "measure the crowd," i.e., to analyze the demographics, characteristics, and habits of crowdworkers. Unfortunately, these statistics are extremely volatile, deeply influenced by the crowdsourcing platforms' policies, and easily biased by the population sampling method. They should therefore be interpreted more as a snapshot of a particular crowdsourcing platform at the time of the survey, rather than as demographics of general validity.

In 2010, Ross et al. [78] presented a demographic description of the workers in Amazon Mechanical Turk (AMT) based on surveys conducted in 2008 and 2009.

The article suggests that in earlier years the population was mostly American, engaging in AMT typically for fun or some extra income, and with a distribution across sex, income, and age that was fairly representative of the U.S. population. Around the time of the survey, there was however a gradual shifting toward an Indian-based population, which presents a strong bias toward young male individuals with a higher reliance on the AMT income for their sustenance. In 2015, Silberman et al.[3] remarked that the demographic presented is outdated for a number of reasons, including changes in Amazon policies, and provided further evidence suggesting the presence of a sampling bias in the previous study.

Fort et al. [37] further analyzed the above data and presented more details on the task distribution. According to the authors, about 80% of the tasks in AMT were carried out by less than 10,000 Turkers, which represented roughly one percent of the registered crowdworkers at that time. Moreover, considerations on the average wage obtainable in AMT, combined with the reasons provided by the Turkers for working on the tasks, made the authors raise ethical issues on the usage of AMT, apparently shared by the legal departments of some universities.

Hirth et al. [46], instead, attempted to provide a more general characterization by studying a platform with no explicit demographic restrictions, called Microworkers. At the time of the study, the majority of the workers on this platform were from Asia, typically from low wage countries. Employers were instead more likely from a western country, with the U.S. representing more than a quarter of the total number of employers. The distribution of reward suggests a polarization similar to the finding of Fort et al. for AMT, with a small number of employers and workers covering the vast majority of the tasks available. Their results also indicate major differences in preferences among the workers regarding accepted tasks, with some high-performing workers systematically accepting faster, less paid jobs and others mostly going for longer, better paid ones.

Martin et al. [64] employed a more qualitative approach to the characterization of some highly active Turkers. They detail the living and working conditions on these people, including the reasons why they work on the AMT platform, how they select the HITs to work on, and the possible disagreements between workers and employers. The authors also consider ethical considerations and opportunities for designing a better working platform.

A constantly updated summary of AMT can be found online[4] (gender, income, marital status, household size, etc.). Next we consider topics more specifically related to crowdsourced visualization work.

2.1.1 Visualization Literacy

Visualization literacy is a relatively new term, defined by Boy et al. as *"the ability to confidently use a given data visualization to translate questions specified in the data domain into visual queries in the visual domain, as well as interpreting visual patterns in the visual domain as properties in the data domain"* [19].

---

[3] https://medium.com/@silberman/stop-citing-ross-et-al-2010-who-are-the-crowdwo rkers-b3b9b1e8d300 last accessed 14 Jun 2017.

[4] http://demographics.mturk-tracker.com last accessed 14 Jun 2017.

Related concepts include *graphicacy* [90] as the ability to understand simple bar charts and diagrams, and *visual literacy* [25] as the ability to understand signs. Studies on perception of visual variables (e.g., [33]) and how people associate values to visual variables, provide some general understanding of what to "expect" from a normal participant. However, these studies do not tell how to asses a person's visual understanding, or the ability to build up a methodology to correctly understand and interpret the meaning behind a picture. Assessing visualization literacy of potential crowdworkers can help define the type of studies possible with crowdworkers, design training conditions, and improve the overall experimental design.

According to Bertin [17], there are three levels of understanding visualizations. To understand a visualization on an *elementary level* means to be able to extract basic information from the data, such as to find a maximal value. Understanding on an *intermediate level* means to be able to extract trends and other higher-level structures. Finally, understanding on a *comprehensive level* means to be able to compare structures and make interpretations that involve domain knowledge. Based on Bertin's observations, Boy et al. define a methodology to measure visualization literacy, which involves (a) stimuli (pictures, tables, text, etc.), (b) tasks (e.g., *find maximum*), and (c) a textual formulation (called a "question"). For questions, Boy et al. define the characteristic of *congruency*: a question with high congruency uses words related to the graphical elements (e.g., *"what is the highest bar?"*), while a question with low congruency uses domain language (e.g., *"which country spends the most on health care?"*). Questions with low congruency are expected to be harder to answer. Boy et al. also formulate a set of guidelines to test visual literacy, which include careful design and repetition of conditions.

However, the data gathered from such a visualization literacy test is rather complex to analyze, and the proposed visualization literacy tests require about 30 min, making it difficult to employ such tests in crowdsourcing experiments. Expressive and short tests are still missing. Two simpler examples of tests for visual literacy exist online, which embed simple multiple-choice tests in an HTML frame.[5] While the first test assesses the understanding of bar charts, the second asks questions about which of two representations is more readable, and attempts to determine whether people can spot deceptive charts [72].

Yet every evaluation may want to define their own criteria of what participants' pre-knowledge is expected to be with respect to visualization literacy. Questions related to training Turkers are discussed further in Sect. 2.3. Study authors may want to carefully check the language and explanations of their tasks. It cannot generally be assumed that the average worker is able to translate a question from the domain space (low congruency) into the visual space (high congruency). Perhaps even simple graphics may benefit from explanation and a clarification of terminology. Similar problems may arise when requiring participants to interact with a visualization. Section 3.3 proposes a possible strategy on

---

[5] http://www.quizrevolution.com/act101820/mini/go/ last accessed 14 Jun 2017, http://perceptualedge.com/files/GraphDesignIQ.html last accessed 14 Jun 2017.

how to maximize the outcome of visualization literacy assessments while amortizing costs.

2.1.2   Cultural Codes

Cultural codes define conventions about decoding information that is stored graphically. Some of these conventions are explicitly defined. For example, the *direction of reading* is different in many cultures: right-left, left-right, top-down. This can influence the order in which visual elements in a visualization are decoded (e.g., the orientation of a time axis [3,13,65]). The *formatting of number and date* affects labels and questions (e.g., 1.000 and 22/02/2016 in Europe vs. 1,000 and 02/22/2016 in North America). *Units and measures* as well as their abbreviations change from country to country (e.g., *MO* (MegaOctet) in France, *MB* in other countries). Time units can also be a source of confusion; day times should probably be indicated in both 12 and 24-hours notation (14:00/2 pm), and fuzzy terms such as "semester" and "biweekly" should probably be avoided.

Other conventions such as colors and symbols can vary between sub-groups and with contexts. *Colors* can have, in many cases, more generally agreed upon meaning with respect to their effect [1], but very different symbolic meanings. For example, the colors white and green are associated with nature and well-being in western cultures, but they can be associated with death in Asia and South America, respectively. When using colors in textual descriptions, there may be discrepancies about the colors associated with a term [93], though generally color categorizations are consistent across cultures [16]. Finally, there may exist conventions about colors in the context of InfoVis: including the rainbow color-scale that (wrongly) implies an order of colors, or dual scales ranging from blue (low or negative) via white (middle or zero), to red (high or positive), or vice versa. Such conventions need special explanation.

Symbols are interpreted entirely by convention, according to the studies of semiotics; for example, in Poland a triangle indicates man's bathrooms while a circle indicates woman's. Simplified pictorial representations of an existing object (e.g., a man icon on bathroom doors) are termed *icons*. Icons are more universal than symbols, though they may still rely on cultural conventions (women wearing skirts, men trousers). Though the usage of symbols is generally discouraged in InfoVis, there may be intrinsic visual encodings, related to visualization literacy such as axis labels and scale tick-marks, and visual elements in visualizations (e.g., circles in node-link diagrams, contour lines in maps) are not generally self-explanatory *per se*, but learned by cultural convention.

2.1.3   Color Blindness

Color blindness affects around 10% of the male population and 0.5% of the female population in the world[6], which amounts up to around 70 million affected people world-wide (these numbers are reported for 2016 and they vary across sources).

---

[6] http://www.colourblindawareness.org/colour-blindness/types-of-colour-blindness
last accessed 14 Jun 2017.

Color blindness is a generic term that covers several types of color perception deficiencies that involve almost every color hue (see Footnote 6), and appear on different scales (mild, moderate, high). As Ware notes [93], some people are not aware that they do not perceive color differences like the majority of the population.

The implications of color blindness for crowdsourcing are three-fold: (a) *self assessment* for any type of color blindness may be required to either categorize participants with different abilities or filter participants from the actual study; (b) *qualifying tests* may be required if color is an essential part of the evaluation and adapted color schemes cannot be employed; an ad-hoc test could involve samples of actual study conditions from the experiment with an emphasis on color perception, or standardized tests and images (see Color Blindness Tests[7] for a collection); and (c) *adapted color schemes* designed to work for most color blind people [23,56] can be employed to increase the soundness of a study.

2.1.4   Domain Expertise

Domain expertise of crowdworkers varies as they have different professions, each of which involves different activities and skills related to analysis, visualization, and domain knowledge. The specific domain expertise can influence a crowdworker's interest in a task and the pre-knowledge he or she brings when decoding information (e.g., finance, biology, politics). More general analytical skills required in a certain field of daily work are related to visualization literacy (e.g., reading bar-charts, working with numbers and statistics). Both conditions may have an impact on tasks results and performances.

On the other hand, an evaluation of visualization may require participants with explicit knowledge in a certain domain. The problem at hand is to gain access to such experts. Domain experts may not participate in crowdsourcing platforms on their own and may not voluntarily spend time in evaluations. In working with domain experts, an appropriate compensation with respect to the expert's work or research may be a more promising approach than monetary rewards. For example, possible compensations of this type might include access to novel visualization tools, access to interesting datasets, etc.

2.2   Finding "The Right" Participants

As participants differ across a wide range of characteristics, a study author may want to find participants with certain characteristics, but exclude others from taking the HIT. As described in Sect. 2.1, visualization literacy tests are not yet generally applicable to crowdsourcing. Being aware of the problem should encourage study authors to include simple tests in their studies, and to focus on sufficient training. It is also important to deliver very precise task descriptions upfront, in order to discourage less motivated workers [33].

Some crowdsourcing platforms create participant profiles that allow a study author to directly contact participants after the HIT. This makes it possible

---

[7] http://www.color-blindness.com/color-blindness-tests last accessed 14 Jun 2017.

to invite the participants for a post-study on the same topic (for example, when evaluating memorability), or to invite the participants to a new study that requires expertise and training obtained in earlier studies. However, platforms without such participant profiles make it difficult, if not impossible, to track workers who already have participated in a study.

2.3   Training

Most tasks in user studies require some sort of training (a) to teach participants the goal of a task (*did the participants correctly understand the tasks and were they able to find the correct answers?*), (b) to teach participants how to use a specific visualization or interaction technique (*were the participants able to decode a visualization properly?, were the participants able to correctly interact?*), and (c) to teach participants specific strategies on how to best solve a specific task (e.g., *first look at A, then adjust B, eventually interpret C*).

The main limitation with training in crowdsourcing is the quality assessment. In a lab study, the instructor can supervise the training, answer questions, and provide clarifications. Training represents a crucial aspects of any type of study design, we therefore address this issue in detail in Sect. 4.3.

3   Study Design

3.1   Types of Experiments and Associated Methodologies

The space of experimental designs for visualization studies can be described along multiple dimensions, several of which we describe here:

- **Study goal:** Studies may be employed to determine whether a visualization or visual technique is able to support the goals and tasks it was designed for (*usability*) and to quantify that ability (*quantification*), to understand how a visualization technique can support workflows in practice (*ethnographic*), to compare two visualization techniques in terms of their ability to support different tasks and workflows (*comparative*), and to understand and model mechanisms of human perception (*perceptual*).
- **Study target:** Studies may evaluate static visual encodings, non-interactive animations, visual encodings augmented by interaction, and visual analytic systems (i.e., multiple integrated and interactive visualizations).
- **Study duration:** Studies can be short or extended, and can be conducted over one or multiple experimental sessions. For example, perceptual studies often involve very short tasks [45], while studies that measure participants' ability to memorize visual information for an extended period of time may involve multiple sessions conducted several days apart [81].
- **Type of participants:** Studies may involve naive participants, or participants with a particular expertise or ability. Similarly, they may target either broad populations or populations with specific attributes (e.g., cultural background, visual impairment). A detailed discussion is provided in Sect. 2.

- **Type of methods and constraints:** Different types of studies typically pose unique challenges in the context of crowdsourcing. For example, ethnographic studies rely on participant observation in their environment, and thus need to capture context-data that may be difficult to acquire by a remote experimenter. Quantitative studies need to isolate the evaluated perceptual or data-reading tasks from other, non-related activities and processes. This can be difficult in crowdsourced environments, as unmonitored participants may engage in activities that experimenters are unaware of, and network, device, and browser variability can translate into recorded performance measures and significantly impact the study's outcome (also see Sect. 7). It is also only recently that complex interactive visualizations and visual analytics systems can be distributed online, making them amenable to crowdsourcing. New research is required to understand the impact of such crowdsourcing particularities on different types of user studies, to create evaluation methods that can isolate the evaluated effects from the evaluation process, and to implement the tools to allow experimenters to conduct a wide range of study types with minimal overhead.

Lam et al. [51] provide a more comprehensive discussion on visualization evaluation, and we detail four examples of crowdsourcing-based studies in Sect. 8. Ideally, crowdsourcing technologies would eventually support the design and deployment of studies spanning this space with minimal overhead on the experimenter.

3.2   Study Design Considerations in Crowdsourced Environments

3.2.1   Study Design

Visualization studies are typically designed as between-subjects, within-subjects, or a mixture of the two [77]. Traditionally, researchers gave preference to mixed or within-subjects designs as they were more robust to differences between individuals, and more amenable to the smaller number of participants that lab studies could attract. However, two characteristics of crowdsourcing lead an increasing number of online studies to recently opt for between-subjects designs [5,48,97]. First, unlike lab studies, crowdsourcing gives experimenters access to participant samples considered sufficiently large to offset participants' individual differences (Sect. 2). Second, between-subject studies are shorter, often significantly so, than within-subject ones, and thus fit better with the micro-task paradigm specific to crowdsourcing. Finally, as we will show in Sect. 3.3, because studies employing a between-subjects design are easily extendable (e.g., with new conditions, with additional tasks), they provide unique opportunities for incremental online experimentation.

3.2.2   Study Duration

In line with the micro-task philosophy underlying crowdsourcing, online studies should be kept relatively short. This can be achieved in several ways. First, as mentioned above, between-subjects designs are shorter than within-subject designs. Depending on the study's goals, the evaluation work can be divided across multiple participants by one or a combination of its independent variables (e.g., by visualizations, by datasets, by tasks or groups of tasks). Second, piloting can more reliably inform the choice of reasonable time-limits for tasks, leading to shorter studies with less variance in duration. Finally, participant testing and training, typical components of a visualization study (Sect. 2), can significantly increase the duration of a study. As discussed in Sect. 3.3, allowing participants to save and reuse their demographic information, perceptual markers, and expertise information across multiple studies could significantly shorten the study duration.

3.2.3   Introductions and Task Descriptions

Introductions are perceived as overhead. Long, text-heavy, ambiguous study descriptions frustrate participants. Experimenters should use few words, avoid jargon, and exemplify encodings, interactions, and tasks using clear visual diagrams. Self-explanatory training sessions and task designs that can be picked up without excessive guidance are particularly effective in shortening introductions.

3.2.4   Study Interfaces

Learning and interacting with the interface guiding participants through the study and collecting answers can introduce overhead. Experimenters should minimize this learning overhead by implementing GUI standards and affordances, and building on participants' pre-existing mental models to create study interfaces that can be learned and used without considerable effort. As a community, experimenters should strive to reuse and share study interfaces across their experiments to reduce the learning strain on participants.

3.2.5   Participant Engagement

Unlike participants in laboratory studies, who typically are invited and participate in a limited number of studies, online participants often sift through many posted tasks before they choose one to participate in. While an important consideration in that choice is the amount of compensation, online participants also factor in a study's appeal and fun factor, intellectual reward, and significance of the study's expected results. In fact, there are online communities (e.g., Reddit) who participate in research studies voluntarily and whose members choose studies to participate in solely based on significance and appeal. Moreover, online participants often rate and discuss studies in online forums, building a collective memory and opinion about each study.

Studies that participants can link to their personal experiences can be more engaging. For example, finding paths in an abstract graph visualization is less likely engaging than finding the friends that connect two people in a social network. Micallef et al. [67] report on participants commenting on their interest and engagement in the study, and on things they learned while participating. Section 5 provides a few suggestions on how this could be achieved.

Experimenters can also consider using gamification (e.g., FoldIt[8]) and use one or both of two approaches. First, evaluated tasks could be gamified: participants would solve game-like tasks that are designed to translate or hide a meaningful research question. This is difficult to implement in practice as finding designs that hide meaningful research questions in appealing game-like setups can be challenging, and new creative effort would be necessary for each new studied task or measure. Alternatively, participants' performance on regular, un-gamified tasks could be used in a gaming scheme to motivate and engage participants. For example, based on their participation and performance on user studies, participants could earn points, reach and pass levels, or compete against each other. Since this approach is independent from the particularities of evaluated tasks, it could be integrated into reusable interfaces and platforms that service many diverse studies.

3.2.6 Malicious Behavior

Workers may not take tasks seriously. Gadiraju et al. [38] define five categories of malicious behavior which all apply to evaluation in information visualization. *Ineligible workers* provide wrong pre-conditions about tasks, visualizations, domains, or other skills. *Fast deceivers* give random answers in order to finish a HIT as fast as possible, e.g., randomly selecting visual elements, or entering random numerical values. *Rule breakers* do not provide the required quality of the answer, e.g., giving 1 keyword, when the task requires at least 3 keywords, or by drawing a circle (or a cat) where a more complex drawing may be expected [91]. *Smart deceivers* conform to the rules but give semantically wrong answers. Finally, *Gold standard preys* can only be caught with repeated test questions during the evaluation.

Gadiraju et al. also provide a measure for the maliciousness of a worker and could report that several workers become malicious *during* the study. Fast deceivers can partially be excluded automatically by looking for consistently wrong or invalid answers. Detecting less salient malicious behavior can happen during training (Sect. 2.3) and by repeated tests for attention (Gold standard test) throughout the study. However, as Gadiraju et al. note, those techniques alone are not sufficient and suggest the need to carefully design the tasks to minimize the extent of cheating. Corresponding design guidelines are proposed [38]. However, many tasks in information visualization are very open-ended and hence provide plenty of opportunities for malicious behavior and drawings of cats (Sect. 6).

3.3 Reusable Designs and Results

Controlled experiments often follow standardized procedures and materials. It is, for instance, typical to use entrance and exit questionnaires, to test participants'

---

[8] https://fold.it/portal last accessed 14 Jun 2017.

visual and cognitive abilities and to train them, to control for display or input factors, and to record performance data. In crowdsourced experiments, setting up each of these components involves web-development and requires programming expertise, can consume significant time, and is susceptible to implementation bugs. As such, reusable study components could be assembled into configurable frameworks, purposefully designed to support the crowdsourced evaluation of interactive visualizations in a plug-and-evaluate manner. Developers could connect interactive visualizations to evaluation engines, and specify tasks to be evaluated on those visualizations, data that should be collected, and the number and profiles of participants to be recruited. Creating studies interactively, by assembling existing building block components and workflows, would reduce the overhead of creating online content programmatically.

Such frameworks already exist to support the creation of computer based lab experiments (e.g., Touchstone [57], EvalBench [2]) and for very specific research domains (e.g., HVTE [9]). They have also started to emerge for web-based studies. For example, online interactive forms have gained considerable popularity and enabled a wide range of studies by simplifying the process of fielding a questionnaire and collecting data. Lightweight frameworks provide infrastructure for data collection (e.g., Experimentr[9]) or result visualization (e.g., VEEVVIE [73]). Much closer to our envisioned workflow is the GraphUnit [70] system, which allows even interactive web-content to be connected and evaluated online with minimal overhead. Additional work is necessary to fully realize the objective described here.

3.3.1 Shareable, Reusable, and Extendable Online Designs

Let us consider the following scenario. A visualization researcher or developer creates a new visualization design and evaluates it against its matching state of the art in a controlled experiment. The creators of a third design should be able to reuse as much as possible of this experiment's materials to compare their own solution to the previous two. Moreover, if the initial experiment was conducted using a between-subject methodology, and the second experiment can leverage the same or a similar crowd, then the possibility of simply extending the previous study with an additional condition, corresponding to the latest design, would be ideal.

Similar scenarios include extending the range of tasks evaluated by existing studies, increasing their sample size or diversity, or replicating the studies with modified conditions. By and large, supporting such workflows would allow researchers to incrementally build on top of their own and their colleagues' findings in an unprecedented way.

Two significant technological advancements are necessary to lead towards this goal. First, storing studies online, both in terms of their designs and in terms of their data, in public or shareable repositories, would provide direct access for researchers and developers interested in understanding the design and results of

---

[9] https://github.com/codementum/experimentr last accessed 14 Jun 2017.

studies or in replicating and extending them. Second, a standardization of the technologies and procedures used to create and deploy online user studies would allow a more seamless integration of new conditions or study components into existing ones.

3.3.2   Reusable Participant Profiles and Qualifications

When evaluating visual and interactive content, it is often imperative to test participants on their perceptual, motor, and cognitive abilities (e.g., testing for color blindness) and on their general visual literacy, and train them to understand or use specific visual encodings or interactive visualizations. But it can also be prohibitively time consuming. An ability to allow habitual study participants to create profiles in which to input demographic information and store results and certifications of their testing and training, and an ability to allow them to reuse this data in subsequent studies, would allow researchers to capture more data and make better use of their participants' time. Some existing crowdsourcing platforms (e.g., Amazon Mechanical Turk) provide such features, but additional support needs to be researched and implemented to support the evaluation of visual and interactive content.

4   Study Procedure

Following the principles for standard laboratory experiments, the study procedure in a crowdsourced context involves four stages: experiment setup, pre-experiment activities, experiment activities, and post-experiment activities. Similar to brick-and-mortar experiments (e.g., [63]), the study procedure in crowdsourced settings should be carefully planned and systematically executed. The study procedure follows directly from a concrete research question, and is the result of the operationalization of an experimental study design. Experimental procedures also need to be adapted to the selected crowdsourcing platform (i.e., technical requirements, invitation and task assignment of registered crowdworkers, selection of desired participant sample, etc.). This needs to be carefully tested before the actual study is executed. For this reason, pilot experiments are especially critical in crowdsourced contexts, so as to achieve high internal validity of the study, despite of the limited experimental control compared to traditional lab studies. Information visualization empirical studies are characterized by tasks relying on both perceptual and cognitive abilities of participants. The nature of such tasks demand care in validation of aspects that might hinder the soundness of the collected results. These aspects include not only design but also study deployment (i.e. platform type vs. architecture used) and participant selection (i.e. spatial and visual abilities).

4.1   Experiment Setup

The limitation of experimental control in online studies that are executed without the presence of an experimenter can of course affect participants' responses irrespective of their actual ability, and thus influence the quality of collected performance data. As mentioned in Sect. 2, one of the main differences with online studies in general, and crowdsourced experiments in particular, is that the experimenter cannot ensure that the intended experiment procedure is followed, and thus is identical for each participant, as intended for a laboratory study. The still open research question for crowdsourced studies is thus how procedural control can be achieved in crowdsourced studies. For example, one solution could be the development of detailed standardized instructions, and the inclusion of automatic setup and procedure checks for crowdsourced experiments.

The experimental design, experiment setup, and its deployment on a crowd-sourcing platform should be equally well documented, as is the norm for traditional experiments, as to ensure transparency, and reproducibility for given crowdsourcing platforms. For instance, items to report relate to full disclosure of specification details of the computing environment, such as the type and location of the server used, the type of crowdsourcing platform, and any technical details of the apparatus used to run the study. This might include the specifications of the employed video camera, eye-movement, mouse tracking or other equipment, or any other remote participant behavior tracking technology. Another important procedural control includes the recording and reporting of how and when micro-tasks were uploaded on the crowdsourcing platform, and to whom. Procedural information to report would have to further include whether offered micro-tasks were presented in batch mode or in a particular sequence, at which exact date and time of the day, and whether participants had to satisfy certain prerequisites for participation (e.g., response quality record, geolocation, cultural background, specific work environment, language, etc.). The exact duration of the micro-task, the specific mechanism adopted to engage with participants before the study, or motivate participants to stay focused on the tasks during the study, and what type of reward was offered to them, also needs to be reported.

4.2 Pre-experiment Activities

Similar to laboratory experiments, pilot experiments should be conducted with the target population of crowdworkers. These participants need to be recruited in identical ways as for the main experiment, including the same reward type. This is especially important for crowdsourced experiments, as the availability of crowdworkers is more volatile, and the crowdworkers' backgrounds are more diverse. More importantly, crowdworkers' motivations for participating in an online experiment are likely to be different from those in typical laboratory experiments, for example, carried out with students at universities. Professional crowdworkers might engage in a crowdsourced experiment as part of their job, and thus might wish to finish as many micro-tasks as quickly as possible, even in parallel, so as to increase their income. Study participants recruited for laboratory studies typically do not depend on participation rewards as their sole source of income. For many traditional experiments, especially those carried out at universities, participation is either required for degree completion (i.e., psychology), or for small rewards such as course credits, or some such. Moreover, participants in controlled experiment settings are closely monitored to stay focused on one experiment task at a time.

Collected data from pilot experiments should be analyzed as thoroughly as for laboratory experiments, so as to ensure that the planned procedure is appropriate for targeted participants, task formulations are comprehensible, enough time is allocated for study completion, and that the reward for study participation is fair. Additionally, for pilot studies in crowdsourced contexts it is particularly important to ensure that:

- task instructions are clear and understood for the diverse set of online participants;
- participant attention checks are robust, to ensure that participants stay focused on tasks;
- apparatus checks are robust, to ensure the experiment setup works as planned on the crowdsourcing platform, and crowdworkers' devices;
- participants are able to run the study apparatus as intended and instructed;
- online micro-tasks work as expected on different display types and web interfaces;
- anticipated target group is reached, i.e., language, geo-location, and other sorts of study requirements are met.

As for controlled laboratory studies, full disclosure of pilot study details and respective sample analysis is necessary in study publications and reports, including when, how and with whom pilots were conducted, the reward offered and given, and why and how the experiment procedures were modified due to pilot experiments.

4.3   Experiment Activities

As the experimenter or study supervisor is not physically present during a crowdsourced study, the experiment introduction and respective instructions need to be carefully designed, complete, and unambiguous for the diverse set of potential crowdworkers. Compared to laboratory studies, the following expectations need particular consideration and communication to participants, and respective mechanisms for removal of participants when study expectations are not met:

- screening for repeated study participation by crowdworkers;
- information about attentional demands (i.e., lighting conditions, noise levels, interruptions, etc.);
- required skills and abilities (i.e., language, expertise);
- technology configuration requirements (e.g., speed of CPU, plugins, browser type and versions, screen size, resolution, and color depth);
- anticipated response time limits (i.e., entire study, sections, and micro tasks);
- expected reward structure including minimal response standards;
- consent for participation in the study.

The crowdsourced study should always include warm-up trials and/or a training session with analysis of the response quality before the actual experiment can be run. Training could be complemented with tests that have to be passed before the actual data is recorded. Training could then, theoretically, be repeated until a certain test is passed, provided that proper feedback is given to the participant, explaining mistakes and pointing out how to arrive at the correct answer. Eventually, more training could be provided on demand. This can be useful to assure that participants understand the expected type of questions and experiment tasks, and that the expected experiment procedures stated in the recruitment phase of the study are met (e.g., check of display type, device type, browser configuration, etc.) and thus are identical across participants and repeatable for future studies. However, long training leads to participant fatigue and crowd-workers may complain and discredit the campaign among their peers.

The response procedures should be well explained and amply practiced before the actual experiment, i.e., whether the response type is active (i.e., participants need to complete a task and the answer is displayed later) or passive (i.e., questions and answers are provided jointly). It should also be communicated ahead of time and documented whether participants are allowed to revise answers by going backwards in the study, skip trials, or whether and when they are allowed to take a break.

The experiment trials portion in a crowdsourced study basically follows the standards for laboratory experiments. However, participants' response behaviors must also be carefully monitored and compared to the planned procedures. Hence, a full account of what happened, when, how, and by whom needs to be documented automatically, and digitally recorded such as, an anonymized identifier for the participant, the number, order, and type of trials; how, when, and where the response was recorded; and possibly any other user interaction logs with the system during the entire experiment (i.e., whether a participant revised answers of previous trials, or moved on to the next trials without completing a prior trial, idle times, etc.), so as to be able to trace what exactly happened during the experiment. In crowdsourcing studies, participants' task-relevant attention needs to be monitored remotely. Procedures can include forced breaks and distractor tasks to monitor participant attentional demands throughout the study.

4.4   Post-experiment Activities

As with traditional experiments, post-test questionnaires might include a series of recruitment checks or tests of control variables, such as the assessment of individual differences (e.g., spatial abilities, numeracy abilities, visual literacy, color blindness, etc.), group differences (i.e., gender, age group, expertise levels, etc.), and/or any other user background or demographic assessments and self reports. Also, experiment-related questionnaires for study monitoring purposes might be very useful (e.g., whether participants used additional tools beyond instruction to solve a task; whether participants were confident in their answers; and/or self-reports on strategies used to complete the task). Other aspects such as debriefings, thank you, and free-form comments, simply follow traditional experiment procedures, but need to be built-in in the online experiment.

In laboratory experiments, participants are sometimes compensated at the start of the study to ensure that they could stop anytime they want. However, in crowdsourced studies, the participants are typically compensated after completion of the experiment, as a means to assure response quality.

4.4.1 Processing and Filtering of Collected Data

A special aspect of crowdsourcing experiments is to systematically validate the collected data, so as to assure that anticipated procedures based on a specific experimental design were indeed followed. For that, the quality of the response data needs to be carefully assessed before it can be statistically analyzed. Data from inattentive participants, participants who did not follow the stated instructions, or did not meet experiment requirements (such as a specific language or similar) need be removed from the analysis, and possibly replaced. Such participants could be identified through mechanisms proposed and discussed in Sect. 2. Data from participants who did not complete the entire experiment as stated (i.e., repeating participants, participants who took long breaks between sections, or similar) need be removed too. In specific task types, such as with image tagging, outlier analysis could be performed on the response data, and responses that are beyond 2–3 standard errors above and below the response mean for the sample could be removed. Besides filtering the response data, one could also perform other kinds of validation assessments such as, response error pattern analysis, response time pattern analysis, etc. Any post-test filtering or data validation analysis need to be additionally reported together with the rationale for adopting such approaches, and a description of the final data used for the actual statistical analysis.

4.4.2 Participant Compensation and Experiment Completion

Researchers wishing to run crowdsourced studies especially with well-established crowdsourcing platforms should strive for a high online reputation with crowdsourced workers, such that their profile with the workers is enhanced, so as to attract reliable crowdworkers. A good reputation can be built first and foremost by being honest with study participants, and by compensating them rapidly after completion of the experiment with the promised award or bonus, stated in the experiment instructions. Experimenters need to clearly indicate in the experiment instructions what the expectations for compensations are (i.e., following task instructions, satisfaction of study prerequisites and requirements, etc.). In a crowdsourced setting, where experiment participation might be considered as "employment for a micro task," one might debate about the ethical basis for compensation conditions based on task quality. This is because in regular employment settings, once a person is employed for a given job, the prior agreed pay might not be as easily revoked due to low quality of delivered work. It would simply be at the employer's discretion not to employ that person again for future tasks.

Conversely, crowdworkers also have an incentive to keep up their reputation on crowdsourcing platforms with micro-task providers. Various crowdsourcing platforms provide assessment measures of a crowdworker's reliability, for example, based on the percentage of the completed tasks that were approved by a task provider, including any comments or feedback on the quality of the performed tasks by task providers. Crowdworkers' reliability data are then perused by other task providers to decide upon selection of study participants. This also means that task providers should carefully consider quality of their assessments of crowdworkers, as this could have a great impact on crowdworkers' profiles, and thus might in extreme cases lead to the blocking of a crowdworker's account.

A simple strategy for researchers to avoid the collection of poor response data for future crowdsourced studies is to keep a log of all the participants that did not complete the task appropriately, or not with the desired focus of attention, and thus disallowing these crowdworkers to participate in future crowdsourced experiments. It is generally good practice to keep a log of the study participant IDs in case these crowdworkers need to be contacted again for follow-up questionnaires or tasks, or who might actually be interested in receiving the publication of study results. A log of IDs might also be useful for cross-checks to exclude crowdworkers from participation in studies that are too similar, as to avoid potential learning or knowledge transfer effects.

Once the study participants are compensated and the necessary information is logged, the micro-task should be removed from the crowdsourcing platform.

5   Study Data

Study data forms an important part of the study design as the tasks are performed on the visualized data. Data specifics substantially influence the visualization and interaction techniques used as well as the tasks to be performed. In addition, the meaning and size of the data can influence the incentives for task completion. Thus, an appropriate choice of data, with respect to study tasks and research questions, is crucial to the success of the entire crowdsourcing experiment and of gaining new findings.

Selecting suitable data for crowdsourcing experiments is a challenging core step in the experiment design. For a specific data type, the study designers need to consider several factors when choosing suitable datasets. For instance, they need to decide upon usage of real or controlled data; they also need to consider data suitability for the crowdsourcing studies. This may include data size, data confidentiality, or privacy issues. Moreover, they should take into consideration data attractiveness which influences the participant's engagement and willingness to conduct the study properly.

5.1   Data Source: Real Versus Controlled Data

The dataset should suit the goal of the study and the tasks to be performed. Depending on the study goal, the designers may decide among the following main data sources: *real-world data, controlled data.*

5.1.1   Real-World Data

Real-world data is gained from domain-specific applications. Therefore, this type of data reflects real user problems. Their closeness to real-world situations may raise the attractiveness of the data for the participants. At the same time, real world datasets may be very domain specific. They may require domain expertise, too. This may reduce the suitability of real data for crowdsourcing.

The datasets offer interpretability and thus also are appropriate for testing insight-focused tasks. Often, real data does not include a "ground truth" and hence is not usable for crowdsourced perception studies. Moreover, real datasets are often very limited with respect to variability. Often, only one dataset of a kind is available. This limits the tasks and designs to open-end questions.

Real datasets may be difficult to obtain and to use in crowdsourcing studies. Frequently, they also have confidentiality and privacy constraints making them unusable in crowdsourcing studies, where the participants can freely access and possibly also share the data without access control. Real datasets are often very large and complex. The data size may increase loading times and hardware requirements. This may be problematic in crowdsourcing studies, where the participants have only limited internet access or only simple hardware available (e.g., crowdsourcing participants in India). Data complexity and size may also lead to long task completion times, thus distracting and frustrating many crowdsourcing participants (see Sect. 5.2 for a more detailed discussion of such issues).

5.1.2   Controlled Data

Controlled data differs from real datasets in one main feature: they have specific "controlled" properties and often provide a variability of these features. These are often more suitable for crowdsourcing studies (e.g., can be created such that they are small and simple and non-confidential). However, there are only limited ways of obtaining controlled data, such that they are suitable for the study design at hand. In the following, we present the advantages and disadvantages of controlled data for crowdsourcing studies. We also provide several pointers to sources of these datasets. Here, we focus on three types of controlled data sources: benchmarks, synthetic data creation, and curated real data.

- **Benchmark datasets:** Benchmark data repositories offer public datasets that have specific properties. They are often used in both laboratory and crowdsourcing studies, thus they support comparability across studies.
  The main advantages of benchmark datasets are their public availability and re-usability in research. In contrast to real-world datasets, they have well-known properties that can be tested for task accuracy and completion time. Many benchmark datasets have small sizes and often have real-world interpretation. This may make them favorable for crowdsourcing studies.
  The main drawbacks of benchmark datasets are their limited number and often specialized focus, of which the UC Irvine Machine Learning

Repository[10] is an example. Nevertheless, data from benchmarks are often used in various studies. This brings along an additional problem for crowdsourcing: dataset reuse may potentially lead to repeated participation. The participation in various studies using the same dataset may lead to learning effects and thus skew the collected results. As a general issue to bear in mind for both crowdsourcing and laboratory studies is that benchmark datasets have a limited set of specific properties. While they are suitable for comparability across approaches using standardized tasks, they may not be suitable for novel tasks or for testing novel visualizations (especially visualizations of complex data types). Such datasets may not be available in benchmarks, or may be very difficult to find. For example, the analysis of dynamic geo-located networks requires specific properties, while many benchmark network datasets are static or do not have geo-location at all.

- **Synthetic data creation:** As an alternative, the study designers can develop proprietary datasets specifically for the study at hand. A clear advantage would be that the individual creation of datasets can consider all requirements of the crowdsourcing study. This, however, requires the careful consideration of all criteria including study tasks, dataset specifics, possible target participants, attractiveness, as well as statistically-significant variability (see sections on Tasks, Design, Metrics and Requirements).
Creating such datasets manually can be cumbersome and time consuming. In many cases, study designers can use automatic or visual-interactive data generation tools. For example, the PCDC System [22], SketchPadN-D [92] or the system developed by Albuquerque et al. [4] allow for visual-interactive creation of multivariate data with specified properties. Random data generators, such as graph generators, can automatically create data with special properties (e.g., [6,7,24,98]). This can be joined with visual-interactive means, for instance, Bach et al. [14] developed an evolutionary graph generation algorithm. Another data type – geographic data – can be generated using spatio-temporal patterns [82–84,87].
- **Curating real datasets:** Pre-processing real data for crowdsourcing experiments can bring advantages of both real and synthetic datasets. The resulting datasets are close to reality and, at the same time, have properties needed in a specific crowdsourcing study. For example, the study designers may select a suitably small subset that can be tackled also in a crowdsourcing study on small screens or with slow internet connection. Moreover, the study designers may encode ground truth into it, which is then suitable for measuring accuracy with large number of participants. This is an advantage for crowdsourcing studies, where other assessment methods such as think aloud protocols are not feasible. However, the data curation process can be tedious. In addition to the above-mentioned requirements, in order to be able to use real datasets in crowdsourcing studies, often also data anonymization is needed. Anonymization needs to ensure that the study participants cannot reveal

---

private or confidential information in the original data. This may be difficult to ensure. But, visualization may help to check anonymity and privacy issues in the data. For example, anonymity in multivariate data can be analyzed with the tool by Dagsputa [32], and spatio-temporal data privacy issues can be revealed by data mining and visualization approaches [10,41,68].

5.2 Data Specifics

In this subsection, we highlight specific issues and characteristics of the data used in crowdsourcing experiments. Our assumption is that the data specifics have a great influence on the design and results of the planned experiments. Thus, the dataset should be carefully chosen. For example, the larger and more complex the data, the less likely it is to be suitable for crowdsourcing due to the fact that the participants need to invest considerably more time and effort to understand the data itself. In addition, domain-specific knowledge often plays an important role when using complex datasets, for instance, consider data coming from biochemistry (e.g., biological networks with experimental data attached to the network elements [50]). We briefly describe the most important data specifics in the following.

5.2.1 Data Type and Complexity
In context of information visualization, people usually differentiate between several data types: univariate data (1D), bivariate data (2D), trivariate data (3D), multidimensional or multivariate data (nD), temporal data, tree or hierarchical data, and network or graph data [49]. The data values themselves can be classified according to diverse scales: nominal, ordinal, and quantitative. The different data types lead to various data complexities, e.g., univariate data is surely easier to understand and visualize compared to network data. When using real datasets (see the previous Sect. 5.1), their structure is mostly more demanding because those data is often a mixture between the above mentioned data types. All these properties have a great influence on which visualization (visual encoding) and interaction technique should be chosen. They also have an effect on the tasks that the participants have to cope with (cf. the next Sect. 6).

5.2.2 Data Size
So-called *data scalability*, i.e., the capability of a visualization to handle an increasing amount of data, is a well-known challenge in information visualization [52]. This applies also to crowdsourcing experiments. On the one hand, the chosen visual encoding and visualization in general must be able to efficiently deal with a large dataset. On the other hand, large datasets may be a problem for the crowdsourcing infrastructure and the technical equipment of the participants as they may be difficult for small screens, slow internet connections, or small computing power.

5.2.3 Data Familiarity

Depending on the tasks to solve in an experiment, familiarity with the data is of crucial importance. Participants normally should have enough knowledge about the data domain (there might be study designs where this is not the case) so that they can understand and interpret the data. If this is the case, we can also assume that we have selected the "right" people for the experiment who have a relationship to the data. But, the data may have unexpected effects. For instance, the data can contain information which may be problematic for participants due to cultural differences.

Another factor not to be ignored is the language used in textual or audio-visual data sources, such as extracted text parts from newspapers. Designers of crowdsourcing experiments should either take care to carefully select participants who are able to understand such data or translate the data.

5.2.4 Data Attractiveness

Generally, it is believed that suitable data can improve participants' motivation and engagement in studies. Data attractiveness can be raised by familiarity and by including a "fun" or "game" factor in the data and the tasks. For example, a task of finding a shortest path in an abstract graph may be less engaging than finding a shortest way to a home of a friend. Another factor that can improve attractiveness is reward from solving a task, especially, educational reward. When the participants see that they also learn by solving the task with special data, this can improve their motivation to participate in a study. A great challenge is to provide attractive datasets and tasks. This may involve long data curation or synthetic data creation processes. Yet whether a dataset is attractive depends on a particular participant. So, a right match of participants and the data is crucial.

5.2.5 Data Confidentiality

A special case of data characteristics are privacy and confidentiality issues, for instance, when real data from medical records are used. Generally, confidential data and/or private data are not suitable for crowdsourcing, because we cannot protect them. A natural way of dealing with private or confidential data is anonymization. However, a full anonymization is a difficult challenge. Therefore, crowdsourcing platforms should also provide additional technical support for dealing with confidential data. For example, they should hinder data download and its subsequent distribution. Moreover, they should enable access only to selected participants.

6 Study Tasks

Many taxonomies have been suggested to organize tasks performed by participants working with visualizations (e.g., [8,21,54,85,88]). The purpose of these taxonomies is to support visualization experts in creating the visualization design and to support the evaluation of visualizations.

The purpose of this section is to help researchers determine *if* their tasks are suited to a crowdsourcing-based evaluation, and *how* they may instead construct their evaluation tasks. Note that this does not mean that every task *can* be made suitable to crowdworkers. Some tasks may be simply too difficult, even in lab studies. We provide a list of considerations to help determine whether or not a task is suitable for a crowdsourcing-based evaluation. This is not a new taxonomy, but rather a new dimension of categorization to be considered in addition to those offered by existing taxonomies.

6.1   Tasks in Existing Studies

In this section, we briefly describe some of the visualization tasks that have been successfully used in crowdsourcing-based evaluations. The type of evaluation that can leverage crowdsourcing is usually referred to as a participant performance evaluation. Lam et al. [51] identify two question types for these studies:

- *What are the limits of human perception for a technique?*
- *How does one technique compare to another, in terms of human performance?*

A perfect example of the first question is provided by Harrison et al. [44]. The authors use a Mechanical Turk study to determine the perception of correlation in commonly used visualizations. They use a staircase methodology to infer the Just Noticeable Differences (JNDs) for perception of correlation in each visualization type. For each trial, the participants were shown two visualization of the same type with different datasets and asked which one was most correlated. As part of the staircase methodology, the data displayed for a new trial depends on the result of the previous trial. If a trial is answered correctly the next trial is more difficult, if it is answered incorrectly the next trial is easier.

Jianu et al. [48] perform the type of study suggested in the the second question in their study on displaying community information on node link diagrams. The authors performed ten different experiments each with a different task. Their tasks are inspired by the graph task taxonomy of Lee et al. [54] which is in turn inspired by the information visualization task taxonomy of Amar et al. [8]. Neither of these taxonomies has any consideration about the impact of using crowdsourcing for an evaluation.

The two questions are not mutually exclusive. Heer and Bostock [45], in their pioneering mechanical turk studies (also discussed in Sect. 8.1) perform perceptual experiments, replicating earlier studies. They applied both types of the above questions in their study, quantifying perceptual distortion of area estimates, and providing information about which area representation was superior in terms of accuracy of human perception.

6.2   A Crowdsourcing Dimension for Task Taxonomies

6.2.1   Task Complexity and Task Effort

Similar to Bertin [17], several other taxonomies distinguish between simpler and more complex tasks. For example, Amar et al. [8] name *low-level* and *high-level*, where low-level tasks being smaller units related to unique actions in analytic activity: *Retrieve Value, Filter, Compute Derived Value, Find Extremum, Sort, Determine Range, Characterize Distribution, Find Anomalies, Cluster,* and *Correlate*. These low level tasks are very concrete and cover a wide range of tasks which people try to solve with information visualizations. They focus on identifying specific entities or finding clear correlations. High level tasks, on the other hand, are more general and may involve complex decision making, uncertainty, identifying trends and outliers, and domain knowledge.

While it may be tempting to use the notion of task complexity as a category for determining suitability for a crowdsourcing evaluation, there are many different interpretations of complexity. The notion of complexity can refer to the perceptual complexity of the task and visualization itself, or the cognitive complexity of the task. These are very much participant-based considerations, which may have a different impact on different participants in an experiment. Therefore, rather than task complexity, we suggest task effort as a consideration for crowdsourcing. Effort can be used to not just characterize the task, but also how that task is performed in a crowdsourcing evaluation.

Consider the task of path-tracing as an example. Path tracing is a frequently used task for graph evaluation [48,66,76,94], and would be considered a connectivity task in the graph task taxonomy of Lee et al. [54]. If the task is to determine if the shortest path between two nodes is 1, 2, or 3 hops between a pair of nodes, in [66], the participant may find the shortest path, but have to continue searching to verify that it is indeed the shortest. This may lead to a longer experiment time and frustration if they have to spend a long time verifying that an initial answer was correct. The approach to path tracing taken by Jianu et al. [48] provides the participant with a series of node titles and asks if these titles form a path. This format of the question allows the participant to quickly see if the path is invalid, and does not result them in searching for potential alternatives. In a crowdsourced approach, which is usually a between-subjects evaluation, this allows for quicker answers and more trials.

There may be cases where a researcher desires the participant to search many possible alternatives, but in evaluations where this is not a goal of the task, the shorter validation approach, in which the participant has to determine whether or not the given information is true, is a more desirable approach. In summary, to reduce task effort for crowd workers, and avoid fatigue and distraction, low-level tasks may be preferred. Studies that involve higher-level tasks may benefit from a reduced number of trials, careful explanations, training (Sect. 2.3) and additional motivation (Sect. 3.2.5).

6.2.2   Task Expertise

Related to task complexity and visualization literacy is the level of expertise required to perform a task. However, complexity and expertise are not mutual. For example, sometimes complex tasks can be explained in a simple way, by breaking down the description into low-level and high-congruent [19] (Sect. 2.1) task and formulation. Often this happens by explaining a specific strategy to the participant, such as *"To compare the two datasets, you could first look at X, then filter Y until you find diverging values, and finally report how often you found different values"*. However, other high-level tasks are much harder to break down in to low-level tasks and the study instructor cannot or does not want to reveal specific strategies.

Finding the right participants can be a challenge in performing a crowdsourced-based evaluation. Even if a pre-qualified set of participants is available, care must be taken in the selection and definition of tasks. In use cases where specific tasks are used to determine if participants are qualified, as discussed in Sect. 2.2, care must be taken to ensure the qualification task guarantees the correct minimum level of expertise. Eventually, study authors may want to carefully train participants to perform specific tasks or instead report on the different strategies participants invent and apply.

6.2.3   Technical Task Feasibility

The heterogeneous nature of computer hardware and software means that researchers cannot assume that all experiment participants will have a similar environment to perform the experiment tasks. This may affect the task performance and may influence the results. Especially, screen size, input devices and calibration, and hardware performance influence task performance. For example, perception or interaction studies may result in different accuracy depending on the used screen size and hardware. Other technical issues related to display capability can also be a factor. An experiment that involves human perception of color requires careful consideration of the fact that different display devices have different color gamuts. Depending on the level of accuracy required it may be possible to calibrate response based on some initial questions, asked for this purpose.

In addition, Internet connection speed, affecting page loading times, can interfere with reported measurement times. For some experiments these delays may not interfere with results; however for others the reporting functionality of a crowdsourcing platform may not offer enough accuracy. Heer and Bostock [45] recommend that if researchers require fine grained timing, that they use their own technical implementation of a task interface which participants can access through Mechanical Turk.

7   Study Measures and Metrics

In visualization, quantitative evaluation usually entails measuring the participants' performance of tasks in terms of accuracy (how many tasks were solved correctly) and time (how long did it take to complete the tasks). More recently, there has been a concerted effort to take into account aspects beyond time and error. For example, the BELIV workshop series is a well-known venue created to encourage the study of novel evaluation methods, such as memorability of visualizations, memorability of the underlying data, subjective preferences, engagement and enjoyment. Visualization researchers have also started to include psycho-physiological and neuro-biological measures to study the effectiveness and efficiency in their visualization evaluations. Measures include eye tracking, galvanic skin response measures (GSR) [60], and Electroencephalogram (EEG) recordings [59]. Video cameras help further assess the process with which participants arrive at a certain response. Facial expressions can reveal the emotional state of the participants, and these can be further analyzed using standardized questionnaires [58].

In the context of crowdsourcing, most types of measurements pose interesting challenges, mostly due to the lack of experimental control. For example, response time can be affected by participants' use of different hardware configurations (e.g., desktop computer, laptop, or mobile device). When measuring long-term memorability (e.g., days after initial visualization interaction), ensuring that the same participants are again available for a second assessment can be difficult. Similarly, measuring enjoyment and engagement by observing behavior, or via think-aloud protocols, poses additional challenges in a crowdsourced setting.

Self-reporting methods are possible alternatives and there is good evidence that people are capable of giving numerical or graphical indication of their emotions [71]. Similarly, interaction logging and basic eye-tracking (e.g., via laptop cameras) might be possible.

Attention to the correctness of the experimental procedure in a crowdsourced context, as described in Sect. 4, is crucial, especially when attempting non conventional types of measurements and novel metrics as described in Sect. 7.4.

7.1   Methodological Background

Borrowing from usability studies in human-computer interaction (HCI) research, visualization designers typically employ one or a combination of two evaluation approaches, broadly categorized in formative and summative evaluation methods. Formative evaluation approaches involve human participants early in the design cycle and are often of a more qualitative or quantitative, but subjective, nature such as Likert-style self-reports, preference ratings, and response questionnaires. Summative evaluation methods include more typically controlled, laboratory-based methods, borrowed from empirical research in psychology such as response time (e.g., efficiency) and response accuracy (e.g., effectiveness). Formative and summative methods can help guide what decision has been made with a visualization, and then validate the effectiveness of resulting visualizations.

The evaluation approaches, measures and metrics above are similar to those used for crowdsourcing studies, yet there are certain differences; we next address the topic of measures and metrics in the crowdsourcing context.

7.2   Measure Types

As mentioned above, there are two major types of measures: quantitative (e.g., time and error) and qualitative (e.g., think-aloud protocols, self-reports, focus group discussions, interviews, observations). Each respective measure type has its own advantages and disadvantages in a typical laboratory setting. In the context of crowdsourced visualization studies, there are additional considerations due to the greater lack of experimental control.

7.2.1   Quantitative Measurements

Quantitative measurements consist of counts, frequencies, rates, and percentages that document the actual existence or absence of occurrences and participants' behavior, beliefs, preferences, or attitudes. These methods are considered objective, although they require standardization in order to fit answers into a response scale and/or a number of predetermined response categories. Examples for such standardized measures are standardized questionnaires, psycho-physiological measures, or success and error rate. Quantitative methods are often used to evaluate new visualization methods in laboratory studies, as well as in crowdsourced evaluations, as they are typically easy to administer, may include many questions, may yield a large amount of clearly structured responses that can be easily summarized and statistically evaluated. But clearly, the actual choice of a particular quantitative measure also includes a subjective component and is dependent on the expertise of the experimenter. Furthermore, sometimes difficulties arise, for instance, if the "correct response" cannot sufficiently be specified [26, 95].

7.2.2   Qualitative Measurements

Qualitative measurements consist of descriptions or lists of recorded visualization use events, unstructured text from questionnaires, interviews, or transcribed focus group discussions, video and audio tapes, or observed behaviors. Qualitative measures can provide rich information about thought processes, as well as opinions, experiences, feelings, and attitudes. Qualitative methods can be very valuable for understanding how and why visualizations are used in realistic and meaningful contexts [75]. Qualitative methods, such as those that apply grounded theory, can provide a useful and holistic analysis of visual analytics applications [47]. Since qualitative data are typically collected through direct observation, interviews, and talk-aloud protocols, they are well-suited to laboratory studies. However, qualitative measures have certain drawbacks in laboratory studies. Beyond the difficulty of systematic evaluation, due to the individuality inherent in such data, there is the time consuming nature of qualitative questions for the participants. In addition to the already mentioned challenges, qualitative measures pose further significant challenges in crowdsourced evaluations. For example, in crowdsourced settings it is more difficult to follow talk-aloud protocols, to collect audio and video of the experiment, or to conduct 1-on-1 interviews with the participants.

In a nutshell, qualitative methods can provide deeper insights and can help clarify quantitative data by providing missing explanatory details and semantic nuances which are not inherent in quantitative data [27]. This, however, makes the systematic evaluation of qualitative data distinctly harder. Vice versa, it is easier to evaluate quantitative data systematically. The combination of quantitative and qualitative data can help to tackle qualitative systematization issues and give the quantitative data an enriched context. However, even in controlled laboratory studies, qualitative data is considered to be more subjective and may be difficult to summarize and compare systematically. The challenges increase in the crowdsourced environment, where the choice of qualitative measures that are easily deployed and analyzed is limited to response questionnaires, while quantitative, yet subjective, measures allow for the use of Likert-style self reports and preference ratings.

7.3   Standard Measures

The most commonly collected performance data in visualization evaluations is task performance data (efficiency (e.g., response time), effectiveness (e.g., response accuracy)), measured in terms of time to complete the tasks and errors made. Most often the time to complete a task is measured directly in seconds or minutes. Alternatively, tasks can be given a fixed amount of time and then analyzed for completion within the given time limits (e.g., count of the completed tasks, percentage of completed tasks, ratios of success to failure). Errors can similarly be measured via counts of (in)correctly completed tasks, percentage of (in)correctly completed tasks, and ratios of success to failure [77].

7.4   Measures Beyond the Standard

While controlled laboratory studies using standard evaluation measures are typical in InfoVis, over the last decade there has been the desire to design and implement new methods of evaluation, from longitudinal field studies, insight based evaluation and other metrics adapted to the perceptual aspects of visualization as well as the exploratory nature of discovery. This desire is embodied in the BELIV workshop, which began in 2006, and which aims to collect and discuss innovative ideas about InfoVis evaluation methods, including new ways of conducting user studies, definition and assessment of InfoVis effectiveness through the formal characterization of perceptual and cognitive tasks and insights, and definition of quality criteria and metrics. Several of the proposed measures can be applied in crowdsourced settings.

Recently there has been an increased interest in measuring recognizability and memorability. A number of studies investigate the effect of embellishments on visualization memorability and comprehension. Bateman et al. [15] conducted a study to test the comprehension and recall of charts using an embellished version and a plain version. Bateman's study has been somewhat controversial, and Li et al. [55] recently reported a replication, limiting their selection to those charts that consisted of datasets with 10 or more observations. They found that the presence of a time limit affected comprehension and short-term recall performance, while the type of chart significantly affected short-term recall. Borgo et al. [18] showed that visual embellishment improves information retention in terms of both accuracy of and time required for memory recall. Since their focus was on "visual perception and cognitive speed-focused tasks" that leverage cognitive abilities, they used analytical tasks, where they enforced attention to switch from one task to another. Another study by Vande Moere et al. [89] showed that visual metaphors do not have a significant impact on perception and comprehension. Short term recall can be measured just as well in crowdsourced studies as in laboratory studies.

Ghani and Elmqvist [39] studied the effect of visual landmarking in node-link diagrams and found that landmarking is generally promising for *graph revisitation,* i.e., the "task of remembering where nodes in the graph are and how they can be reached." Marriott et al. [62] investigated the cognitive impact of various layout features, such as symmetry and alignment, on the recall of graphs. They asked participants to look at drawings and redraw them. Perceptual characteristics and memorability in dynamic graphs have also been studied [11,12,36,40]. As a part of an experiment measuring the effectiveness of four visualizations (BubbleSets, Node-link, LineSets, and GMap) Jianu et al. [48] asked participants to perform ten different tasks, including one task related to the memorability of the data.

Graph revisitation tasks and simple memorability tests can be performed in crowdsourced settings, although drawing tasks will likely be much more difficult. Saket et al. [81] present evidence that different visual designs can significantly impact the recall accuracy of the data being visualized, specifically, comparing *node-link* visualizations to *map-based* visualizations. This was measured by asking participants to perform certain tasks with both types of visualizations and later on asking them again to perform a subset of the tasks without the visualization. This type of data recall experiment can be performed in crowdsourced settings.

Other aspects, such as enjoyment and engagement, are not as well explored, even though enjoyment is often given as a reason to consume visualizations [21]. Enjoyment has been carefully studied in psychology. One of the most well-known models for understanding and measuring enjoyment in psychology is the flow model of Csikszentmihalyi [31]. Elmqvist et al. [34] define fluid interaction in the context of information visualization. In a recent study, Haroz et al. [43] assessed user engagement with ISOTYPES by measuring the total amount of time participants spent looking at different visualizations. Boy et al. [20] investigated the effects of initial narrative visualization techniques and storytelling on user engagement by examining interaction logs (e.g., amount of time spent on exploration, number of meaningful interactions). Recently, Mahyar et al. [61], Tanahashi et al. [86], and Saket et al. [79] proposed models of enjoyment in visualization. In particular, Saket et al. considered different elements of flow (challenge, focus, clarity, feedback, control, immersion) and argued that these elements correspond to specific levels of Munzner's nested model [69]. Later

Saket et al. [80] used the flow-based evaluation in a study of the enjoyment of two different visualization methods of the same relational data: node-link and node-link-group visualizations. The results indicated that the participants in this study found node-link-group visualizations more enjoyable than node-link visualizations.

Measuring time spent looking at different visualizations might be difficult in crowdsourced setting when there is a financial incentive to complete the job as fast as possible. However, in crowdsourced setting it should be possible to measure flow elements via Likert-style self reports, preference ratings, and response questionnaires.

Alternative methods for measuring enjoyment and engagement in visualizations have also been considered. Cernea et al. [28,29] employed a mobile electroencephalographic headset for detecting emotional responses, when working with a visualization [58]. Peck et al. [74] argue that functional, near-infrared spectroscopy is a viable technology for understanding the effect of visual design on a person's cognition processes. Fabrikant et al. [35,58–60] measured the emotional responses of participants in a cartographic experiment about interactions with maps, using sensors that monitor psycho-physiological responses and eye movement data. Novel approaches to include eye tracking methodologies [53,96] also in crowdsourcing contexts provide interesting future possibilities in the assessment toolbox of the empirical visualization researcher.

7.5 Challenges for Study Measures and Metrics in Crowdsourcing Studies

There are increased difficulties in performing both quantitative and qualitative evaluations via crowdsourcing. From differences in hardware (desktop, laptop, mobile device) to differences in viewing capabilities (screen size and resolution), and the availability of camera and microphone, such variations can dramatically affect most measurements. Variations in the crowdsourcing platform (which place different restrictions on the experimenter and the participants), as well as environmental conditions (e.g., light conditions, distractions such as noise level, help from another person) that cannot be controlled, pose additional challenges. Consequently, the validity of such experiments and the associated experimental conclusions can be widely open to debate and challenges.

Various strategies to address some of these issues can be employed. If a minimum hardware standard is needed, qualification tasks can be used to select participants with devices that meet the standard (e.g., spoken responses to establish access to microphone, video responses to establish access to camera, etc.). The standard timing of tasks, which can be affected by many factors (e.g., device type, internet connection quality, screen size, etc.) can be replaced by timed tasks, where each task has a time limit (and if the answer is not given within that time limit the result is recorded as incorrect). Crowdsourcing platforms that allow the experimenter to identify and contact the participants can be used for evaluations that require repeated sessions (e.g., memorability).

8   Case Studies

This section discusses four case studies that demonstrate diverse ways in which crowdsourcing can be used for visualization research. Not only can crowdsourcing be used to perform simple visual perceptual micro-tasks as described in case study 1, but it can also be used to understand users' complex visual comprehension of composite visualizations as summarized in case study 2. While the first two studies demonstrate the use of crowdsourcing for evaluating and comparing static visualizations, the third case study shows how different user individual traits can be assessed and included in the visualization study, and the last case study indicates the use of crowdsourcing for interactive visualizations, including data collection for informing the design of visualization techniques and algorithms. Below, we summarize the four case studies by their participants, procedures, data, tasks, and measures. For each case study, we also discuss their take-away points and limitations.

8.1   Case Study 1: Assessing Graphical Perception

Jeffrey Heer and Michael Bostock (2010). *Crowdsourcing graphical perception: using mechanical turk to assess visualization design.* In Proceedings of the SIGCHI Conference on Human Factors in Computing Systems (pp. 203–212). ACM.

- **Crowdsourcing usage:** Used Amazon Mechanical Turk to replicate previous laboratory studies in spatial coding and luminance contrast and then compare the results of the two.
- **Design:** The study design follows the design of previous laboratory studies where a user is asked to accomplish various visual perception tasks, ranging from ranking visual variables by their effectiveness for conveying quantitative values to judging how a chart size may affect visual comparison accuracy.
- **Participants:** For task 1's sub-task 1, there are 70 trials and 50 Turkers per trial; a total of 3481 responses are received and each trial is paid $0.05. For task 1's sub-task 2, there are 108 trials and 24 Turkers per trial; each trial is paid $0.02 (10 s per trial). For task 2, there are 60 trials and 24 Turkers per trial; each trial is paid $0.02 per trial. Task 3 includes 48 trials and 24 Turkers per trial; each trial is paid $0.04.
- **Procedure:** For each task, a Turker first performs a qualifying task and then the perceptual task.
- **Data:** The data used to create the visualization used in the experiments are gathered from the previous laboratory studies.
- **Tasks:** The study includes three main tasks. The first task is to replicate Cleveland and McGill's studies on spatial coding. The task includes two sub-tasks: Proportional Judgment and Rectangular Area Judgment. The second task is another perceptual task: separation and layering via luminance contrast. It replicates an alpha contrast experiment by Stone and Bartram. The third task is on the effects of chart size and gridline spacing on the accuracy of visual comparison.

- **Measures and metrics:** The study collects the Turkers' judgment from a set of visual perception tasks and compares the crowdsourced judgment with that obtained from previous laboratory studies. Depending on the task, the metrics/measure are different. For example, for the alpha contrast task, the alpha value, time to completion, and the Turker's screen resolution, color depth, and browser type are recorded.
- **Take-Away points:** (1) Since this is an early crowdsourced study for visual perception tasks, it demonstrates the viability of such studies, since the study successfully replicated prior experiments in three visual perceptual tasks. (2) The study also demonstrates the use of crowd to gain new insights into visualization design. (3) It also characterizes the use of Mechanical Turk for conducting web-based experiments. (4) It shows certain advantages of using crowdsourced studies over laboratory studies, including its low cost, speed, as well as participant diversity.
- **Limitations:** The main limitations lie in the type of visual perceptual tasks being investigated. When such tasks become more complex and require more visual literacy, it is unknown how the crowd would perform.

8.2   Case Study 2: Understanding Users' Comprehension and Preferences for Complex Information Visualization

Huahai Yang, Yunyao Li, and Michelle X. Zhou (2014). *Understanding users' comprehension and preferences for composing information visualization.* ACM Transactions on Computer-Human Interaction (TOCHI), 21(1), 6.

- **Crowdsourcing usage:** Used Amazon Mechanical Turk to crowdsource participants' insights and preferences for using complex information visualization to accomplish real-world visual analytic tasks.
- **Design:** The paper presents two crowdsourced between participant-design studies. The first study aims at soliciting the participants' comprehension of a typical information visualization by asking the participant to articulate the insights s/he has derived from the visualization given a specific, realistic analytic task with real datasets. This study contains a total of ten sets of visualization, each of which contains three visualizations, two simple visualizations that present the same dataset in different ways and one composite visualization that is supposed to provide additional insight compared to the two simple ones. The second study aims at soliciting the user's preferences when using a composite information visualization to accomplish an analytic task. This study consists of eight groups of visualizations, each of which includes five different composite visualizations of a dataset. And each participant is asked to assess the five composite visualizations by accomplishing an analytic task, as well as rank his/her preference amongst the five composite designs.
- **Participants:** In the first study, 50 Turkers were recruited for each of 10 sets of visualization; a total of 524 responses were received and each response was paid $1.50 (about 20-minute per response). In the second study, thirty Turkers were recruited for each of eight groups of visualization; a total of 240 responses received.

- **Procedure:** In the first study, each Turker is asked to articulate the insights that they derive from each visualization in free text. In the second study, each Turker is asked to rank his/her preferences for each composite visualization that s/he uses to accomplish an analytic task.
- **Data:** Six real-world datasets from SPSS associated with real-world analysis tasks were used in both studies.
- **Tasks:** In both studies, Turkers are asked to perform visual analytic tasks by deriving certain types of insights from a given visualization. The Turkers were also asked to describe any derived insights in free text.
- **Measures and metrics:** Both studies collected rich data, ranging from free text to ranked user preferences. A set of measures and metrics is also derived from extensive data analysis. In study 1, from user-articulated visual insights in free text, a taxonomy of user-perceived visual insights is derived. A set of metrics is also derived to measure the taxonomy, including the quality of insights (accuracy + depth), ease of comprehension, usefulness of insights, and distribution of insights. In Study 2, user preferences of composite visualization are derived from the collected data.
- **Take-Away points:** (a) This is an early study that crowdsources users' complex, high-level comprehension of information visualization beyond simple visual perception experiments. It thus provides methods to systematically instrument such crowdsourced studies for complex visual cognitive tasks and rigorously analyses the quality and reliability of free-text-based crowdsourced results beyond structured, multi-choice survey answers. (b) The study also presents a systematic content analysis method for other researchers to harvest insights from such crowdsourced rich content in free text. The collected raw text as well as the derived visual insight taxonomy establishes the connections between one's verbal expressions and information visualization, which lays a foundation to develop more advanced information visualization systems, e.g., natural-language-based visualization retrieval and generation.
- **Limitations:** The main limitations lie in the type of visualizations and analytic insights being investigated. When interactive visualization is involved, deriving insights from such an interactive visualization may introduce unknown challenges (e.g., a wide diversity of actions amongst participants) that this study has not addressed.

8.3   Case Study 3: Analyzing Deceptive Visualizations

Anshul Vikram Pandey, Katharina Rall, Margaret L. Satterthwaite, Oded Nov, and Enrico Bertini (2015). *How deceptive are deceptive visualizations?: An empirical analysis of common distortion techniques.* In Proceedings of the SIGCHI Conference on Human Factors in Computing Systems (pp. 1469–1478). ACM.

- **Crowdsourcing usage:** Used Amazon Mechanical Turk (AMT) to study deceptive visualizations, assessing in particular: (a) the deceptiveness of different distortion techniques in visualization; (b) the type of questions for which such visualizations are mostly deceptive; (c) the effect of users' various individual traits on the deceptive effect.

- **Design:** Four within-group experiments were conducted to assess four different types of deception caused by different distortion techniques ("truncated axis," "aspect ratio," "area," "inverted axis") and evaluate the deception effect on the users' responses. The deception type was the independent variable, while the user response was the dependent variable.
- **Participants:** Recruited 330 unique AMT workers who reported to be located in the Unites States and who had a task approval rate of at least 99%. Participants were paid $0.30 for a 5 to 10-minute experiment.
- **Procedure:** An experiment website was hosted on a server external to AMT, and a link to the webpage was provided in AMT's task description. The experiment stages, shown as different webpage pages, included: (a) consent form; (b) personal information form; (c) chart familiarity test; (d) visual abilities test; (e) deception test, including a chart overview, the chart, the deception test question and an attention check question; and (f) need for cognition scale.
- **Data:** The context and the axes of the charts were made up for the study but non-abstract. Example of a chart title, 'Access to safe drinking water by minority ethnic group over time'. The type of data used is not clearly explained in the paper.
- **Tasks:** Two types of tasks in accordance with the type of deception: (a) "how much" questions ("how much better is A compared to B"), when the visualization message is exaggerated or understated; (b) "what" questions ("what does chart A show?") with multiple-choice answers, when the visualization message is reversed.
- **Measures and metrics:** (a) user response, including response accuracy (percentage of correct answers) and mean user response; (b) measures of the deceptive effect occurring when the visualization message is exaggerated or understated (results of the correctly and incorrectly represented charts were compared in a between-participants analysis) and when the message is reversed (response accuracy was compared in a between-participants analysis); (c) measures of individual traits, including their familiarity with basic charts, their visual literacy, their need for cognition, age, gender and education, used to regulate the user response.
- **Take-away points:** (a) To our knowledge, this is the only crowdsourced visualization study which takes into account the effect of various user individual traits on the collected responses. As shown in previous laboratory user studies (e.g., [99]), user individual traits influence the effectiveness of visualizations, yet such traits are often not tested in crowdsourced experience due to the need to keep online experiments short. (b) This study indicated that good quality results could be achieved by employing attentive check questions, which are then used to filter out the data before analysis, and by testing various individual traits such as visual literacy which can then be used to regulate the user response accordingly.

- **Limitations:** The data collected for the user individual traits did not provide any statistically significant results, possibly indicating that these trait tests should be redesigned and adapted for crowdsourced experiments.

8.4   Case Study 4: Identifying Graph Layout Aesthetics

Steve Kieffer, Tim Dwyer, Kim Marriott, and Michael Wybrow (2016). *Hola: Human-like orthogonal network layout*. IEEE Transactions on Visualization and Computer Graphics, 22(1), 349–358.

- **Crowdsourcing usage:** Built an online system (using HTML5/Javascript) named Orthowontist to conduct two studies: (a) collecting data about the aesthetic criteria a graph layout algorithm should optimize to ensure the generation of human-readable network layouts with a comparable quality to manual layouts produced by hand, and (b) evaluating the effectiveness of the layouts generated by the proposed automatic orthogonal network layout algorithm, HOLA, that took into account the aesthetic criteria collected in the first phase.
- **Design:** Both studies adopted a within-group design.
- **Participants:** Both studies were advertised on a university-wide bulletin. For study 1, part 1 had 17 participants who could have won one of three $50 gift cards if their layouts were ranked high in part 2, and part 2 had 66 participants who could have won a $50 gift card only if their answers were the closest to the aggregated answers of other participants. For study 2, 89 participants completed part 1, 84 completed part 2, and 83 continued through parts 3 and 4.
- **Procedure:** The overall procedure for both studies involved: (a) consent form and instructions; (b) questionnaire about their experience in using node-link diagrams; (c) technical training on how to use Orthowontist along with training tasks; (d) the study tasks; and (e) comments about the study.
- **Data:** Study 1 used small random abstract graphs with an incomprehensible layout for part 1, and the layouts used in part 1 together with the participants' improved layouts in part 1 for part 2. Study 2 used graphs with diverse number of nodes and edges. A few graphs depicted real-data (e.g., Sydney's metro map, the Glycolysis-Gluconeogenesis pathway), others were random graphs. None of the nodes and edges were labeled and no context was provided for any of the graphs.
- **Tasks:** In study 1, the participants were asked to (1a) manually edit the layout of graphs to make them more human-readable, and (1b) choose the best layout with respect to their aesthetic preference. In study 2, the participants were asked to (2a) rank graph layouts based on their aesthetic preference, (2b) find the shortest path between two nodes in a graph, (2c) identify all neighbouring nodes of a highlighted node by clicking on the nodes, and (2d) choose the best of two layouts for the same graph and explain why.
- **Measures and metrics:** For both studies, user preference, response accuracy and response time were recorded. For some tasks, the participants were asked to explain in writing their response.

- **Take-Away Points:** (a) Crowdsourcing is not only useful to evaluate visualization, but also to collect data to inform the design of novel visualization algorithms. (b) It is possible to use crowdsourcing for interactive tasks, such as manually editing the layout of graphs (e.g., moving nodes or edges, adding or deleting edges) or interacting (e.g., clicking) with parts of the visualization (e.g., the nodes of a graph) to provide an answer. (c) It is also possible to log complex interactions when crowdsourcing user studies.
- **Limitations:** It is unclear whether the study included participant attentive checks and how the experimenter ensured the data reliability.

8.5 Summary

As described above, the four case studies have used crowdsourcing for different aspects of visualization research. Case study 1 demonstrates that crowdsourcing can be used to replicate previous laboratory studies on understanding people's visual perceptions. Moreover, a crowdsourced approach greatly reduces the cost and time required to perform such studies, let alone having access to the large, diverse participant population. Case study 2 goes further to demonstrate that crowdsourcing can also be used to understand participants' comprehension in composite visualizations. It also indicates how to crowdsource rich participant input in free text and harvest insights from such input beyond crowdsourcing and analyzing just simple micro-task data. Case study 3 further shows the power of crowdsourcing in understanding participants' perception of complex and potentially deceptive visualizations. It also shows how various individual traits can be measured and assessed in crowdsourced studies. Case study 4 solicits the crowd's aesthetic criteria for network layout and then incorporates the crowdsourced results into layout algorithms. It demonstrates the effectiveness of harvesting the crowd's creativity to inform new visual designs beyond studying participants' visual perceptions.

While the four case studies demonstrate the effectiveness of crowdsourcing in visualization research, they also point out the challenges and limitations in such studies. In particular, the difficulty in instrumenting interactive visualizations for a diverse crowd as well as acquiring comprehensive participant behavioral data during the study (e.g., a participant's attentiveness and experimental condition) that might be easier to control or observe in a traditional laboratory condition.

9 Conclusion

In this chapter, we have highlighted what can be considered the most relevant dimensions in the use of crowdsourcing for Information Visualization research and application development, to which its use brings some genuine advantages and challenges.

9.1   Strengths and Opportunities

Literature shows how access to a larger and diverse cohort enriches the amount of information that can be collected as well as the types of data analysis that can be conducted. Financial effectiveness is one of the most mentioned features especially for research on a budget, and crowdsourcing supports easy scaling to large samples that would otherwise be prohibitive, greatly expanding the space of feasible study designs. Crowdsourcing provides opportunities beyond simple cost-cutting, and support from crowdsourcing platforms considerably reduces recruiting effort, which is an extremely time consuming task.

Crowdsourcing as a concept is still evolving. The diversity of approaches deployed on existing platforms and interpretations of the concept itself, which transcends off the shelf environments like Amazon Mechanical Turk, provide the opportunity for the research community to tap into dimensions not yet explored. First and foremost is the development of platforms capable of supporting InfoVis-type experiments. The literature shows how community requirements go beyond simple data collection typical of marketing research, for which most of the existing platforms have been initially developed. Literature also shows how the ability to scale to a large cohort and to increase user community diversity can lead to new analytical methods which might strengthen existing or lead to new findings. Comparison of traditional laboratory based studies and crowdsourcing based studies is a powerful means to replicate and compare results which can lead to consolidate or question field knowledge foundations. Challenges posed by crowdsourcing environments also represent an opportunity to re-think study settings and propose novel designs.

9.2   Weaknesses and Threats

Scalability to large cohorts comes at a loss in ability to control two aspects of a study execution: recruitment and filtering of participants, and monitoring of task execution from both experimental setting and participants' level of involvement. These aspects imply a considerable increase in the complexity of designing a study; more factors need to be taken into account to avoid confounding effects and guarantee reliability of the collected data. Cost-effectiveness carries also non-negligible ethical issues when monetary transactions are involved. Work ethics is not only an ethical issue but a fundamental aspect in research, therefore this book devotes an entire chapter to its role in crowdsourcing (see Chap. 3).

Crowdsourcing provides access to the power of the crowd which is a fascinating phenomenon. The crowd itself is, however, a very complex entity and as such not suited for each and every task. Threats that might be looming at the horizon include the fallacious perception that quantity implies quality. Crowdsourcing-based studies should not be interpreted as a replacement for traditional laboratory studies and neither a requirement to support research findings. It is also easy to overestimate a crowd's knowledge basis; when tasks demand specific skills the chance of overestimation is a highly dangerous threat to the soundness of a study's results.

References

1. Adams, F.M., Osgood, C.E.: A cross-cultural study of the affective meanings of color. J. Cross Cult. Psychol. **4**(2), 135–156 (1973)
2. Aigner, W., Hoffmann, S., Rind, A.: EvalBench: a software library for visualization evaluation. Comput. Graph. Forum **32**(3pt1), 41–50 (2013)
3. Aigner, W., Miksch, S., Schumann, H., Tominski, C.: Visualization of Time-Oriented Data. Human-Computer Interaction. Springer, London (2011). doi:10.1007/978-0-85729-079-3
4. Albuquerque, G., Lowe, T., Magnor, M.: Synthetic generation of high-dimensional datasets. IEEE Trans. Vis. Comput. Graph. **17**(12), 2317–2324 (2011)
5. Alsallakh, B., Micallef, L., Aigner, W., Hauser, H., Miksch, S., Rodgers, P.: Visualizing sets and set-typed data: state-of-the-art and future challenges. In: Eurographics conference on Visualization (EuroVis)-State of The Art Reports, pp. 1–21 (2014)
6. Alvarez-Garcia, S., Baeza-Yates, R., Brisaboa, N.R., Larriba-Pey, J., Pedreira, O.: Graphgen: a tool for automatic generation of multipartite graphs from arbitrary data. In: 2012 Eighth Latin American Web Congress (LA-WEB), pp. 87–94. IEEE (2012)
7. Álvarez-García, S., Baeza-Yates, R., Brisaboa, N.R., Larriba-Pey, J.L., Pedreira, O.: Automatic multi-partite graph generation from arbitrary data. J. Syst. Softw. **94**, 72–86 (2014)
8. Amar, R., Eagan, J., Stasko, J.: Low-level components of analytic activity in information visualization. In: IEEE Symposium on Information Visualization (INFOVIS 2005), pp. 111–117. IEEE (2005)
9. Andrews, K., Kasanicka, J.: A comparative study of four hierarchy browsers using the hierarchical visualisation testing environment (HVTE). In: 11th International Conference Information Visualization (IV 2007), pp. 81–86. IEEE (2007)
10. Andrienko, G., Andrienko, N.: Privacy issues in geospatial visual analytics. In: Gartner, G., Ortag, F. (eds.) Advances in Location-Based Services. Lecture Notes in Geoinformation and Cartography. Springer, Heidelberg (2012). doi:10.1007/978-3-642-24198-7_16
11. Archambault, D., Purchase, H.C.: The mental map and memorability in dynamic graphs. In: Pacific Visualization Symposium (PacificVis), pp. 89–96. IEEE (2012)
12. Archambault, D., Purchase, H.C.: Mental map preservation helps user orientation in dynamic graphs. In: Didimo, W., Patrignani, M. (eds.) GD 2012. LNCS, vol. 7704, pp. 475–486. Springer, Heidelberg (2013). doi:10.1007/978-3-642-36763-2_42
13. Bach, B., Dragicevic, P., Archambault, D., Hurter, C., Carpendale, S.: A descriptive framework for temporal data visualizations based on generalized space-time cubes. Comput. Graph. Forum (2016). http://dx.doi.org/10.1111/cgf.12804
14. Bach, B., Spritzer, A., Lutton, E., Fekete, J.-D.: Interactive random graph generation with evolutionary algorithms. In: Didimo, W., Patrignani, M. (eds.) GD 2012. LNCS, vol. 7704, pp. 541–552. Springer, Heidelberg (2013). doi:10.1007/978-3-642-36763-2_48
15. Bateman, S., Mandryk, R.L., Gutwin, C., Genest, A., McDine, D., Brooks, C.: Useful junk? The effects of visual embellishment on comprehension and memorability of charts. In: Proceedings of the SIGCHI Conference on Human Factors in Computing Systems, pp. 2573–2582. ACM (2010)
16. Berlin, B., Kay, P.: Basic Color Terms. University of California Press, Berkeley (1969)

17. Bertin, J.: Sémiologie graphique: Les diagrammes-Les réseaux-Les cartes. Gauthier-VillarsMouton & Cie (1973)
18. Borgo, R., Abdul-Rahman, A., Mohamed, F., Grant, P.W., Reppa, I., Floridi, L., Chen, M.: An empirical study on using visual embellishments in visualization. IEEE Trans. Vis. Comput. Graph. **18**(12), 2759–2768 (2012)
19. Boy, J., Rensink, R.A., Bertini, E., Fekete, J.D.: A principled way of assessing visualization literacy. IEEE Trans. Vis. Comput. Graph. **20**(12), 1963–1972 (2014)
20. Boy, J., Detienne, F., Fekete, J.D.: Storytelling in information visualizations: does it engage users to explore data? In: Proceedings of the SIGCHI Conference on Human Factors in Computing Systems, pp. 1449–1458. ACM (2015)
21. Brehmer, M., Munzner, T.: A multi-level typology of abstract visualization tasks. IEEE Trans. Vis. Comput. Graph. **19**(12), 2376–2385 (2013)
22. Bremm, S., Von Landesberger, T., Heß, M., Fellner, D.: PCDC-on the highway to data-a tool for the fast generation of large synthetic data sets. In: EuroVis Workshop on Visual Analytics, pp. 7–11 (2012)
23. Brewer, C.A., MacEachren, A.M., Pickle, L.W., Herrmann, D.: Mapping mortality: evaluating color schemes for choropleth maps. Ann. Assoc. Am. Geograph. **87**(3), 411–438 (1997)
24. Brinkmann, G., McKay, B.D.: Fast generation of planar graphs. MATCH Commun. Math. Comput. Chem. **58**(2), 323–357 (2007)
25. Bristor, V.J., Drake, S.V.: Linking the language arts and content areas through visual technology. THE J. **22**(2), 74–77 (1994)
26. Çöltekin, A., Fabrikant, S.I., Lacayo, M.: Exploring the efficiency of users' visual analytics strategies based on sequence analysis of eye movement recordings. Int. J. Geograph. Inf. Sci. **24**(10), 1559–1575 (2010)
27. Çöltekin, A., Heil, B., Garlandini, S., Fabrikant, S.I.: Evaluating the effectiveness of interactive map interface designs: a case study integrating usability metrics with eye-movement analysis. Cartography Geogr. Inf. Sci. **36**(1), 5–17 (2009)
28. Cernea, D., Kerren, A., Ebert, A.: Detecting insight and emotion in visualization applications with a commercial EEG headset. In: SIGRAD 2011 Conference on Evaluations of Graphics and Visualization-Efficiency, Usefulness, Accessibility, Usability, pp. 53–60 (2011)
29. Cernea, D., Weber, C., Ebert, A., Kerren, A.: Emotion scents - a method of representing user emotions on GUI widgets. In: Proceedings of the SPIE 2013 Conference on Visualization and Data Analysis (VDA 2013). IS&T/SPIE (2013)
30. Cole, F., Sanik, K., DeCarlo, D., Finkelstein, A., Funkhouser, T., Rusinkiewicz, S., Singh, M.: How well do line drawings depict shape? ACM Trans. Graph. **28**(3), 28:1–28:9 (2009)
31. Csikszentmihalyi, M.: Flow: The Psychology of Optimal Experience. Harper Perennia, New York (1990)
32. Dasgupta, A., Kosara, R.: Privacy-preserving data visualization using parallel coordinates. In: IS&T/SPIE Electronic Imaging, pp. 786800-1–786800-12. International Society for Optics and Photonics (2011)
33. Demiralp, Ç., Bernstein, M.S., Heer, J.: Learning perceptual kernels for visualization design. IEEE Trans. Vis. Comput. Graph. **20**(12), 1933–1942 (2014)
34. Elmqvist, N., Vande Moere, A., Jetter, H.C., Cernea, D., Reiterer, H., Jankun-Kelly, T.J.: Fluid interaction for information visualization. Inf. Vis. **10**(4), 327–340 (2011)
35. Fabrikant, S.I., Christophe, S., Papastefanou, G., Maggi, S.: Emotional response to map design aesthetics. In: 7th International Conference on Geographical Information Science, pp. 18–21 (2012)

36. Farrugia, M., Quigley, A.: Effective temporal graph layout: a comparative study of animation versus static display methods. Inf. Vis. **10**(1), 47–64 (2011)
37. Fort, K., Adda, G., Cohen, K.B.: Amazon mechanical turk: gold mine or coal mine? Comput. Linguist. **37**(2), 413–420 (2011)
38. Gadiraju, U., Kawase, R., Dietze, S., Demartini, G.: Understanding malicious behavior in crowdsourcing platforms: the case of online surveys. In: Proceedings of the SIGCHI Conference on Human Factors in Computing Systems, pp. 1631–1640. ACM (2015)
39. Ghani, S., Elmqvist, N.: Improving revisitation in graphs through static spatial features. In: Graphic Interface (GI 2011), pp. 737–743 (2011)
40. Ghani, S., Elmqvist, N., Yi, J.S.: Perception of animated node-link diagrams for dynamic graphs. Comput. Graph. Forum **31**(1), 1205–1214 (2012)
41. Giannotti, F., Pedreschi, D.: Mobility, Data Mining and Privacy: Geographic Knowledge Discovery, p. 410. Springer, Heidelberg (2008). doi:10.1007/978-3-540-75177-9
42. van Ham, F., Rogowitz, B.: Perceptual organization in user-generated graph layouts. IEEE Trans. Vis. Comput. Graph. **14**(6), 1333–1339 (2008)
43. Haroz, S., Kosara, R., Franconeri, S.L.: Isotype visualization-working memory, performance, and engagement with pictographs. In: Proceedings of the SIGCHI Conference on Human Factors in Computing Systems, pp. 1191–1200. ACM (2015)
44. Harrison, L., Yang, F., Franconeri, S., Chang, R.: Ranking visualizations of correlation using Weber's law. IEEE Trans. Vis. Comput. Graph. **20**(12), 1943–1952 (2014)
45. Heer, J., Bostock, M.: Crowdsourcing graphical perception: using mechanical turk to assess visualization design. In: Proceedings of the SIGCHI Conference on Human Factors in Computing Systems, pp. 203–212. ACM (2010)
46. Hirth, M., Hoßfeld, T., Tran-Gia, P.: Anatomy of a crowdsourcing platform-using the example of microworkers.com. In: 2011 Fifth International Conference on Innovative Mobile and Internet Services in Ubiquitous Computing (IMIS), pp. 322–329. IEEE (2011)
47. Isenberg, P., Zuk, T., Collins, C., Carpendale, S.: Grounded evaluation of information visualizations. In: Proceedings of the 2008 Workshop on BEyond Time and Errors: Novel Evaluation Methods for Information Visualization (BELIV 2008) pp. 6:1–6:8. ACM (2008)
48. Jianu, R., Rusu, A., Hu, Y., Taggart, D.: How to display group information on node-link diagrams: an evaluation. IEEE Trans. Vis. Comput. Graph. **20**(11), 1530–1541 (2014)
49. Kerren, A., Ebert, A., Meyer, J. (eds.): Human-Centered Visualization Environments. LNCS, vol. 4417. Springer, Heidelberg (2007). doi:10.1007/978-3-540-71949-6
50. Kerren, A., Schreiber, F.: Network visualization for integrative bioinformatics. In: Chen, M., Hofestädt, R. (eds.) Approaches in Integrative Bioinformatics, pp. 173–202. Springer, Heidelberg (2014). doi:10.1007/978-3-642-41281-3_7
51. Lam, H., Bertini, E., Isenberg, P., Plaisant, C., Carpendale, S.: Empirical studies in information visualization: seven scenarios. IEEE Trans. Vis. Comput. Graph. **18**(9), 1520–1536 (2012)
52. Laramee, R.S., Kosara, R.: Challenges and Unsolved Problems. In: Kerren et al. [49], pp. 231–254
53. Lebreton, P., Mäki, T., Skodras, E., Hupont, I., Hirth, M.: Bridging the gap between eye tracking and crowdsourcing. In: Proceedings of SPIE, vol. 9394, pp. 93940W–93940W-14 (2015)

54. Lee, B., Plaisant, C., Parr, C.S., Fekete, J.D., Henry, N.: Task taxonomy for graph visualization. In: Proceedings of the 2006 AVI Workshop on Beyond Time and Rrrors: Novel Evaluation Methods for Information Visualization, pp. 1–5. ACM (2006)
55. Li, H., Moacdieh, N.: Is "chart junk" useful? An extended examination of visual embellishment. Proc. Hum. Factors Ergon. Soc. Annual Meeting **58**(1), 1516–1520 (2014)
56. Light, A., Bartlein, P.J.: The end of the rainbow? Color schemes for improved data graphics. EOS **85**(40), 385–391 (2004)
57. Mackay, W.E., Appert, C., Beaudouin-Lafon, M., Chapuis, O., Du, Y., Fekete, J.D., Guiard, Y.: Touchstone: exploratory design of experiments. In: Proceedings of the SIGCHI Conference on Human Factors in Computing Systems, pp. 1425–1434. ACM (2007)
58. Maggi, S., Fabrikant, S.: Embodied decision making with animations. In: Proceedings of International Conference on Geographic Information Science 2014 (2014)
59. Maggi, S., Fabrikant, S.I.: Triangulating eye movement data of animated displays. In: ET4S@GIScience, pp. 27–31 (2014)
60. Maggi, S., Fabrikant, S.I., Imbert, J.P., Hurter, C.: How do display design and user characteristics matter in animations? An empirical study with air traffic control displays. Cartographica **51**(1), 25–37 (2016)
61. Mahyar, N., Kim, S.H., Kwon, B.C.: Towards a taxonomy for evaluating user engagement in information visualization. In: Workshop on Personal Visualization: Exploring Everyday Life (2015)
62. Marriott, K., Purchase, H., Wybrow, M., Goncu, C.: Memorability of visual features in network diagrams. IEEE Trans. Vis. Comput. Graph. **18**(12), 2477–2485 (2012)
63. Martin, D.: Doing Psychology Experiments, 7th edn. Thomson Wadsworth, Belmont (2008)
64. Martin, D., Hanrahan, B.V., O'Neill, J., Gupta, N.: Being a turker. In: Proceedings of the 17th ACM Conference on Computer Supported Cooperative Work & Social Computing, pp. 224–235. ACM (2014)
65. McCloud, S.: Understanding Comics: The Invisible Art. HarperPerennial, New York (1994)
66. McGee, F., Dingliana, J.: An empirical study on the impact of edge bundling on user comprehension of graphs. In: Proceedings of the International Working Conference on Advanced Visual Interfaces, pp. 620–627. ACM (2012)
67. Micallef, L., Dragicevic, P., Fekete, J.D.: Assessing the effect of visualizations on bayesian reasoning through crowdsourcing. IEEE Trans. Vis. Comput. Graph. **18**(12), 2536–2545 (2012)
68. Monreale, A., Andrienko, G.L., Andrienko, N.V., Giannotti, F., Pedreschi, D., Rinzivillo, S., Wrobel, S.: Movement data anonymity through generalization. Trans. Data Priv. **3**(2), 91–121 (2010)
69. Munzner, T.: A nested model for visualization design and validation. IEEE Trans. Vis. Comput. Graph. **15**(6), 921–928 (2009)
70. Okoe, M., Jianu, R.: Graphunit: evaluating interactive graph visualizations using crowdsourcing. Comput. Graph. Forum **34**(3), 451–460 (2015)
71. Paas, F., Tuovinen, J.E., Tabbers, H., Van Gerven, P.W.: Cognitive load measurement as a means to advance cognitive load theory. Educ. Psychol. **38**(1), 63–71 (2003)

72. Pandey, A.V., Rall, K., Satterthwaite, M.L., Nov, O., Bertini, E.: How deceptive are deceptive visualizations? An empirical analysis of common distortion techniques. In: Proceedings of the SIGCHI Conference on Human Factors in Computing Systems, pp. 1469–1478. ACM (2015)

73. Papadopoulos, C., Gutenko, I., Kaufman, A.: VEEVVIE: visual explorer for empirical visualization, VR and interaction experiments. IEEE Trans. Vis. Comput. Graph. **22**(1), 111–120 (2016)

74. Peck, E.M.M., Yuksel, B.F., Ottley, A., Jacob, R.J., Chang, R.: Using fNIRS brain sensing to evaluate information visualization interfaces. In: Proceedings of the SIGCHI Conference on Human Factors in Computing Systems, pp. 473–482. ACM (2013)

75. Plaisant, C.: The challenge of information visualization evaluation. In: Proceedings of the Working Conference on Advanced Visual Interfaces (AVI 2004), pp. 109–116. ACM (2004)

76. Purchase, H.: Which aesthetic has the greatest effect on human understanding? In: DiBattista, G. (ed.) GD 1997. LNCS, vol. 1353, pp. 248–261. Springer, Heidelberg (1997). doi:10.1007/3-540-63938-1_67

77. Purchase, H.C.: Experimental Human-Computer Interaction: A Practical Guide with Visual Examples. Cambridge University Press, Cambridge (2012)

78. Ross, J., Irani, L., Silberman, M., Zaldivar, A., Tomlinson, B.: Who are the crowdworkers? Shifting demographics in mechanical turk. In: CHI 2010 Extended Abstracts on Human Factors in Computing Systems, pp. 2863–2872. ACM (2010)

79. Saket, B., Scheidegger, C., Kobourov, S.: Towards understanding enjoyment and flow in information visualization. In: EuroVis. The Eurographics Association (Short Paper) (2015)

80. Saket, B., Scheidegger, C., Kobourov, S.: Comparing node-link and node-link-group visualizations from an enjoyment perspective. Comput. Graph. Forum **35**(3), 41–50 (2016)

81. Saket, B., Scheidegger, C., Kobourov, S.G., Börner, K.: Map-based visualizations increase recall accuracy of data. Comput. Graph. Forum **34**(3), 441–450. http://dx.doi.org/10.1111/cgf.12656

82. Sakshaug, J.W., Raghunathan, T.E.: Synthetic data for small area estimation. In: Domingo-Ferrer, J., Magkos, E. (eds.) PSD 2010. LNCS, vol. 6344, pp. 162–173. Springer, Heidelberg (2010). doi:10.1007/978-3-642-15838-4_15

83. Sakshaug, J.W., Raghunathan, T.E.: Generating synthetic data to produce public-use microdata for small geographic areas based on complex sample survey data with application to the national health interview survey. J. Appl. Stat. **41**(10), 2103–2122 (2014)

84. Sakshaug, J.W., Raghunathan, T.E.: Nonparametric generation of synthetic data for small geographic areas. In: Domingo-Ferrer, J. (ed.) PSD 2014. LNCS, vol. 8744, pp. 213–231. Springer, Cham (2014). doi:10.1007/978-3-319-11257-2_17

85. Shneiderman, B.: The eyes have it: a task by data type taxonomy for information visualizations. In: Proceedings of the 1996 IEEE Symposium on Visual Languages, Boulder, Colorado, USA, 3–6 September 1996, pp. 336–343. IEEE Computer Society (1996)

86. Tanahashi, Y., Ma, K.L.: Stock lamp: an engagement-versatile visualization design. In: Proceedings of the 33rd Annual ACM Conference on Human Factors in Computing Systems, pp. 595–604. ACM (2015)

87. Theodoridis, Y., Silva, J.R.O., Nascimento, M.A.: On the generation of spatiotemporal datasets. In: Güting, R.H., Papadias, D., Lochovsky, F. (eds.) SSD 1999. LNCS, vol. 1651, pp. 147–164. Springer, Heidelberg (1999). doi:10.1007/3-540-48482-5_11

88. Valiati, E.R., Pimenta, M.S., Freitas, C.M.: A taxonomy of tasks for guiding the evaluation of multidimensional visualizations. In: Proceedings of the 2006 AVI Workshop on Beyond Time and Errors: Novel Evaluation Methods for Information Visualization, pp. 1–6. ACM (2006)

89. Vande Moere, A., Tomitsch, M., Wimmer, C., Christoph, B., Grechenig, T.: Evaluating the effect of style in information visualization. IEEE Trans. Vis. Comput. Graph. 18(12), 2739–2748 (2012)

90. Wainer, H.: A test of graphicacy in children. Appl. Psychol. Measure. 4(3), 331–340 (1980)

91. Walny, J., Huron, S., Carpendale, S.: An exploratory study of data sketching for visual representation. Comput. Graph. Forum 34(3), 231–240 (2015)

92. Wang, B., Ruchikachorn, P., Mueller, K.: SketchPadN-D: WYDIWYG sculpting and editing in high-dimensional space. IEEE Trans. Vis. Comput. Graph. 19(12), 2060–2069 (2013)

93. Ware, C.: Information Visualization: Preception for Design, 3rd edn. Elsevier, Amsterdam (2013)

94. Ware, C., Mitchell, P.: Visualizing graphs in three dimensions. ACM Trans. Appl. Percept. 5(1), 2:1–2:15 (2008)

95. Wilkening, J., Fabrikant, S.I.: How users interact with a 3d geo-browser under time pressure. Cartography Geogr. Inf. Sci. 40(1), 40–52 (2013)

96. Xu, P., Ehinger, K.A., Zhang, Y., Finkelstein, A., Kulkarni, S.R., Xiao, J.: TurkerGaze: crowdsourcing saliency with webcam based eye tracking. CoRR abs/1504.06755 (2015)

97. Yang, H., Li, Y., Zhou, M.X.: Understand users' comprehension and preferences for composing information visualizations. ACM Trans. Comput. Hum. Interact. 21(1), 6:1–6:30 (2014)

98. Ying, X., Wu, X.: Graph generation with prescribed feature constraints. In: SDM, vol. 9, pp. 966–977. SIAM (2009)

99. Ziemkiewicz, C., Kosara, R.: Preconceptions and individual differences in understanding visual metaphors. Comput. Graph. Forum 28(3), 911–918 (2009)

Cognitive Information Theories of Psychology and Applications with Visualization and HCI Through Crowdsourcing Platforms

Darren J. Edwards[1]([✉]), Linda T. Kaastra[2], Brian Fisher[2], Remco Chang[3], and Min Chen[4]

[1] Swansea University, Swansea, UK
d.j.edwards@swansea.ac.uk
[2] Simon Fraser University, Burnaby, Canada
[3] Tufts University, Medford, USA
[4] University of Oxford, Oxford, UK

1 Introduction

This chapter introduces information processing perspectives from cognitive psychology, providing historical background content where it might prove useful. The hope is that this will provide readers enough of an understanding of psychology perspectives, theories, and methods that they can better apply crowdsourcing methods to understand the cognitive outcomes of interaction within visualization environments and other computer interfaces.

Readers who are interested in a comprehensive understanding of cognitive psychology theory and methods would do well to refer to one of the many textbooks or online resources (such as the Noba Project[1]) on psychology history, theory and methods. Here we will limit ourselves to touching on key perspectives with an emphasis on the diversity of approaches that have been used to study cognition.

2 Introduction to Psychology and Its Subdomains

It is important to understand that the field of cognitive psychology did not emerge from a single methodological or conceptual framework. Rather, it grew out of a number of different approaches to understand the nature of mental life. Some theoretical work in early psychology was not based on scientific observation at all, but on the clinical work of trained practitioners through subjective introspection, and without objective verification. Other researchers developed lines of inquiry based on methodological approaches from scientific disciplines such as chemistry, biology, physics, and engineering [24]. This diversity of approaches led to much disagreement as to what methods would be most effective, and what kind of theory would provide the best understanding of human cognition.

---

[1] http://novaproject.com last accessed 14 Jun 2017.

© Springer International Publishing AG 2017
D. Archambault et al. (Eds.): Evaluation in the Crowd, LNCS 10264, pp. 139–153, 2017.
DOI: 10.1007/978-3-319-66435-4_6

2.1   Structrualism

One of the first conceptual approaches to psychology, developed in the early 1900s, was Structuralism [71]. This was founded in part by Wilhelm Wundt and later developed by E. Bradford Titchener. Structuralism was in part inspired by methodological advancements in the field of chemistry. In a way analogous to research on chemical compounds, Structuralists aimed to use introspective methods to identify and catalog a diverse set of mental properties, and then to discover how those properties combined to make up more complex mental operations. When applied by chemists, this approach produced a manageable set of elements and compounds. The same approach taken by Structuralist researchers led to claims of at least 40,000 elements of sensation alone [71]. However, the work drew criticism from contemporaries such as William James, who claimed that the profusion of elements was the result of the "psychologist's fallacy" of introspective methods. He concluded that introspection could not be used to discover elements of sensation and perception without distortion [36].

2.2   Functionalism

Another contemporary movement in psychology was the Functionalist movement. Functionalists examined the role of mind, or mental activity, in the life of an organism [8]. This approach drew from Darwin's theory of natural selection. Early Functionalists aimed to explore consciousness [36] through studying mental operations, and to identify psychophysical relations [1] that transform physical phenomena (e.g. an image projected on the retina) with their psychological outcomes (e.g. the perception of the stimulus).

2.3   Gestalt Psychology

A third contemporary approach, Gestalt psychology, was inspired by the physics of the day. Gestalt psychologists employed third-person phenomenological inquiry to discover principles of perceptual organization [75]. One driving idea behind this methodological approach was the insight that mental properties combine to create something new in the same way that physical particles organize into new wholes. Wertheimer put it this way, "I stand at the window and see a house, trees, sky. Theoretically, I might say there were 327 brightnesses and nuances of color. Do I have '327'? No. I have sky, house, and trees" [75]. As this quote suggests, Gestalt psychologists were aware of the challenges of identifying the units and levels of mind that could be empirically investigated. From the Gestalt perspective, our perception of events in the world is better explained by regularities in the environment itself rather than by an information processing method.

2.4   Behavioral Psychology

These competing ontologies made it difficult for a unified approach to understanding human cognition to emerge. Lacking any common ground of concepts, reconciling structuralism and functionalism proved impossible.

A different approach altogether was taken by behavioral psychologists, who avoided conflicts between competing ontologies, arguing that any conceptual approach would have to be based on subjective evidence and so fail to rise to the level of a true science. In order to avoid what they considered to be a subjective approach to science Behaviorists instead chose to empirically study actions, i.e., what people and animals do in response to different environmental situations (e.g. [51]).

Behavioral psychology became the dominant approach of psychology in the 1950s with its use of classical and operant conditioning methods to understand human and animal behavior. Classical conditioning experiments [51], demonstrated that through pairing the sound of a bell with food, associative learning could occur, a process now called classical conditioning. To demonstrate this, Pavlov measured the levels of saliva a dog produced when exposed to these stimuli. With the presence of food the dog would salivate, and after some training the food was removed and the dog would continue to salivate on the sound of the bell. This classically conditioned response coupled the presence of food with the sound of the bell, leading to the same result regardless of which stimulus was used. Skinner [23], expanded this work in an approach called operant conditioning. Operant conditioning proposed that any behavior which led to a pleasant outcome was likely to be repeated, and any behavior which led to an unpleasant outcome would be less likely to be repeated. Individual behaviors that led to positive outcomes could be combined, resulting in complex patterns of behavior that could be reliably produced in animals and humans.

Behaviorism produced many interesting findings. However, by the late 1960s it was no longer the dominant theory in psychology. The challenge came from studies demonstrating characteristics of behavior that were not easily explained by conditioning. Notable among these was Chomsky's transformative generative grammar, as described in his book 'Syntactic Structures' published in 1957 [10]. Chomsky argued that Skinner's operant conditioning was not adequate to explain the emergence of language. Instead, there were innate components to language in the form of a universal grammar. Chomsky suggested that all cultures, even in remote regions, have the same basic components of language such as verbs and nouns, and that language could be generated in an almost infinite amount of ways. Without the conceptual core of universal grammar it would be unlikely that language could be explained through conditioning alone (see [17], for a more complete historical perspective).

2.5 The Beginnings of Cognitive Psychology

Through challenges such as Chomsky's, it became apparent that understanding cognition would require researchers to study mental representations and ways in which they were generated, processed, stored and recalled. Thus Cognitive Psychology gradually replaced Behaviorism as the dominant paradigm of psychology, and it was then incorporated in early Human-Computer Interaction (HCI). It remains central to HCI and visualization research today.

Cognitive psychology was used by Ulric Neisser in 1967 [47] to describe the processing of sensory input, how it is transduced from physical stimuli into sensation, elaborated and stored in mental representations, recovered from memory and used in cognitive task performance. Rather than focusing purely on the behavioral outputs in response to reinforcement provided, cognitive psychology uses constructs that describe regularities in mental representations and methods by which those representations are processed that can be confirmed by experiments. In keeping with the focus on human information processing, Neisser proposed that people could be considered dynamic information processing systems whose mental operations can be given in computational terms (e.g. Shannon's information theory [64]). Today, cognitive psychology is a large subject area which bases theories on mental representations and processes such as implicit and explicit memory, focal attention, visuospatial processing, object and event categorization etc.

Although its focus is on information representation and processing, cognitive psychology was able to characterize a range of human capabilities and limitations that hold true over a variety of cognitive tasks. Examples of these are the working memory model (WMM) [3] and the multi-store model for human memory [2], which includes a central executive with a role in processing short term memory information from two kinds of short-term "working" memory – a visual-spatial sketchpad for spatial information and an articulatory-phonological (AP) loop for sounds, especially language – into long term storage through rehearsal.

Another well-known piece of work was Miller's 1956 [44], which applied Claude Shannon's information theory to [64] propose that the capacity limitation of the AP loop was "seven plus or minus two" or 2.5 bits of information. Because the AP loop was a key component of many information processing pathways it was claimed that its capacity would limit performance of a variety of cognitive tasks.

Computer science researchers are increasingly knowledgeable about the key points of these important older works. They are often less aware of newer, more progressive models of human cognition that might also impact their work. For example, a great deal of attention has been given to devising categorization theories that utilize information theory to describe processes of category formation and its use in cognition [38, 39].

Studies of categorization give rise to two distinct theoretical traditions, supervised categorization (e.g. [48, 69, 74]); and unsupervised categorization, e.g. the simplicity model [55–58]. A third emerging area, relational representation in categorization, proposes theories which claim that relational properties are important in categorizing information [20, 70, 79]. Categorization models have been applied to many areas of psychology, including clinical and developmental psychology, for example, as a diagnostic tool for autism [19], and for traumatic brain injury [21], as well as a way of understanding cognitive development in children [18].

Other modern cognitive theories are based on information theory as well. Unitization Theory specifies information reduction in implicit memory. Experiments conducted by Unitization theorists show that through the training of a consistent sequence of events the individual events that make up this sequence eventually become part of a whole and lose their individual identity. Through unitization, information contained in a string of numbers is reduced from multiple bits of information in memory to a single bit, or "chunk" of information [30,52,53]. Theories such a Unitization Theory demonstrate that our processing of information can be altered by the sequences in which they take place. This theory may be particularly relevant to experiments where there is less control of the specific stimuli and presentation order, as is typically the case in crowdsourcing studies.

2.6 Cognition and Computer Science

Attempts to develop computer models of human performance had a deep impact on cognitive psychology. Work by David Marr [41] led to his tri-level hypothesis. This hypothesis was based on the early thinking about visual representation and was influenced in part on Shepard and Metzler's, 1971, mental rotation [68]. Marr proposed that there are three levels of description of information processing in the visual system. The 'computational theoretic level' describes the operating requirements for the system— what the system computes, what are its outputs used for, and what problem it solves. The 'algorithmic representation level' specifies the operations that take place to enable the system to solve the problem. Finally, the 'physical level' specifies the mechanisms that are responsible for the processing, e.g., which neurons process a visual stimulus and how they operate.

Applying this approach to human vision, Marr suggested that the reason for seeing places constraints on the nature of seeing. This can be considered an ecological approach to perception theory, in that it specifies that the properties of an organism's visual system are determined by the operations that vision must perform in order for that creature to survive. Finding food, escaping predation etc. place requirements on visual processing that must be operationalized algorithmically and operationalized on the physical infrastructure, i.e. the neurons.

At the algorithmic level, processing a representation can take many forms. For example, the number three can be represented in binary (11), Roman (III) or Arabic (3) numerals, by the word "three", saying "du du da", showing three fingers, using a triangle, holding three acorns, and so on. It should be obvious by looking at the different representations of three, that each representation privileges a certain algorithm, or computational process. Take, for example, the case of a lost person seeking to find their location. Different individuals may approach the problem of being lost very differently. One might navigate based on the position of the sun and shade from buildings or lampposts to determine which direction to walk. Another might look for address numbers on buildings and street signs. Yet another might look for friendly people to approach and ask for directions. In these instances the same goal can be supported by algorithmic level processes that are quite different. Each of these algorithms is constrained not only by the need to achieve the goal of the computation but also the operating characteristics of the physical neurons that perform the computation.

Marr's Tri-Level Hypothesis of vision serves as an example of how the information-processing model of mind can address the transformation between the physical world and cognitive task performance in the context of human behavior in the environment. It does this by bridging from a computational theory of the organism in its environment to the creation of representations of information and algorithms by which they can be processed. These algorithms in turn are mapped onto neural substrates for processing. Through specification of these three levels it becomes possible to generate powerful explanations for cognition in humans and in human-computer cognitive systems.

Marr's Tri-Level approach to understanding cognition was later extended to distributed cognition by Edwin Hutchins [34,35] in his theory of human interactions with external events. Hutchins' work has been a key contributor to the development of HCI work today.

2.7   Crowdsourcing Psychology Studies

In recent years, psychologists have begun to explore crowdsourced forms of data collection such as Survey Monkey, Crowd Flower and Amazon Mechanical Turk (AMT) [16]. What may be important to note is that all of these studies have taken place within the last decade. Because the use of crowdsourced experiments in psychology is quite recent, its use is still controversial and the methods used are continually being refined.

3   The Influence of Psychology on Visualization and HCI Research

This section introduces some of the ways in which psychology has been utilized in visualization and HCI research, including recent studies using crowdsourcing methods. This is done as a basic overview. The next two sections explore the advantages and limitations, as well as future directions for crowdsourcing research in these areas.

3.1   The Influence of Psychology on Visualization Research

As an applied science, visualization has benefited tremendously from the discoveries in psychology. For example, in visual design, the understanding about the ordering of some commonly used visual channels, such as color, size, shape, orientation, and symbols [28], is derived from a large collection of studies on visual search [59,76]. The phenomenon of visual multiplexing [9], which has been utilized to create effective visualization, can be ratiocinated using literary evidence in psychology, such as the multi-store model for human memory [2], Gestalt principles of organization [32], and dimensionality of the stimulus space [66]. Many recent advances in psychology are waiting to be applied in visualization, as will be discussed in the Future Directions section of this chapter.

As a way of evaluating scientific theory, visualization offers a platform by which theories of psychology can be tested and potentially disconfirmed. Fundamental questions about how people perceive complex graphical representations and reason about the information they contain may yield discoveries that are critical to both visualization and psychology. For example, how do humans adapt to constructed environments such as visualization to perform analytical tasks and decision processes? How do humans interpret, and are influenced by, uncertainty depicted in visualization? How do humans learn to interpret static patterns (e.g., a time series plot) as temporal events, and how can such skills be extended in other scenarios (e.g., visualizing a video using static imagery)?

Cognition researchers have embraced crowdsourcing platforms for a variety of empirical studies [29]. For example, there have been crowdsourcing studies on color naming [45], human visual computing [26], uncertainty encoding [5], Bayesian reasoning charts [43], and orderability judgment [11]. In each of these applications experiment design and analysis must contend with potential confounding effects in empirical data collected from these less controllable environments. It is likely that the visualization community will support this effort by contributing new visual analytics tools for observing large volumes of crowdsourced data, analyzing confounding effects and their impact, removing outliers and anomalies, and presenting analytical results. For these reasons, crowdsourcing seems to be a reasonable platform for data collection in terms of visualization research and will continue to be in the future.

3.2   Distributed Cognition in HCI Research

As discussed in Sect. 2.6, Marr's Tri-Level Hypothesis helped to give rise to a perspective on cognition that viewed it as distributed across multiple human agents, or across a human and a responsive external system. This approach to cognition proposed the use of cognitive ethnography to study human collaboration and interaction with external events by Edwin Hutchins and colleagues [31,34,35]. By viewing cognition as the interaction of representation and algorithm, Hutchins was able to develop ethnographic methods to explore cognitive processing across different kinds of cognitive systems and at different scales of observation.

In an example of this human interaction application with cognitive distribution, Hutchins compared Western and Micronesian flight navigation systems along Marr's three levels. The computational level was characterized by the self-positioning of the aircraft with respect to the task and the travel goals. While it may seem like the problem would be the same for both groups, Hutchins demonstrated key differences in the representation and algorithms employed in both groups [33]. First, in Western navigation, the ship was moving across the ocean from one location to another. The path could be drawn and calculated on a small-scale chart that represents the Earth. In the Mirconesian system, the navigator was at the center, and his position was fixed with reference to the stars and sun. There were islands he could not see which also had fixed positions with respect to the stars and sun. When the Micronesian navigator traveled in a canoe, he was aiming for a certain fixed bearing with respect to the stars and sun, by moving the Earth past him. So, while the Micronesian navigator moved the Earth past him, the Western navigator moved along the Earth.

These are very different ways of representing aspects of the environment for the purposes of navigation, and these differences continue to the hardware level. The hardware level of Marr's tri-level hypothesis includes the substrate in which the cognitive processing takes place. For the field of vision, this includes the structures of the eye and the firing of neurons in all of the systems involved in vision. For Hutchins, the hardware level includes aspects of the environment that play a role in cognition, for example, the nomograph and ruler used to calculate ship speed. Hutchins called these 'cognitive artefacts' as they perform the task of organizing functional skills into cognitive functional systems.

In parallel with the growing interest in distributed cognition in the cognitive science community, HCI research has moved beyond studies of individual task based interaction to examine groups of individuals communicating through technology [77] e.g. in computer supported cooperative work (CSCW). The psychological theory of distributed cognition has been an important component used to bridge HCI with CSCW [46].

One example of this comes from Scaife and Rogers [63]. These researchers explored how external properties of graphical representations can affect thinking and reasoning through their influence on the users' mental representations.

In another example, Mayers et al. [42] assessed user knowledge of Macintosh applications. They found that even expert users could not recall all of the menu headings. Despite their lack of recall, these users encountered no difficulties in using the menus and the application as a whole. From this, Mayers believed that users did not commit all of the applications components to memory. Rather the users relied on cues to select the correct menu. Young et al. [78], suggested that these findings challenged the well-known 'Goals, Operators, Methods, Selection rules' (GOMS; e.g., [37]) family of interaction. In Young's view the display, through cueing the user, played a more central role in controlling interaction with the graphical user interface than did the user's memory.

We find that work in psychology and HCI can be quite complimentary. Working from Mayers' findings in HCI can lead us to seek further explanations by focusing on theories in psychology involving visual cues, limits in memory stores, attentional saliency, and categorical efficiency in reducing information. While promising, these approaches of bridging HCI and Psychology work have not been sufficiently utilized. We discuss this in our Future Directions section, with an emphasis on crowdsourcing approaches.

4   Advantages and Disadvantages of Using Crowdsourcing in Psychology

This section takes a psychological perspective in exploring some of the advantages and disadvantages of crowdsourcing platforms for research. These include self-selection, response bias, representativeness of the population, and the reliability of crowdsourced experiments. We address responses to these threats in our Future Directions section by proposing an information theoretical approach to cognition with application to crowdsourcing studies.

Given the similarities between the two disciplines, the advantages and disadvantages of crowdsourced data for HCI and psychology may be similar. From the psychology literature, Crump et al. [16] suggests that one of the major concerns about laboratory experiments is the challenge of obtaining quick, large and reliable samples. As well, the lack of diversity of the population obtained threatens the external validity of the study results. This view is supported by other psychologists, for example, Reips [60] suggests that the advantages of using crowdsourcing over laboratory experiments is the ability to generate a large sample and diverse demographic, whilst the disadvantages are the loss of control and self-selection in subject recruitment. Other concerns about laboratory studies, include the pygmalion effect, where the experimenter's expectations lead to higher performance by the participant [6,62]; low power due to unavailability of students wishing to participate [12,25]; and demand characteristics [49,61], where participants, often students of the same subject area, believe that the experiment demands a certain outcome. In contrast, crowdsourcing data gathering provides access to a more diverse participant pool, with lower costs [29,65]. Other advantages and disadvantages are discussed below.

4.1 Self-selection and Completion Rates

Shawver et al. [65] suggested that the completion rates and how the experiments are completed may play a role in the success and accuracy of findings. Their findings demonstrated a higher completion rate for participants in face-to-face (laboratory) settings when compared to online settings. However, the higher completion rate in the face-to-face setting did not result in better data. The greater accuracy of the online data could be due to the self-selection nature of the online platform, with individuals dropping out of the survey based on some internal cue about the quality of their own responses and without pressure to remain in the study until the end. These pressures may exist in laboratory settings and may affect the quality of the data, with less accurate data generated as a result.

4.2 Representativeness of the Data

Using AMT or other online platforms to gather data does not automatically ensure that the participants or their responses will be representative of a diverse population. Researchers can take measures to strengthen the diversity of the data pool by using a filter or clustering procedure [15]. However, simply being open to the general public means that crowdsourcing has the potential to attract a more diverse population in comparison to university-based laboratory studies that draw from a student population.

4.3   Reliability of Crowdsourced Experiments

Concerns about lack of control in studies conducted using crowdsourcing can be ameliorated in the same way that laboratory studies are, through replication in other studies and by other researchers. The test-retest validity of crowdsourcing found high test-retest reliability when using an AMT population for psychometric tests [7]. This was also the case for Gosling et al. [27] who found good reliability in questionnaire surveys conducted using an internet population. In addition to this, Paolacci et al. [50] replicated several one-shot decision-making experiments on AMT. These studies used well-researched tasks such as the Asian disease problem test for framing effects [73], the Linda problem test for the conjunction fallacy [72], the Physician problem test of outcome bias [4] and the Prisoner's dilemma game [13]. However, these experiments do all involve the participant making a single decision about a question, so these were not cognitively demanding.

Despite the fact that AMT has been demonstrated as useful and reliable for simple, and cognitively non-demanding tasks, very little work had been conducted in the psychology community to evaluate the usefulness of crowdsourcing for more complex cognitively demanding experiments.

Many cognitive psychology experiments require accurate (typically millisecond) measurement of subject reaction times. This level of accuracy is common in studies of attention. These studies may also require multi-trial designs and complex instructions, making them challenging for crowdsourcing methods. Crump et al. [16] replicated several of these cognitively demanding reaction time studies using crowdsourcing: the Stroop task-switching experiment [40]; the Flanker task [22]; the Simon task [14]; the Posner cuing tasks [54]; and the category learning task [67] with good results in a series of short 5 min studies. To our knowledge no replications have been conducted for longer scale cognitive psychology experiments that are typical for laboratory studies.

5   Future Directions for Improving Visualization and HCI Crowdsourced Experiments

We will conclude this chapter by suggesting how recent information processing theories and models from psychology could support more effective use of crowdsourcing for visualization and HCI research.

While classical theories from cognitive psychology, such as the multi-store model for human memory [2], Gestalt principles of organization [32], and dimensionality of the stimulus space [66] are a good starting point for design and analysis of HCI laboratory studies, they are not well suited for crowdsourcing methods.

When using crowdsourced methods experimenters should be aware that they have less control over what is being presented to the participant than in laboratory studies. More recent modeling approaches to understanding human cognition may prove more useful in guiding the design and analysis of these studies. One example of this is the Relative Judgment Model of categorization (RJM [70]). This model specifies how the order of stimuli presented to the participant will affect the decision-making process and the accuracy of the subject responses. Through the use of RJM it may be possible to factor out the effects of variability of stimulus presentation encountered in crowdsourcing studies, reducing their ability to obscure the effects of interest.

Other recent information processing models could prove useful for HCI work. Mayers et al. [42] explored the information processing nature of cognition. Theories of unitization and contextual locking [52,53] can predict how user procedures can become unitized in memory as a conceptual "chunk" and as a perceptuomotor procedural "script". A string of procedures – e.g. 'press start' then 'press menu', then 'press select application' – initially require multiple discrete decisions, taking up several bits of information stored in working memory. According to unitization theory these bits of information can be reduced to a single bit of information after learning. Through procedural learning, the number of bits in working memory can reduce to a single bit of information capturing the entire procedure. As Mayers et al. [42] suggest, an explicit (i.e. conscious) memory of each of these steps is not needed once the sequence of actions has been learned.

Models of chunking and procedural learning could play an important role in interpreting crowdsourced experiments. As with RJM, these models may be able to be used in crowdsourcing to both study their phenomena of interest and to factor out these learning effects, thus enabling analysis of other variables of interest.

For studies conducted in relatively contaminated and uncontrolled environments, computational and mathematical models of human cognition can be used to model complex data and to factor out known effects, producing a clean dataset for subsequent statistical and modeling analysis.

6   Conclusion

This chapter has sought to (1) introduce the broad nature of psychology; (2) offer some examples of how psychology has been applied to visualization and HCI; (3) explain some of the advantages of using crowdsourced experiments, as identified through the psychology literature; and (4) to offer some new approaches from contemporary information theories of psychology that can be applied to crowdsourced experiments.

As crowdsourced research grows in importance we must continue to advance new methods for designing, validating, and analyzing results from complex experiments. We believe that the advantages of crowdsourcing will make this effort worthwhile.

Acknowledgment. We would like to express gratitude to Dagstuhl for facilitating the seminar (titled, 'Evaluation in the Crowd: Crowdsourcing and Human-Centred Experiments'), which has allowed this collaboration to develop.

References

1. Angell, J.R.: The province of functional psychology. Psychol. Rev. **14**(2), 61 (1907)
2. Atkinson, R.C., Shiffrin, R.M.: Human memory: a proposed system and its control processes. Psychol. Learn. Motiv. **2**, 89–195 (1968)˙
3. Baddeley, A.D., Hitch, G.: Working memory. Psychol. Learn. Motivation **8**, 47–89 (1974)
4. Baron, J., Hershey, J.C.: Outcome bias in decision evaluation. J. Pers. Soc. Psychol. **54**(4), 569 (1988)
5. Boukhelifa, N., Bezerianos, A., Isenberg, T., Fekete, J.D.: Evaluating sketchiness as a visual variable for the depiction of qualitative uncertainty. IEEE Trans. Visual Comput. Graphics **18**(12), 2769–2778 (2012)
6. Brophy, J.E., Good, T.L.: Teacher-Student Relationships: Causes and Consequences. Holt, Rinehart & Winston, New York (1974)
7. Buhrmester, M., Kwang, T., Gosling, S.D.: Amazon's mechanical turk a new source of inexpensive, yet high-quality, data? Perspect. Psychol. Sci. **6**(1), 3–5 (2011)
8. Carr, H.A.: Psychology: A Study of Mental Activity. American Psychological Association (1925)
9. Chen, M., Walton, S., Berger, K., Thiyagalingam, J., Duffy, B., Fang, H., Holloway, C., Trefethen, A.E.: Visual multiplexing. Comput. Graph. Forum **33**(3), 241–250 (2014)
10. Chomsky, N.: Syntactic Structures. Mouton & Co., The hague (1957)
11. Chung, D.H., Archambault, D., Borgo, R., Edwards, D.J., Laramee, R.S., Chen, M.: How ordered is it? on the perceptual orderability of visual channel. In: INFOVIS (2016)
12. Cohen, J.: Statistical power analysis for the behavioral sciences (revised edn.) (1977)
13. Cooper, R., DeJong, D.V., Forsythe, R., Ross, T.W.: Cooperation without reputation: experimental evidence from prisoner's dilemma games. Games Econ. Behav. **12**(2), 187–218 (1996)
14. Craft, J.L., Simon, J.R.: Processing symbolic information from a visual display: interference from an irrelevant directional cue. J. Exp. Psychol. **83**(3p1), 415 (1970)
15. Creswell, J.W., Plano Clark, V.L., Gutmann, M.L., Hanson, W.E.: Advanced mixed methods research designs. In: Handbook of Mixed Methods in Social and Behavioral Research, pp. 209–240 (2003)
16. Crump, M.J., McDonnell, J.V., Gureckis, T.M.: Evaluating amazon's mechanical turk as a tool for experimental behavioral research. PLoS ONE **8**(3), e57410 (2013)
17. Edwards, D.J.: Integrating Behavioural and Cognitive Psychology: A Modern Categorization Theoretical Approach. Nova Science Publishers, Hauppauge (2015)
18. Edwards, D.J.: Unsupervised categorization with a child sample: category cohesion development. Eur. J. Dev. Psychol. **14**(1), 1–12 (2016)
19. Edwards, D.J., Perlman, A., Reed, P.: Unsupervised categorization in a sample of children with autism spectrum disorders. Res. Dev. Disabil. **33**(4), 1264–1269 (2012)
20. Edwards, D.J., Pothos, E.M., Perlman, A.: Relational versus absolute representation in categorization. Am. J. Psychol. **125**(4), 481–497 (2012)
21. Edwards, D.J., Wood, R.: Unsupervised categorization with individuals diagnosed as having moderate traumatic brain injury: over-selective responding. Brain Injury **30**(13–14), 1–5 (2016)

22. Eriksen, C.W.: The flankers task and response competition: a useful tool for investigating a variety of cognitive problems. Visual Cogn. **2**(2–3), 101–118 (1995)
23. Ferster, C.B., Skinner, B.F.: Schedules of Reinforcement (1957)
24. Friedenberg, J., Silverman, G.: Cognitive Science: An Introduction to the Study of Mind. Sage, California (2011)
25. Gigerenzer, G., Porter, T.: The Empire of Chance: How Probability Changed Science and Everyday Life, vol. 12. Cambridge University Press, New York (1990)
26. Gingold, Y., Shamir, A., Cohen-Or, D.: Micro perceptual human computation for visual tasks. ACM Trans. Graph. (TOG) **31**(5), 119 (2012)
27. Gosling, S.D., Vazire, S., Srivastava, S., John, O.P.: Should we trust web-based studies? A comparative analysis of six preconceptions about internet questionnaires. Am. Psychol. **59**(2), 93 (2004)
28. Healey, C., Enns, J.: Attention and visual memory in visualization and computer graphics. IEEE Trans. Visual Comput. Graphics **18**(7), 1170–1188 (2012)
29. Heer, J., Bostock, M.: Crowdsourcing graphical perception: using mechanical turk to assess visualization design. In: Proceedings of the SIGCHI Conference on Human Factors in Computing Systems, pp. 203–212. ACM (2010)
30. Hoffman, Y., Perlman, A., Orr-Urtreger, B., Tzelgov, J., Pothos, E.M., Edwards, D.J.: Psychological Research. Springer, Heidelberg (2016)
31. Hollan, J., Hutchins, E., Kirsh, D.: Distributed cognition: toward a new foundation for human-computer interaction research. ACM Trans. Comput.-Hum. Interact. (TOCHI) **7**(2), 174–196 (2000)
32. Humphrey, G.: The psychology of the gestalt. J. Educ. Psychol. **15**(7), 401 (1924)
33. Hutchins, E.: Cognition in the Wild. MIT Press, Cambridge (1995)
34. Hutchins, E.: How a cockpit remembers its speeds. Cogn. Sci. **19**(3), 265–288 (1995)
35. Hutchins, E., Holder, B.: Conceptual models for understanding an encounter with a mountain wave. In: HCI-Aero 2000 (2000)
36. James, W.: The Principles of Psychology, vol. 2 (1890)
37. Kieras, D., Polson, P.G.: An approach to the formal analysis of user complexity. Int. J. Hum. Comput. Stud. **51**(2), 405–434 (1999)
38. Lakoff, G.: Women, Fire, and Dangerous Things: What Categories Reveal About the Mind. Cambridge University Press, Cambridge (1990)
39. Laurence, S., Margolis, E.: Concepts and cognitive science. In: Concepts: Core Readings, pp. 3–81 (1999)
40. Logan, G.D., Zbrodoff, N.J.: Stroop-type interference: congruity effects in color naming with typewritten responses. J. Exp. Psychol. Hum. Percept. Perform. **24**(3), 978 (1998)
41. Marr, D., Vaina, L.: Representation and recognition of the movements of shapes. Proc. Royal Soc. London B: Biol. Sci. **214**(1197), 501–524 (1982)
42. Mayes, J.T., Draper, S.W., McGregor, A.M., Oatley, K.: Information flow in a user interface: the effect of experience and context on the recall of macwrite screens. In: Human-computer interaction. pp. 222–234. Prentice Hall Press (1990)
43. Micallef, L., Dragicevic, P., Fekete, J.D.: Assessing the effect of visualizations on Bayesian reasoning through crowdsourcing. IEEE Trans. Visual Comput. Graph. **18**(12), 2536–2545 (2012)
44. Miller, G.A.: The magical number seven, plus or minus two: some limits on our capacity for processing information. Psychol. Rev. **63**(2), 81 (1956)
45. Moroney, N.: Unconstrained web-based color naming experiment. In: Electronic Imaging 2003, pp. 36–46. International Society for Optics and Photonics (2003)
46. Nardi, B.A.: Context and Consciousness: Activity Theory and Human-Computer Interaction. MIT Press, Cambridge (1996)

47. Neisser, U.: Cognitive Psychology. Appleton-Century-Crofts, New York (1967)
48. Nosofsky, R.M.: Exemplar-based accounts of relations between classification, recognition, and typicality. J. Exp. Psychol. Learn. Mem. Cogn. **14**(4), 700 (1988)
49. Orne, M.T.: On the social psychology of the psychological experiment: with particular reference to demand characteristics and their implications. Am. Psychol. **17**(11), 776 (1962)
50. Paolacci, G., Chandler, J.: Inside the turk understanding mechanical turk as a participant pool. Curr. Dir. Psychol. Sci. **23**(3), 184–188 (2014)
51. Pavlov, A.P.: ... Le crétacé inférieur de la Russie et sa faune, vol. 16. Typolithographie de la Société IN Kouchnéreff & c-ie (1901)
52. Perlman, A., Hoffman, Y., Tzelgov, J., Pothos, E.M., Edwards, D.J.: The notion of contextual locking: previously learnt items are not accessible as such when appearing in a less common context. Q. J. Exp. Psychol. **69**(3), 410–431 (2016)
53. Perlman, A., Pothos, E.M., Edwards, D.J., Tzelgov, J.: Task-relevant chunking in sequence learning. J. Exp. Psychol. Hum. Percept. Perform. **36**(3), 649 (2010)
54. Posner, M.I., Cohen, Y.: Components of visual orienting. Attention Perform. X: Control Lang. Processes **32**, 531–556 (1984)
55. Pothos, E.M., Chater, N.: A simplicity principle in unsupervised human categorization. Cogn. Sci. **26**(3), 303–343 (2002)
56. Pothos, E.M., Edwards, D.J., Perlman, A.: Supervised versus unsupervised categorization: two sides of the same coin? Q. J. Exp. Psychol. **64**(9), 1692–1713 (2011)
57. Pothos, E.M., Perlman, A., Bailey, T.M., Kurtz, K., Edwards, D.J., Hines, P., McDonnell, J.V.: Measuring category intuitiveness in unconstrained categorization tasks. Cognition **121**(1), 83–100 (2011)
58. Pothos, E.M., Perlman, A., Edwards, D.J., Gureckis, T.M., Hines, P.M., Chater, N.: Modeling category intuitiveness. In: Proceedings of the 30th Annual Conference of the Cognitive Science Society. LEA, Mahwah (2008)
59. Quinlan, P.T., Humphreys, G.W.: Visual search for targets defined by combinations of color, shape, and size: an examination of the task constraints on feature and conjunction searches. Percept. Psychophysics **41**(5), 455–472 (1987)
60. Reips, U.D.: The web experiment method: advantages, disadvantages, and solutions. In: Psychological Experiments on the Internet, pp. 89–117 (2000)
61. Rosenthal, R., Fode, K.L.: The effect of experimenter bias on the performance of the albino rat. Behav. Sci. **8**(3), 183–189 (1963)
62. Rosenthal, R., Jacobson, L.: Pygmalion in the Classroom: Teacher Expectation and Pupils' Intellectual Development. Holt, Rinehart & Winston, New York (1968)
63. Scaife, M., Rogers, Y.: External cognition: how do graphical representations work? Int. J. Hum. Comput. Stud. **45**(2), 185–213 (1996)
64. Shannon, C.E., Weaver, W.: The mathematical theory of communication (1949)
65. Shawver, Z., Griffith, J.D., Adams, L.T., Evans, J.V., Benchoff, B., Sargent, R.: An examination of the WHOQOL-BREF using four popular data collection methods. Comput. Hum. Behav. **55**, 446–454 (2016)
66. Shepard, R.N.: Attention and the metric structure of the stimulus space. J. Math. Psychol. **1**(1), 54–87 (1964)
67. Shepard, R.N., Hovland, C.I., Jenkins, H.M.: Learning and memorization of classifications. Psychol. Monogr. General Appl. **75**(13), 1 (1961)
68. Shepard, S., Metzler, D.: Mental rotation: effects of dimensionality of objects and type of task. J. Exp. Psychol. Hum. Percept. Perform. **14**(1), 3 (1988)
69. Smith, D.J., Minda, J.P.: Thirty categorization results in search of a model. J. Exp. Psychol. Learn. Mem. Cogn. **26**(1), 3 (2000)

70. Stewart, N., Brown, G.D., Chater, N.: Absolute identification by relative judgment. Psychol. Rev. **112**(4), 881 (2005)
71. Titchener, E.B.: The 'type-theory' of the simple reaction. Mind **18**, 236–241 (1896)
72. Tversky, A., Kahneman, D.: Extensional versus intuitive reasoning: the conjunction fallacy in probability judgment. Psychol. Rev. **90**(4), 293 (1983)
73. Tversky, A., Kahneman, D.: The framing of decisions and the psychology of choice. In: Wright, G. (ed.) Environmental Impact Assessment, Technology Assessment, and Risk Analysis, pp. 107–129. Springer, Boston (1985)
74. Vanpaemel, W., Storms, G.: In search of abstraction: the varying abstraction model of categorization. Psychon. Bull. Rev. **15**(4), 732–749 (2008)
75. Wertheimer, M.: Laws of Organization in Perceptual Forms. A Source Book of Gestalt Psychology. Routledge & Kegan Paul, London (1923)
76. Williams, L.G.: The effects of target specification on objects fixated during visual search. Acta Psychol. **27**, 355–360 (1967)
77. Wright, P.C., Fields, R.E., Harrison, M.D.: Analyzing human-computer interaction as distributed cognition: the resources model. Hum.-Comput. Interact. **15**(1), 1–41 (2000)
78. Young, R.M., Howes, A., Whittington, J.: A knowledge analysis of interactivity. In: Proceedings of the IFIP TC13 Third Interational Conference on Human-Computer Interaction, pp. 115–120. North-Holland Publishing Co. (1990)
79. Zentall, T.R., Galizio, M., Critchfield, T.S.: Categorization, concept learning, and behavior analysis: an introduction. J. Exp. Anal. Behav. **78**(3), 237–248 (2002)

Crowdsourcing Quality
of Experience Experiments

Sebastian Egger-Lampl[1]($\boxtimes$), Judith Redi[2], Tobias Hoßfeld[3], Matthias Hirth[4],
Sebastian Möller[5], Babak Naderi[5], Christian Keimel[6], and Dietmar Saupe[7]

[1] Austrian Institute of Technology, Vienna, Austria
sebastian.egger-lampl@ait.ac.at
[2] Delft University of Technology, Delft, Netherlands
[3] University of Duisburg-Essen, Duisburg, Germany
[4] University of Würzburg, Würzburg, Germany
[5] TU Berlin, Berlin, Germany
[6] Technische Universität München, Munich, Germany
[7] University of Konstanz, Konstanz, Germany

1 Introduction

Understanding and measuring quality of multimedia and communication services
and underlying communication networks from an end-user perspective (Quality
of Experience, QoE) has attracted increased attention over the course of the
last decade. For a better understanding of the QoE concept and its progression
towards its actual conception and execution, it is helpful to make a brief review
of the recent history of communications quality assessment.

In the early 1990s, the notion of Quality of Service (QoS) attracted considerable attention in telecommunications, nurtured by articles, for example,
Parasuraman [76], in which the authors described their conceptual model of service quality and in which the ultimative instance for the service quality judgment
was the respective customer. This user or customer centricity is also reflected in
the ITU-T definition of QoS[1], which underlines the subjective roots of the service
quality concept despite being oriented rather towards the view of a telecommunications provider or manufacturer:

> *Quality of Service is the totality of characteristics of a telecommunications*
> *service that bear on its ability to satisfy stated and implied needs of the*
> *user of the service.* [46]

However, contrary to this original definition, most QoS-related work actually
focused on the investigation of purely technical, objectively measurable network
and service performance factors such as delay, jitter, bitrate, packet loss etc.,
thereby effectively reducing quality to a purely technology-centric perspective
[7,85].

---

[1] ITU-T standards and work are frequently referred to in this introduction, as a number of initial and ongoing work in QoE is carried out within ITU-T study group
12.

D. Archambault et al. (Eds.): Evaluation in the Crowd, LNCS 10264, pp. 154–190, 2017.
DOI: 10.1007/978-3-319-66435-4_7

Due to this deviance from its subjective focus the concept of QoS got less attractive to domains such as audio and video research, where historically subjective quality assessment played a major role in comparing, for example, codec performance. A countermovement gained momentum which took up the notion of *Quality of Experience*, which was initially introduced in the context of broadcast technologies and television systems by Kubey and Csikszentmihalyi [62][2]. The notion of QoE was rapidly adopted not only in the context of mobile communications [99] but also in the domains of audio and video quality assessment [71,79,91,107]. However, each service type (voice, video, data services, etc.) tended to develop its own QoE community with its own research tradition and flavor. In addition, it has to be noted that some domains do not even use the notion of QoE but rather use the terms "subjective quality" or "user-perceived quality" although utilizing the conceptual model that goes back to QoE [3,5,27].

This has resulted in a number of parallel attempts to define QoE, as outlined by Reichl [85], accompanied by an equally large number of QoE frameworks and taxonomies (see Laghari et al. for a comprehensive overview [63]). However, today the definition by ITU-T Rec. P.10 (Amendment 2, 2008) is still the most widely used formulation of QoE, defining the concept as:

QoE is the overall acceptability of an application or service, as perceived subjectively by the end user. [45]
Note 1: includes the complete end-to-end system effects.
Note 2: may be influenced by user expectations and context.

During discussions at the Dagstuhl Seminar 09192 in May 2009 it was pointed out that among others the notion of "acceptability" in the above definition is problematic as the concept of acceptability demands a certain (usage) context of the service [94] to yield reproducible results across different assessments of QoE or acceptability respectively. In addition, a new definition of acceptability was proposed as follows:

Acceptability is the outcome of a decision [yes/no] which is partially based on the Quality of Experience. [70]

In an attempt to overcome this patchwork of definitions and additions, the COST Action IC 1003 has published a QoE definition whitepaper [7]. Version 1.2 of this whitepaper defines:

QoE is the degree of delight or annoyance of the user of an application or service. It results from the fulfillment of his or her expectations with respect to the utility and / or enjoyment of the application or service in the light of the user's personality and current state.

---

[2] It can not be figured out with 100% certainty who introduced the notion of QoE into the domain of multimedia quality assessment, however the work by Kubey and Csikszentmihalyi is one of the earliest ones that used the notion in the same understanding as it is still used nowadays [62].

Thus, it advances the ITU-T definition by going beyond merely binary acceptability and by emphasizing the importance of both pragmatic (utility) and hedonic (enjoyment) aspects of quality judgment formation[3].

In this respect, the above definition captures the essence of QoE by highlighting some of its main characteristics: subjectivity, user-centricity, and multidimensionality. Particularly concerning the latter aspect, most frameworks and definitions found in the literature highlight the fact that QoE is determined by a number of hard and soft *influence factors*: (a) user factors, (attributable either to the user him/herself), (b) system factors and (c) context factors (see Fig. 1 and [7]). This means that whether a user judges the quality of, for example, a mobile video service as good (or even excellent) not only depends on the user her- or himself (expectations, personal background, etc.), the performance of the technical system (including traditional network QoS as well as client and server performance),[4] but to a large extent also on the context (task, location, urgency, etc.) of the experience. The resulting level of complexity and broadness turns reliable and exact QoE assessment into a challenging problem.

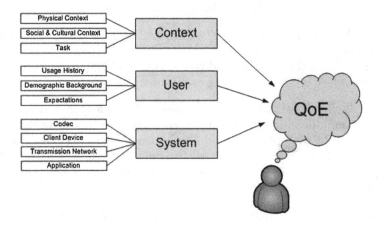

Fig. 1. QoE influence factors belonging to context, human user, and the technical system itself [95].

The very first and core step towards implementing this concept is the measurement of QoE.

In this respect, the QoE research and industrial community has typically favored a quantitative approach versus, for example, a more qualitative approach

---

[3] The definitions of the terms used as well as further details can be found in the QoE definition whitepaper [7] itself.

[4] Note that the technical system generally comprises of a chain of components (sender, transmission network elements, receiver) that connect the service provider with the end-user. All these elements can influence service quality (and thus QoE) on different layers, predominantly in terms of network- and application-level QoS.

taken towards User Experience (UX) in the Human Computer Interaction (HCI) domain. Psychometric techniques have been adapted to measure perceptions and preferences with respect to QoE, in what has been called QoE subjective testing. Subjective testing is, to date, the most common way to quantify users' QoE. Nevertheless, it is typically performed in highly controlled laboratory environments, to avoid bias and noise in the measurement due to undesired influence factors (see Fig. 1). This, of course, poses a limit to the quantity of test participants that can be involved, as well as on their diversity. For this reason, lately the community has started looking at crowdsourcing as an alternative approach to conduct large scale QoE experiments.

This chapter provides an overview of recent advances for QoE research in a crowdsourcing setting. To this end, it has firstly provided a general background to the QoE concept in the introduction above. The remainder of this chapter provides first an overview of QoE experiment types and commonly used scaling methodologies, followed by a discussion of specific QoE issues and experimental challenges for three different service categories: voice communication, audio-visual multimedia and web applications. Furthermore, specific challenges for transferring laboratory based experiments to the crowdsourcing context are reviewed for these three service categories. Finally, lessons learned are summarized in order to provide guidelines for setting up crowdsourced QoE tests to the interested reader. In the appendix to this chapter a novel approach towards using paired comparison in the crowdsourcing environment and related technologies for subsequent reconstruction of absolute category ratings is discussed.

2   Subjective QoE Experiments

The main goal of subjective QoE experiments is to sort stimuli (e.g., speech segments, audio tracks, images, videos,...) according to their perceived properties or attributes on a given scale, as defined by Engeldrum [19]. The scaling can be obtained by directly asking participants to (numerically) quantify QoE (in the so-called "direct" tests), or by deriving indices related to quality on the basis of other, intermediate measures ("indirect" tests). Such measures could for example be thresholds of perception (in classical psychophysics), physiological responses (such as skin conductance, EEG or EMG), or performance indicators (such as task success for an interaction task). All such tests can in principle be carried out both in a laboratory as well as in a crowd environment. However, different types of tests may set different requirements to the influence factors.

There are a number of criteria according to which experiments addressing the QoE of a system or service can be differentiated. A common classification is one used for standard psychophysical experiments, distinguishing amongst the following:

- Perceptual modality: Viewing tests, listening tests, viewing and listening tests, etc.
- Degree of activity: Passive (e.g. listening-only or viewing-only tests), active (e.g. speaking tests), interactive (e.g. conversation tests with different degree of interactivity)

- Presentation method: presentation of constant stimuli, with or without explicit reference (e.g. Absolute Category Rating tests, Paired Comparison tests, Comparison Category Ratings, Degradation Category Ratings) vs. adjustment of stimuli by the test participants
- Scaling method: Quantitative scaling of stimuli on a nominal, ordinal, interval or ratio scale

Whereas the first two items above do differ for different types of services and stimuli (discussed in Sects. 2.1, 2.2, and 2.3) the latter two items (and their variations) are rather common for all types of QoE experiments as they deal with the mapping of subjective experiences on certain (quantitative) descriptors. In the following a number of scaling methodologies that quantify subjective experiences are discussed.

The Paired Comparison (PC) method as described by David, Thurstone and Engeldrum is a classic psychometric technique that allows to precisely measure distances among stimuli in terms of Just Noticeable Differences (JNDs) [13, 19, 100]. The experimental procedure consists of asking participants to compare each stimulus with all other stimuli in the set. As a result, even small differences between the stimuli can be detected, which makes the method particularly useful when stimuli close together in quality are to be sorted. On the other hand, the judgment effort grows as the square of the number of stimuli, hence this number must be limited.

Direct scaling techniques overcome this limitation by presenting the participant with a numerical (or categorical) scale on which each stimulus is evaluated (effort grows only linear with the number of stimuli). Participants have to quantify the QoE of the stimulus on such a scale; this judgment can depend on the comparison of the stimulus with a reference (Double Stimulus Methodology) or not (Single Stimulus Methodology). The Double Stimulus Impairment Scaling (DSIS) methodology as described in ITU-R BT-500 is often chosen for the assessment of audio or visual impairments [48]. DSIS judgments are expressed on an interval scale (typically, a five-point Absolute Category Rating - ACR - scale or a Degradation Category Rating scale [48]), as a (conscious) comparison of each impaired stimulus with its undistorted version. Being a double stimulus method, DSIS requires a moderate effort per judgment, but still allows the assessment of large datasets. A possible drawback of the method may be the categorical scale used for the assessment: the boundaries among categories (for example, "good" and "fair") are blurred and depend on the participant; this may result in low inter-participant agreement as indicated by Engeldrum and Keelan [19, 54]. Redi et al. have shown that to date the ACR scale is however the most widely used one in image and video subjective testing, also in a Single Stimulus settings (i.e., without an explicit reference to be presented to the participant) [82]. Both DSIS and Single Stimulus scaling can be performed also with numerical scales, both discrete or continuous as described in ITU-R BT-500 and Huynh-Thu et al. [42, 48]. In all cases, the results of the tests are reported in terms of average score per stimulus (Mean Opinion Scores), expressed in the scale used for the experiment. These scores reflect human preference, though do not have a precise psychophysical meaning. Indeed, the obtained scores may vary with the definition of the scale as shown by Engeldrum [19], as well as with the quality range spanned by the stimuli as shown by de Ridder [89]. This suggests that comparing results of different experiments may be problematic, possibly inducing inconsistencies when merging these data in a single, larger dataset.

The methods briefly described above are commonly used across the media domains considered in this chapter: audio, image/video and web. On the other hand, for each of these domains, the dominant influencing factors may change; as such, specific methodological choices and recommendations to conduct subjective QoE experiments were developed. In the following subsection we cover this specificity, separately per domain.

2.1 Experiments Addressing Speech and Audio QoE

2.1.1 Experiments Addressing Speech QoE

Speech quality has been an object of investigation for more than a century, and the corresponding methodologies assessing speech QoE are rather well established. Common types of experiments include listening-only tests (Absolute Category Rating, Paired Comparison, Comparison Category Rating, Degradation Category Rating), third-party listening tests (listening to a conversation between two other persons), speaking-only tests, as well as conversation tests. More recently, diagnostic tests targeting individual listening-quality dimensions, conversational dimensions, as well as technical sources of quality degradations, have been a focus of research. The most common methods are described in the P.800 series of Recommendations issued by the International telecommunication Union, ITU-T, in particular ITU-T Rec. P.800 for listening-only and conversation tests, ITU-T Rec. P.805 for conversation tests with differing degree of interactivity, ITU-T Rec. P.806 for multi-dimensional assessment of listening-only quality, or ITU-T Rec. P.830 regarding quality assessment of coded speech. All of these methods can be considered as good practice for speech related QoE assessment and are frequently used for the different speech application fields.

These recommendations also specify a number of influence factors. User influence factors that have to be controlled are the participants' hearing ability, their language skill, and potentially their expertise with the domain of speech quality in the case that diagnostic listening for identifying technical sources of degradations is of interest. Whereas these characteristics can easily be controlled in a laboratory setting, they are more difficult to verify in a crowd setting, where participants may have the possibility to cheat in the case that self-reported abilities are used.

System influence factors are the ones most frequently under study. They include the source speech material (commonly collected from a variety of speakers, using different types of text material), the technical characteristics of the signal processing chain as well as the presentation device used by the listening participant. In the case of speaking or conversational tests, this deletes the source material from the list of influence factors which can be controlled for, however this puts additional requirements for the speaking and listening devices. Context factors which can be expected to carry an impact on the results are the listening environment (especially the background noise and reverberation), as well as the test task given to the participants. The latter has shown to significantly impact quality judgments in the case of conversational test situations.

2.1.2   Experiments Addressing Audio QoE

Audio quality is in principle addressed similarly to speech quality. However, as the level of quality is commonly expected to be much higher, the test methodologies are commonly focusing on a more sensitive distinction between different processing chains of reproduction devices, and the requirements for the test equipment and listening situation are commonly higher. Test paradigms which are followed in audio quality assessment are, for example, double-blind triple-stimulus tests with hidden anchor, where test participants first have to distinguish between a degraded stimulus and a hidden reference, and then have to rate the perceived degradation on a category scale; or the multiple-stimulus test with hidden reference and anchor (MUSHRA), where the quality of multiple stimuli presented in parallel to the test participants has to be rated in relationship to each other, and is anchored by the use of a scale with absolute labels. With respect to factors influencing audio QoE, the same influence factors do apply as mentioned for speech above.

2.2   Experiments Addressing Image and Video QoE

Research on subjective image and video quality has, so far, mostly focused on determining user sensitivity to visual impairments and quantifying the annoyance generated by their visible presence. Multiple psychometric methodologies have been developed for this purpose, and adapted for the measurement of image and video quality in standardized conditions [44, 47, 48, 50, 55].

Methodologies such as DSIS, Paired Comparison and Single Stimulus evaluation with an ACR scale defined in ITU-R BT-500 and ITU-T P.910 are typically used to conduct both image and video subjective QoE assessments [47, 48]. In addition, the Quality Ruler (QR) method deserves a mention, as an middleground alternative between the direct scaling methodologies (DSIS, Single Stimulus) and Paired Comparison. The QR method was first described by Keelan in [54], and subsequently adopted as an international ISO standard for psychometric experiments for image quality estimation [55] and video quality estimation in ITU-R BT-500 [48]. The core idea of the QR method is to provide the participant with a set of reference images, anchored along a calibrated quality scale, to compare a test image with. The task of the participant is to find the reference image closest in quality to the test image by visual matching. Reference images (1) depict a single scene and vary in only one perceptual attribute (i.e., blur, blockiness, color saturation); (2) are closely spaced in quality, but altogether span a wide range of quality. They are presented in a way that easily allows detection of the quality difference between them, and their close spacing in quality should allow the participant to score with higher confidence, decreasing the risk of inversions and range effects. In practice, participants perform several comparisons of reference-test stimuli to complete a single assessment, until they find the reference stimulus that matches the quality of the test one. The advantage of this procedure is that, as long as the reference stimuli are kept the same, subjective scores obtained from a QR experiment always refer to the ruler scale, and not to the quality range spanned by the test stimuli. This minimizes range effects. Furthermore, Redi et al. have shown that the visual matching procedure reduces inter-participant variability [82]. This method has been successfully implemented for images, and recently Freitas et al. have proposed to use it for video quality assessment with promising results [22].

As mentioned earlier for audio and speech quality assessment, recommendations and standards enlist a series of influencing factors that impact on subjective quality assessment of images and videos. Among user influencing factors, we can distinguish between physiological (e.g. visual acuity, color blindness, stereo blindness) and psychological factors (preference for image material, personality and culture). To limit the influence of physiological factors on the test outcomes, ITU-R BT-500 advises to screen participants for (corrected to) normal visual acuity (e.g. by means of the Snellen or Landolt charts), and for normal color vision (e.g. via the Ishihara test) [48]. Limiting the influence of psychological factors is more complex; questionnaires investigating individual characteristics (e.g. personality) can be administered pre- or post-test and their outcomes used as co-variates in the rating analysis; a large number of observers and the careful selection of diverse image material can also help averaging out individual differences. Due to the visual nature of the stimuli, their physical representation towards the human participants is crucial. Hence, representation characteristics of the display device are the most important system influence factor. Examples of such characteristics are the achievable contrast ratio, the representable color space as well as the dynamic range of the display. Depending on the independent variable varied, one of these characteristics might be of utmost importance, for example, dynamic range for experiments addressing HDR representations of images or videos. With respect to context influencing factors, visibility conditions (monitor resolution and calibration, distance to screen, lighting) need to be controlled for and made uniform (most recommendations prescribe specific settings in this respect). The ambience (or context) in which the experiment is carried out also influences evaluations: Jumisko-Pyykkö and Hannukselausers found users to be more tolerant towards visual artifacts when evaluating them in realistic viewing conditions (laboratories with a living room appearance, bus, cafes) than in traditional laboratories [53].

2.3   Experiments Addressing Web QoE

Web-QoE, defined as "Quality of Experience of interactive services that are based on the HTTP protocol and accessed via a browser" by Hossfeld et al. [39], focuses on the optimization of web services by understanding the end-users' perception of overall system performance. The critical issue in this context are perceived waiting durations which occur after requesting a web-site until it has been fully loaded in the visible browser window.

Therefore, it is important to instrument waiting durations as the key metric for assessing Quality of Experience for web-based services. Furthermore, it is important to go beyond single page requests to a series of consecutive page views in order to accommodate for the interactive nature of web browsing activities. Especially interactivity and the related tasks which users want to accomplish are major QoE influencing factors beyond network-related performance parameters and have to be accounted for. The main characteristics of such subjective web browsing QoE tests as described in ITU-T P.1501 are [49] to simulate realistic web browsing where users are browsing and interacting with webpages in order to acquire certain information. The procedure they go through within this methodology has to ensure that users get into a browsing mode rather than a pure page loading mode. From a system factor perspective it must be ensured that participants are exposed to a certain QoS level over a period of time rather than for one event, in order to grasp several request-response cycles for the subjective evaluation. Additionally, it has to be ensured that the manipulated parameters (e.g., delay, packet loss, downlink bandwidth) can be set to the desired values and that these settings can be verified by *a posteriori* analysis (e.g., traffic traces). Accommodating for all these characteristics and at the same time ensuring that waiting times are properly instrumented is typically addressed by two approaches: (a) utilizing network emulators [16,94] that shape traffic such that the loading behavior of normal webpages is manipulated or (b) developing special webpages where waiting times are directly instrumented via, for example, Javascript [12,17,20,112].

With respect to the context of use, Strohmeier et al. showed that the task assigned (i.e. context of use) to the test participants has a considerable impact on QoE [12]. This is important to keep in mind when using certain tasks to stimulate the interaction between the webpage and the participant for each test condition. In addition to the assigned task, the webpage must be interactive and has to provide sufficient content such that the participant can browse through it over several conditions, without getting bored. As for the other services discussed above, human influence factors have to be considered for Web QoE as well. Varela et al. have shown that despite the ubiquitous usage of web sites across the globe, there are nevertheless differences with respect to archetypical web site arrangement and structuring as well as web site design and visual appeal [103]. Additionally, Sackl et al. showed that user expectations with respect to downlink performance and web page loading times have to be considered as well [92].

3   Transferring QoE Lab Experiments to the Crowd

The previous section has shown that QoE testing in laboratory environments is an established approach known for producing valid and reliable results. The major disadvantage of such laboratory-based experiments is the fact that they not only require expensive facilities and testing expertise but also incur significant expenses and relatively long campaign setup and turnaround times (typically in the order of weeks). Therefore, laboratory experiments are not suitable for testing a large number of technical conditions in proof of concept tests or for comparing a large number of prototype implementations during the development phase.

Crowdsourcing, with its outreach to thousands of users concurrently, represents a very appealing option for subjective QoE experiments. Nevertheless, crowdsourcing of QoE experiments also faces certain challenges. In order to properly transfer QoE experiments from the laboratory to the crowd testing environment, dedicated solutions and great care has to be put into the test design. Within this section we discuss specific challenges that are connected with QoE experiments in crowdsourcing such as experiment duration and human, system and context influence factors.

3.1 Influence Factors Particularly Relevant for QoE Tests in Crowdsourcing

3.1.1 Test Duration and Design

Independent on the type of media/signal on which the QoE assessment is carried out, QoE testing is typically performed in a within-subjects fashion. In the simplest case, the experimenter wants to evaluate the impact of a set of F system factors s_f, with $f = 1, .., F$, on a specific type of media. To do so, (1) a set of K diverse, unimpaired media contents $O_k, k = 1, ..., K$ is selected and (2) a set of levels L_f is determined per each factor s_f to be applied, in isolation or combination with other levels of other factors, to the K selected contents. This results in a number N of impaired stimuli, which can be described as $O_k(s_1(i_1), s_2(i_2), ...s_F(i_F))$, where $f = 1, ..., F$ and $i_f = 1, ..., L_F$ in case of full factorial design. A pool of M users is then asked to evaluate the quality of *all* impaired stimuli (within-subjects design), within one or multiple sessions. This setup, also denoted as complete block design, allows to control for individual differences in quality perception (by modeling users as a random factor); nevertheless, it results in long experimental sessions, especially when the number of conditions N to be tested is large.

In crowdsourcing, long test sessions should be avoided. As pointed out by Hossfeld et al., short durations will favor engagement of the workers with the tasks, thereby favoring reliable executions and commitment [33,38]. Hour-long crowd-based tests would most likely result in poorly reliable executions and, therefore, poor results. For this reason, crowd-based evaluations see the transformation of complete block designs into incomplete ones. That is, the set of stimuli to be evaluated is divided in subsets, each evaluated by separate groups of workers in different campaigns. While considerably shortening the task duration, this practice has implications for the validity and reliability of the evaluations, namely:

- Redi et al. showed that it increases the risk of context effects, since the quality range spanned by each block of stimuli can hardly be kept constant across blocks [81]

- In the case of interaction between worker and influencing factors (i.e. different impairment perceptions depending on the worker, which quite often occurs), the non-systematic structure of the test will make the results difficult to analyze and interpret
- It further complicates the analysis, given that the incomplete block design becomes unbalanced, and that the same worker may participate to different campaigns (which is often the case, but can be controlled for on certain platforms).

3.1.2   Crowd Diversity and Expectations

With respect to user diversity, crowdsourcing platforms have a different reach-out to the population compared to typical laboratory tests. As crowdsourcing platforms are online platforms, only computer-literate persons will participate in the tasks, and due to the prevailing financial motivator the group will also show certain income characteristics, which certainly will differ from test participants recruited for laboratory tests (e.g. at academic institutions, through marketing companies, through newspapers, etc.).

Furthermore, visual and hearing characteristics, which are important for a number of QoE experiments, are usually rather widespread and can be only controlled to a certain extent in crowdsourcing settings. Due to the shorter crowdsourcing task length compared to the laboratory (see above), a higher number of different crowdworkers is required to collect the same number of ratings. Along with this increased user diversity, the diversity in user ratings increases as well. Another indirect factor of QoE perception on the user level can be the users' expectations: those used to lower quality (e.g. low video resolution) will rate differently than those typically consuming higher quality (e.g. high video resolution). Sackl et al. proved that the expectation level may be closely related to the usage experience of services and to the country of the crowdworkers [92]. In line with these findings, Hirth et al. showed that users from different regions may have different expectations about the provided content quality [32]. As a countermeasure to crowd diversity and expectations, training tasks or jobs can be integrated in crowdsourcing campaigns. In the training job, anchor stimuli (see Sect. 5.1) are presented to the worker and rated by them. Proper identification of such anchor degradations should be clearly visible in the respective worker's ratings. Anchor stimuli act as a standard reference, and their aim is to introduce the entire quality range to the workers with more consistent results in the end. Gardlo, Egger and Hossfeld have shown that proper training sessions help workers to use the entire range of the scale [24]. Another approach of temporarily expiring training certificates as a prerequisite qualification for crowdworkers has been proposed by Polzehl et al. [78]. The authors showed that training certificates valid for 40 min were able to clearly improve the correlation of crowdsourced and laboratory test results. As this subsection has only discussed QoE-related user factors the interested reader is pointed towards Chap. 3 for a more in depth discussion about demographic factors and challenges with respect to crowdsourcing.

3.1.3 Equipment

In contrast to laboratory experiments where presentation hardware can be closely monitored and controlled, workers in crowdsourcing tests typically use their own devices, in their current environments (e.g. wherever they are in case of mobile crowdsourcing). These devices may differ in terms of hardware (e.g. display, brightness sound output device, connected headphone, volume settings), software (e.g. OS, installed codecs) and connectivity (e.g. the bandwidth or delay of the Internet connection may vary). Furthermore workers may use their devices in different ways (e.g. monaural/binaural listening, concurrent use of other devices and/or applications) which can not be controlled and barely monitored. Therefore, it is important to either detect the device type and the device usage, or to ask users about their used hardware and settings. Another limitation (rather than an influence factor) with respect to the equipment are crowdsourced QoE tests of specific technologies, which require dedicated equipment. This might not be feasible, due the lack of diffusion of such equipment, and for the difficulty in emulating it. For example, immersive media technologies such as augmented reality and/or virtual reality, mulsemedia etc. The same holds true for contingent equipment that is often used to assist QoE experiments: eyetrackers and physiological sensors. In the case of eye-tracking, recent developments by Lebreton et al. have made it possible to track eye-movements of the worker while doing the task, although there is room for improvement [64]. Measurements through physiological sensors can not be achieved, for now.

3.1.4 Context

Because of the remoteness of the workers and the heterogeneity of the used soft- and hardware, it is necessary to monitor the users' environment in order to identify additional influence factors on the QoE assessment (see Sect. 1 for QoE influencing factors). Due to the unknown context in which the QoE assessment is performed by the workers in QoE crowdsourcing tests, these influence factors are not known beforehand, but are hidden, yet still influence the users' QoE ratings. In general, we have three options to cope with the unknown context and the resulting hidden influence factors. We can either monitor the appropriate context parameters, adapt the context or try to prevent the undesirable context itself in our test design. The environment in which the workers evaluate the stimuli in QoE crowdsourcing tests may impact the overall QoE and thus the application should be able to detect such factors. For visual stimuli, the general viewing conditions represented by the background illumination or the screen resolution can be influencing factors.

One option to adapt the conditions of the workers' environment is to provide them with simple test patterns that allow them to either calibrate their devices or enable the quantification of the deviation of a device's stimuli representation from the desired target. For visual stimuli, Gardlo et al. showed that basic test patterns similar to the test patterns used for calibration of monitor contrast and illumination in a professional environment can be utilized to quantify the users' viewing conditions, for example by asking how many gray steps on a grayscale step-wedge are visible [25]. Moreover, such patterns can also be used to instruct workers how to calibrate their display.

Similarly, we can prevent an undesirable context from the technical perspective, for example for video QoE assessment, by pre-loading videos with included distortions in the remote browser, so that additional distortions introduced by the transmission do not affect the playback [15,40]. Hence, influence of the users' context with respect to bandwidth is no longer an issue. But even by doing so, the resulting initial delays may also be too long and influence the user rating. In both cases, it is evident that monitoring on system or application level is required. As a possible solution, download speed and latency may also be measured before the actual test, and then only users with suitable connection speed and latency are selected.

3.2   Speech and Audio QoE

As speech and audio QoE tests span a wide range from pure listen-only tests to interactive conversational tests (see Sect. 2.1), the challenges for conducting such tests through crowdsourcing are manifold as well. Therefore, we exemplify only challenges and solutions that are applicable across all these test types. As sound reproduction is key for speech and audio tests, respective human and system characteristics have to be carefully considered. With respect to hearing abilities of the crowdworkers, and when the workers hearing level is not an independent factor under the study design, hearing levels of all participating workers should be examined in screening tasks. Candidates with normal hearing levels should then be qualified for participating in the main campaign. Alternatively, workers with different hearing levels should equally be distributed throughout different campaigns and test conditions. Besides the human hearing characteristics, Cooke et al. showed that system characteristics can be assessed during such screening tasks (e.g. type of hardware, OS, mon- or bi-aural output devices) [10]. With respect to context factors, either question-based or measurement-based context assessment is feasible. Measurement-based approaches as introduced by Naderi et al. on mobile devices allow for identification of worker mobility (or the worker being stationary through motion sensors, location data) or if he is in a silent or noisy environment (through the device microphone) [73].

Initial suggestions on how to design crowdsourcing tasks for subjective speech and audio QoE have been provided by Naderi and Pozehl [74,78], as well as guidelines of resulting data analysis by Ribeiro [88]. Furthermore, within ITU-T study group 12 a work item has been started towards a recommendation on subjective methods for assessing audio quality in crowdsourcing environments.

In the domain of audio and speech quality, crowdsourcing is to date used for subjective speech quality ratings (e.g. listening-only-tests [74,78]), naturalness [88], intelligibility test [68,108] and preference tests of speech synthesis systems, followed by data collection studies (e.g. to explore factors from wireless networks that impact mobile voice quality [75], evaluating voice-over-IP services [93] and Skype call quality assessments [111]).

3.3   Image and Video QoE

Image and video quality assessment is done for a range of different application areas: from the visual quality evaluation of picture and video coding technologies and processing algorithms to the influence of network delays and packet loss in case of video quality. The QoE of image and video is usually determined in a well-defined testing environment with subjective methodologies, as described in standards [47,48,55].

The first challenges we face result from the differences of crowdsourcing compared to the structure and procedures of subjective video quality assessment in an laboratory environment. Crowdsourcing tasks are typically small tasks that can be done by the workers both fast and easily and while image and video quality assessment is usually a comparably easy task, laboratory-based assessment sessions can last up to 30 min as in ITU-R BT-500 and ISO 20462 [48,55]. Hence, it is not possible to just run a test designed for a laboratory environment without modifications; it rather needs to be partitioned into several crowdsourcing campaigns, for example, its basic test cells (BTCs) or only a small subset of BTCs compared to a laboratory-based assessment will be included in each crowdsourcing campaign and its underlying tasks. The necessary breaking up of the structure of the laboratory-based assessment makes the adherence to design rules aiming at avoiding contextual effects, therefore more challenging. Moreover, compared to the approach taken in laboratory-based assessment, Keimel et al. and Redi et al. showed that workers will usually only assess a subset of all image or video sequences under test [56,84].

In contrast to images, video is more challenging from a resource perspective (e.g. bandwidth requirements or download volume for long video sequences) in crowdsourced quality assessments. Obviously, we are neither able to control the setup of the testing environment itself (e.g. room illumination), nor the used equipment (e.g. displays). This, however, also implies that evaluations requiring explicitly a controlled environment, for example, for determining the thresholds of just noticeable differences of stimuli, are not suitable for crowd-based evaluation. Also research questions utilizing new technologies for the visual stimuli are not yet widely deployed in consumer equipment. For example, Hanhart et al. have claimed that questions related to high dynamic range (HDR) displays, can not easily be answered using crowdsourcing as respective displays are not widely available to crowdworkers [28,29]. Even though image downloads and video streaming is nowadays a generally used service, crowdsourced image video quality assessment faces some additionally challenges compared to the laboratory environment. Firstly, we need to consider that in general the worker's web-browser and plug-ins cannot be assumed to support the original encoding format of images and videos, especially lossless compression. On the one hand, this limits the possibility to asses new coding technologies or other processing algorithms which are neither supported nor can be emulated using generic web technologies. On the other hand, double stimulus methodologies requiring an undistorted version of the stimuli under test (e.g. DSIS, as defined in ITU-R BT.500 [48]) can also not be used. Even though this last point can be circumvented by re-encoded images and videos for the delivery with common lossy coding techniques supported by common web-browsers, the test case then differs even stronger from the laboratory setup, as also the artefacts introduced by this additional compression will be implicitly assessed. Secondly, in case of video QoE the bitrate needed for smooth video playback can be substantial and this can limit the pool of potential workers. Buffering the video can help in lifting this limitation, but buffering will extend the time needed per test case, limiting in turn the number of test cases that can be assessed per crowdsourcing task and thus further deviating from the laboratory-based setup.

Despite these differences between crowdsourced and laboratory-based image and video quality assessment, crowdsourced image and video quality assessment has been used so far successfully as a replacement for laboratory-based QoE assessments for a number of different research questions: Image recognizability and aesthetic appeal [81,83,84], selfie portrait images perception in a recruitment context [69], privacy in HDR images and video [59,60,86], QoE of video coding in general [57,58], audio-visual QoE of Internet-based applications in [8,9,109], and influence of stalling events and initial delays [34,36] on the QoE of video streaming applications. In addition, a general discussion using crowdsourcing for image and video QoE is provided by Hossfeld et al. [33,84].

3.4   Web QoE

In the context of interactive services accessed via the browser, waiting times are the key influence factor for the user's perception of performance. Thus, proper manipulation of these waiting times is of utmost importance in evaluation studies. For crowdsourced tests this is a particular challenge. Due to the limited control of the network connection (traffic shaping, as shown by Schatz and Egger [94] or delay of certain page elements in the downlink path as shown by Shaikh et al. [97]), such a manipulation can only be achieved through the development of special web sites that are able to instrument certain page loading behavior and respective waiting times until the content is displayed. A further complicating factor for this aspect is the realistic appeal of the resulting web sites as deemed important in ITU-T P.1501, which necessitates a certain content depth of the created web sites. This results in a large set of content to be acquired for, for example, a news look-a-like web site [49]. Furthermore, comparable to other services such as video and speech, test duration, testing equipment of the worker and crowd diversity do pose certain challenges for conducting Web QoE studies in a crowdsourcing environment. Due to the limited time for the test duration per user and incomplete block designs a large number of workers have to be chosen. Differences in testing equipment can not be *a priori* defined by the nature of crowdsourcing, however logging of numerous equipment factors important for Web QoE (e.g. screen size and resolution, terminal category etc.) is possible. This enables the researcher to consider equipment factors in the data analysis as an additional dimension. Contrary to video and speech services where reproduction fidelity of the end user device is of high importance for resulting media fidelity, reproduction fidelity of web sites is not bound to media fidelity as long as correct rendering can be ensured. Hence, visual characteristics of the display such as color accuracy or brightness of the display are not as important. Diversity of crowd and workers is of course a complicating factor but can be controlled either *a priori* by proper crowd selection or *a posteriori* by respective reliability analysis approaches (see Sect. 5.2). Also context factors do exert certain influences on Web QoE. Strohmeier et al. have shown that the task context while web browsing does impact users' QoE ratings [12]. On the other hand, results from Guse et al. have shown that physical context (laboratory vs. metropolitan transport) did not lead to significant differences in the QoE ratings [26].

Despite these challenges certain successful work on Web QoE in a crowdsourcing context has been presented. In order to overcome the web site content challenge, the work from Egger and Schatz [17], ETSI[5] [20], and Zinner et al. [112] present open source solutions that make it easy to create web sites with instrumentable loading times and realistic appeal [17,20,112]. To date, no crowdsourced results with these solutions have been published but will appear shortly. With respect to crowd and worker diversity the work in Varela et al. has studied the impact of design and visual appeal on web QoE for geographically differing societies and showed that there are different degrees of influence and different preferences of design as well [103]. A further study from Varela et al. showed that changes in visual appeal do impact perceived performance of web sites despite technically identical loading times [104].

4   Crowdsourcing Frameworks for QoE Testing

Crowdsourcing has been widely used by researchers in domains other than QoE so far and consequently numerous different tools (e.g., Turkit [67]), have already been developed to ease the application of Crowdsourcing for their purposes. While some tools, like Turkit, focus on general problems, for example, providing control flow for consecutive crowdsourcing tasks, other software tools or frameworks are designed for a specific use case.

Using crowdsourcing to conduct QoE assessments seems to be a promising way to quickly collect a large number of test results in real world usage settings. However, it imposes new and different challenges compared to similar tests in laboratory environments. The first challenge is to find an appropriate pool of workers for the test and a crowd provider providing a flexible enough interface to run the experimental tasks. The second major challenge is the delivery of the test to the workers. It is often necessary to redesign the test to a web-based version which allows the access for the globally distributed workers and – in the best case – does not require the workers to install any software on their device. During this process a significant software development effort is needed that can be reduced significantly by reusing existing frameworks.

Web-based crowdsourcing frameworks for multimedia quality assessment represent a conceptual approach with programming tools to develop subjective tests that can be executed in a web browser. In particular, such frameworks allow

---

[5] European Telecommunications Standards Institute.

multimedia content to be displayed in a browser for workers to evaluate the quality using web forms. The test logic may be implemented at the client-side (e.g. Javascript) or at the server-side (e.g., PHP). Such frameworks enable the execution of the tests utilizing typical crowd-provider platforms. The basic functionality of a framework includes (a) the creation of the test (by supporting common testing methodologies like ACR, DCR, PC), (b) the execution of the test (by supporting training, task design, task order, screening), and (c) the storage and access to the result data. In the following we give an overview of existing crowdsourcing frameworks that have been specifically developed for QoE tests[6] and their available features.

This overview is structured along specific criteria such as the test design, the applied test methodology, the type of media to evaluate, and the hardware and software environment. In the remainder of this section, we focus on frameworks especially for crowdsourced QoE studies. Hoßfeld et al.provided a survey of widely used frameworks for this purpose in [37]. We summarize the considered frameworks therein and additionally consider Crowdee[7], which has a major focus on quality testing.

Quadrant of Euphoria

Initially proposed by Chen et al. in [9] and extended by Wu et al. in [109], Quadrant of Euphoria mainly focuses on the QoE evaluation of audio, visual, and audio-visual stimuli. It allows for a pairwise comparison of two different stimuli in an interactive web-interface, where the worker can judge which of the two stimuli has a higher QoE. Reliability assessments are based on the actual user ratings under the assumption that the preferences of users are a transitive relation, expressed by the Transitivity Satisfaction Rate.

crowdMOS

The crowdMOS framework for subjective user studies was proposed by Ribeiro et al. [88] and is an open-source project that initially focused on subjective audio testing using the ACR and MUSHRA audio quality assessment methodologies. Ribeiro later extended the crowdMOS framework to image quality assessments [87] with ACR for video from ITU-T P.910 [47]. For assessing the reliability of users, the sample correlation coefficient between the average user rating of a worker and the global average rating is used.

QualityCrowd

QualityCrowd is an open-source project by Keimel et al. that provides a multitude of different options for the test design [57]. In this framework, a test can consist of any number of questions and can contain videos, sounds or images or any combination. Moreover, it allows the use of different testing methodologies

---

[6] As each crowdsourcing test is somewhat unique, it is very difficult to find a framework that can be used directly without any modification. However, using an existing framework as a starting base and modifying it to fit the requirements of the test design needed is a highly valuable alternative.

[7] http://crowdee.de last accessed 14 Jun 2017.

(e.g. single stimulus or double stimulus), and different scales (e.g., discrete or continuous quality or impairment scales). In its latest iteration (QualityCrowd2[8]) a simple scripting language has been introduced that allows for the creation of test campaigns with high flexibility. This is not only achieved by enabling the combination of different stimuli and testing methodologies, but also by the possibility to specify training sessions and/or the introduction of control questions for the identification of reliable user ratings in order to ensure high data quality.

WESP

Rainer et al.describe an open source[9] Web-based subjective evaluation platform (WESP), which was initially developed for subjective quality assessments of sensory experience but can also be used for general-purpose QoE assessments [80]. WESP provides a management and presentation layer for configuring the task design and for the presentation of the actual user study, respectively. The management layer allows the configuration of each component (e.g. pre-questionnaire, voting mechanism, rating scale, and control questions), independently and thus provides enough flexibility for a wide range of different methodologies (e.g., single stimulus, double stimulus, pair comparison or continuous quality evaluation). Additionally, any new methodology can be implemented through the management layer. The presentation layer presents the content (e.g. video using HTML5 or Flash), to the workers and is based on standard HTML elements. In particular, it allows the collection of explicit and implicit user input: the former is entered by the user via explicit user input elements (e.g. voting using a slider for a given rating scale), compared to the latter describing implicit input represented by data from the browser window (e.g. window focus or duration of the test).

BeaqleJS

The BeaqleJS framework is developed by Kraft and Zölzer and focuses on subjective audio studies [61]. It is written in Javascript and PHP, and HTML5 is used to playback the audio clips[10]. Several audio formats are supported, including an uncompressed WAV PCM format. The framework allows the implementation of different testing methodologies via code extensions, with two evaluation methodologies already implemented: the ABX methodology and MUSHRA. Currently, there is no support for reliability detection and evaluation results are emailed to the organizer of an evaluation in a text file.

in-momento crowdsourcing

Gardlo et al. [25] introduced the *in-momento* crowdsourcing framework, combining careful user-interface design together with the best known practices for QoE crowdsourcing tests from Hossfeld et al. [33]. Instead of *a posteriori* data analysis and subsequent removal of unreliable data, this framework aims at live

---

[8] https://github.com/ldvpublic/QualityCrowd2 last accessed 14 Jun 2017.

[9] http://selab.itec.aau.at/ last accessed 14 Jun 2017.

[10] https://github.com/HSU-ANT/beaqlejs last accessed 14 Jun 2017.

or *in-momento* evaluation of the user's behavior: as the user proceeds with the assessment, the reliability of the user is continuously updated and a reliability profile is built which is used for screening. Users are able to quit the assessment task at any point unlike in other frameworks. The aim is to avoid forcing a user to continue with the test even though they are bored or have lost interest, as these two issues are closely related to unreliable behavior. Since the reliability profile is known at each stage of the assessment, it is possible to offer reliable users additional tasks for an increased reward.

Crowdee

Crowdee is a mobile crowdsourcing micro-task platform which is developed and actively supported by a research group of the Quality and Usability Laboratory, Technische Universität Berlin. Besides the fundamental functionalities provided by crowdsourcing platforms, Crowdee brings worker mobility to crowdsourcing user studies. Workers use a mobile application to find and perform micro-tasks available in the platform. As a result they are able to perform QoE tasks wherever and whenever they want, which facilitates conducting QoE studies in field settings [73]. With respect to modalities, crowdee enables image, audio or video content for testing. As a further option for media playout the researcher can force multimedia content to be preloaded before the start of a task to avoid influence of network distortions. Scales and questions can be selected among free text, single or multiple choice, sliders, taking a picture, or recording audio and video.

In addition, the platform supports dynamic worker profiles. Profile values can automatically or manually be assigned on response submission or approval time. Profile keys can be used to specify necessary qualifications and profile values for granting permission to perform a job. Polzehl et al. used these temporal profile entries in order to specify training qualification validity periods and were able to significantly improve the quality of responses in a crowdsourcing speech quality assessment task [78].

Discussion of Frameworks: Pros and Cons

Table 1 compares the different crowdsourcing frameworks for QoE assessment. The frameworks differ mainly in the testing methodology they natively support and which kind of multimedia content can be used.

There are some platforms (CrowdMOS and BeaqleJS), which focus on audio quality assessment and implement specific methodologies for subjective evaluation of audio quality like MUSHRA. Other platforms like WESP or Crowdee allow full flexibility by providing programming interfaces or making the source code publicly available. Concerning the task design and the possibility to add additional reliability questions beyond the rating task (e.g. content questions to check reliability of users), this feature is only provided by CrowdMOS or QualityCrowd2. Others implement basic screening mechanisms instead. Quadrant of Euphoria from Chen et al. uses the transitivity index [9]; CrowdMOS uses 95% confidence intervals which does however not allow to check reliability of workers properly as described by Hossfeld et al. [33]; the *in-momento* approach from

Table 1. Comparison of crowdsourcing frameworks for QoE assessment.

Frame-work Ref.	Euphoria [9]	Crowd MOS [88]	Quality Crowd2 [57]	WESP [80]	BeaqleJS [61]	in-momento [25]	Crowdee [73]
Multimedia types							
Image	x	x	x	x		x	x
Video	x		x	x		x	x
Audio	x	x	x	x	x		x
Testing methodology and scale							
Single		x	x	x		x	x
Double	x		x	x	x		x
Mushra		x			x		x
Cont. Scale			x	x		x	x
Questionnaire and task design							
Add. questions		x	x	x			x
Custom template		x	x				x
Random order	x	x		x		x	x
Screening	x	x				x	x

Gardlo et al. computes a reliability score of a worker during the test used for reliability screening [25]. Crowdee differs as it is a crowdsourcing platform provider and can therefore provide a (historic) reliability profile of its workers.

The frameworks considered here are designed for different purposes: either to support concrete methodologies like MUSHRA or paired comparison, or to evaluate quality of certain multimedia types. However, as each crowdsourcing test is somewhat unique, Hossfeld et al. have shown that it is very difficult to find a framework that can be used directly without any modification [37]. Still, the provided overview may help the researcher to select an existing framework as starting base which may then be modified to the purposes of the own test.

5 Lessons Learned

5.1 Scale and Anchoring

Whereas multiple criteria should be adopted to select the methodology most appropriate to investigate a specific problem, direct scaling via, for example, Absolute Category Rating (ACR), has been extensively used in laboratory-based QoE testing [21] due to its ease in implementation and straightforwardness in the interpretation of results. As mentioned earlier, ACR entails users to visualize the stimulus once (Single Stimulus setup), and quantify its quality/level of impairment on a discrete scale, along which qualitative labels (adjectives) are reported (bad-poor-fair-good-excellent for the quality scale). Workers are required to indicate which of these five adjectives better expresses the quality level of the stimulus.

Although direct scaling fits perfectly many of the requirements of crowdtesting (ease of implementation, task simplicity and fast completion), it is important that the task designer takes into account one of its major drawbacks: the risk of returning scores suffering from context effects as shown by Corriveau et al. and de Ridder [11, 89]. Context effects derive from the cognitive bias that leads subjects to use the entirety of a scoring scale (in case of ACR, until 'bad'), to express the quality range that is visualized in the stimulus set. So, having a stimulus set having true quality values covering a range $[0, A]$, and a second set of stimuli covering the range $[A/2, A]$, it is quite likely that the worst stimulus of the second range will still obtain a Mean Opinion Score (MOS) close to 'bad' (although in reality is not as bad as other stimuli in the first set, with a true quality value $<A/2$). Pitrey et al. showed the solution to this issue is re-alignment [77].

In order to overcome these issues with direct scaling the work by Wu and Chen proposes to use comparison rating procedures instead [9, 109]. An elaborate discussion of this approach can be find in the appendix of this chapter.

A possible solution to context effects derived from the fragmentation of QoE evaluations in crowdsourcing was proposed by Hossfeld et al. and Redi et al. [33, 84]. The authors suggest to introduce a small number of stimuli in each evaluation campaign, kept equal for all sub-tasks and spanning a wide range of quality. These stimuli, named "anchors", have the purpose of limiting context effects by fixing the extreme values of aesthetic appeal to be seen in each sub-task. For this reason, at least one of the anchors should present extremely bad quality, possibly lower than that of the entire stimulus set, and at least one should have excellent quality (as known, for example, from a small pilot study prior to the main campaign). Redi et al. showed that the use of anchors was effectively limiting context effects [84]. The authors had a set of 200 images to be rated with respect to aesthetic quality in a crowdsourcing environment. They divided the set in 13 subsets, to be evaluated in as many campaigns. Then, they added to each campaign five images whose quality values corresponded to the minimum, maximum and 25th, 75th and 50th percentile of the distribution of the quality values of the entire image set (as known from a previous laboratory experiment, see Fig. 2). In analyzing the data, the authors performed a re-alignment of the image MOS across campaigns, only to conclude it was unnecessary and their ordering would not change significantly after realignment, thereby proving the effectiveness of the anchors.

In terms of language and scale design crowdsourcing workers are quite heterogeneous regarding their native language and their cultural background. Therefore, they often receive instructions and scale descriptors different from their native language. As the language cannot be relied on in terms of scale description, different scale designs can influence the scale usage and the resulting mean opinion scores. Therefore, the unambiguous design of rating scales is essential for acquiring proper results from crowdsourcing campaigns.

Based on these assumptions a comparison of different scale types and designs Gardlo, Egger and Hossfeld have revealed that an ACR 5 scale with non-clickable anchor points and traffic-light semaphore design as depicted in Fig. 3 yields reliable results and is most efficient in terms of the relative number of outliers [24].

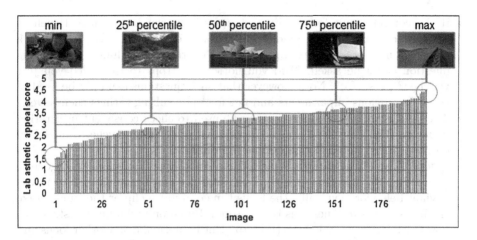

Fig. 2. Anchors used in the crowdsourcing-based image aesthetic quality assessments reported in [84]

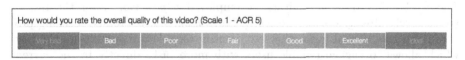

Fig. 3. ACR-5 scale with non clickable anchor points and a traffic-light semaphore design. The scale designs is available under Creative Commons Attribution 3.0 Austria License at https://github.com/St1c/ratings last accessed 14 Jun 2017.

5.2   Reliability Checks

QoE evaluations by their very nature are highly subjective and may differ significantly among the workers. Consequently, it is impossible to categorize subjective ratings as either 'correct' or 'incorrect'. To overcome this issue, reliability checks have to be added to a task in order to estimate the trustworthiness or reliability of a user. In particular, Hossfeld et al. propose to add one of the following elements in the test design to check the reliability of the users.

- Verification tests as reported by Alonso et al. and Downs et al. help in identifying automatization in the form of scripts, but can also be an indicator for sloppy workers and random clickers [1,14]. They include captchas or computation of simple text equations: "two plus 3=?", "Which of these countries contains a major city called Cairo? (Brazil, Canada, Egypt, Japan)".
- Consistency tests estimate the validity of a user's answer by asking, for example, at the beginning of the test, "In which country do you live?", followed later in the test by the question "In which continent do you live?"
- Content questions about the test allow to assess the attention of the user, for example, one can ask after showing a video clip "Which animal did you see in the video? (Lion, Bird, Rabbit, Fish)".

- If the correct result for certain test cases is known in advance, Hsueh et al. showed that so-called gold standard data can by utilized [41]: when a video clip under test, for example, does not contain any stalling, the following question could be asked: "Did you notice any stops to the video you just watched? (Yes, No)". Note, however that such questions can only be used to check for obvious impairments and not for the resulting ratings themselves.
- The repetition of test conditions can be used to check consistent user rating behavior. This can be seen as a special kind of consistency check but based on user ratings instead of additional information.
- Independent of the ratings or additional consistency questions, the general interactions of the user with the task interface can be monitored to unveil deviant behavior. Typically, the focus time of a video clip or the time it take the users to answer questions is monitored. Based on preliminary tests about how trustworthy users behave (used to identify 'normal behavior' or focus and answering times), an additional reliability score based thereon is computed.

Combining these elements also leads to an improved reliability of the results. These reliability tests may either be employed *a posteriori* after the test or alternatively already during the test. The *in momento* reliability checking proposed by Gardlo et al. also allows to identify reliable workers during the test, which allows to engage reliable users with more tasks directly in the current test [25].

After the conclusion of the test, commonly used outlier detection methodologies for the subjective ratings can also be used to detect users whose ratings significantly deviate from the average evaluations as usually represented by the Mean Opinion Scores (MOS), and in a non-systematic way, i.e. their ratings are not systematically above or below the average. For ACR or interval scales, the procedure proposed in ITU-R BT.500 [48] is most suitable. For paired-comparison based tests rating inversions as introduced by Xu and Chen, can be utilized [9,110]. Outlier detection should also include assessing the task execution time since it is a good indicator for the reliable task completion as proposed by Hossfeld, Redi and Korshunov, as workers may skip stimuli too fast without taking the time to properly evaluate them, intertwine the rating task with another task (e.g. web surfing), or get distracted during at least one test case by their environment (e.g. a phone call) [38,60,81]. The first two cases can be identified using the outlier detection from ITU-R BT.500 as workers identified to repeatedly score in an amount of time which is significantly lower or higher than average can be deemed unreliable. The last case can be identified by detecting unusually high evaluation times for a single stimulus. Redi et al. showed that this can be done by observing the standard deviation of the time taken by each worker to evaluate each stimulus as suggested in [81,83].

In their Best Practices for Crowdsourcing paper, Hossfeld et al. note that it is important to filter out all ratings from suspicious workers rather than individual ratings, as there may be hidden, not monitored influence factors for that worker (e.g. bad light conditions) or workers not conducting the task properly (e.g. wrongly understood instructions) [33].

5.3   Duration

In QoE crowdsourcing, Hossfeld et al. recommend campaigns to be fairly short (up to 10 min) to avoid boredom and unreliable behavior [33,38]. Traditional QoE tests typically involve tens or hundreds of stimuli, requiring participants to score for much longer timespans (typically between 30 min and one hour). Thus, to collect QoE scores for a large set of stimuli, researchers usually have to decompose the scoring task in a set of smaller tasks (i.e., campaigns), each one including a sub-set of the stimuli. Redi et al. replicated a laboratory-based experiment in crowdsourcing [81]. In the laboratory experiments, all participants evaluated a total of 200 images in a single session (with three small breaks in between), taking in total 40 min, approximately. Such long task duration could not be replicated in crowdsourcing; hence, the authors split-up the evaluation task into a number of sub-tasks (campaigns) including 20 images each. However, this approach increased tenfold the risk of context effects.

5.4   Payment

There are different motivations for users to participate in crowdsourcing as pointed out in Chap. 3, which aims at understanding the crowd and especially who they are and what their motivations are. As a key result of that chapter, payment is the major motivation for the crowd in commercial crowdsourcing platforms, and all other motivations are secondary. Still, it was observed that higher payments do not guarantee more success or better quality work. Also faster batch completion times cannot be achieved with a higher payment in general, even if some studies indicate that crowdsourcing users tend to choose mainly tasks with high rewards [2,96].

Varela et al. established two identical crowdsourcing campaigns on Web QoE assessment, which only differed in the reward to the workers [102]. In the second campaign, the users earned three times more money than the workers in the first campaign. The higher paid campaign led to significantly shorter completion time (3 h vs. 173 h), but the ratio of reliable users was lower (66% vs. 72%). As a result of the shorter completion times, the demographics of users was narrowed which may be caused by higher motivation of users to participate, time-zones of users, and the start time of the campaign. This effect may be considered when starting a crowdsourced QoE campaign, for example, by possibly throttling the execution, or by selecting users with a certain demographic background in order to obtain more representative population samples.

However, the major observation was that the mean user rating across all test conditions was slightly higher for the higher paid group (3.80 vs 3.60) [102]. A detailed analysis showed that the difference was statistically significant. A possible explanation may be that the users wanted to ensure to earn the reward by 'pleasing' the employer which was leading to higher ratings. In the tests, the normalization of the user ratings based on z-scores lead however to the same main effects and interactions. Thus, the normalized user ratings allowed to properly derive a QoE model. Redi et al. compared paid workers and volunteers when rating the beauty of images and observed that paid users are more likely to commit to the execution of a crowdsourcing task [83]. However, again a bias of paid users to rate quality towards the higher end of the quality scale in contrast to voluntary users was observed.

There are however no general conclusions on payments and incentive design for crowdsourcing studies. For other applications of crowdsourcing beyond QoE testing, different results were observed. Harris et al. used crowdsourcing for screening a number of candidates applying for a job at a company and to conduct resume reviews [31]. Better incentive schemes increased the quality of work.

From these examples we summarize that the influence of payments needs to be considered, (a) in the analysis of the results, for example, using z-scores [57, 102], or removing worker bias [51], and (b) in the test design to ensure that the workers do not want to please the employer and use the entire scale, for example, by proper instructions and training [35, 38]. Further, (c) reporting of payments is crucial in publications of crowdsourced QoE studies.

6   Conclusions

Crowdsourcing for QoE testing has seen a steep take up in numerous crowd-sourced tests due to its promise to reach out to a large, diverse and global crowd in real life environments with short turn-around times. However, research practice has shown that crowdsourcing also hides many pitfalls due to the lack of direct visual and crowdworkers' feedback. Related to these pitfalls, this chapter discusses a number of these issues and their solutions by people that adopted crowdsourcing for QoE testing. Furthermore, a number of existing crowdsourcing platforms are reviewed and discussed with respect to their abilities for different types of QoE tests. The final overview of lessons learned can serve as guidelines for best practices in the experimental setup, data analytics and monetary incentives to be used for QoE testing in the crowd.

Acknowledgement. The authors want to thank Schloss Dagstuhl Leibniz-Zentrum für Informatik, the participants of Dagstuhl Seminar 15481 *Evaluation in the Crowd: Crowdsourcing and Human-Centred Experiments* as well as the Qualinet members that participated in the creation of *Best Practices and Recommendations for Crowdsourced QoE - Lessons learned from the Qualinet Task Force* [38]. Furthermore, this work was supported by the Deutsche Forschungsgemeinschaft (DFG) under Grants HO4770/2-1 and TR257/38-1.

A   Appendix

Absolute vs. Comparative Tasks

In the chapter above we pointed out several weaknesses that are inherent to crowdsourced tests: for example, the lack of control, the diversity of the typically international crowdworker pool and problems with ACR scaling methodologies.

However, the feasibility of large-scale crowdsourced tests motivates to consider other options for judging stimuli besides the single stimulus absolute category rating scheme that is commonly used in QoE crowd testing. In this appendix we discuss the limitations of this traditional approach, and discuss the method of paired comparison as an alternative. We then outline psychometric scaling methods that can reconstruct qualities of stimuli from paired comparisons and conclude by stating the limitations of this approach.

Limitations of Absolute Category Rating

A major category of subjective testing in laboratory environments is aimed at assessing *quality of experience* (QoE) that commonly is defined as an expression of human expectations, feelings, perceptions, cognition and satisfaction with respect to a particular product, service or application. For such tasks where subjects are directly asked to express their subjective perception of a sensory event (visual or auditory event, encounter with a certain system etc.), it is necessary to assign (numerical) values to the related event. Typically, such assignments are achieved by using certain scales. As events can differ strongly, a number of different scales can be used. Among these, absolute category rating (ACR) scales [43] and Comparison Category Rating (CCR) scales [43] have emerged as well established examples for absolute rating or comparative rating tasks in laboratory settings. However, in recent years industry and research has rather shifted towards absolute category ratings (ACR) as they compare well to several other customer satisfaction measures that are typically used to assess product offerings, as well as questions about various aspects of customer interaction with services, products or companies [90]. Such ACR scales have several drawbacks:

- Their usage often varies between different users as they have different understandings of how to map their personal perception on the ACR scale.
- Users tend to avoid both ends of the scale, thus the votes tend to saturate before reaching the end points as shown by Keimel et al. and Gardlo et al. [23,56].
- Language and cultural differences regarding the 'distance' between scale labels for a given International Telecommunication Union (ITU) scale as reported by Jones et al. and Virtanen et al. make it difficult to compare results across cultural or international boundaries [52,105]. Rossi et al. termed these different usage patterns the *scale usage heterogeneity problem* [90].
- There is no well established method for detection of unreliable ratings (in the QoE domain; in other domains such as image labeling, there are established methods to build and use ground truths). Crowdworkers of a study may lack the necessary care and attention to give proper ratings.

One solution to address such issues is the usage of appropriate scale design as reported by Gardlo et al. that have shown to overcome certain limitations of ACR scales [24]. Possible other solutions can be the usage of training sessions within a task as described by Hossfeld et al. that help to align rating diversity and scales usage across different subjects [38]. With such measures and controlled laboratory setups, MOS (mean opinion score) test results can be reproduced quite well in different laboratories.

Crowdsourcing has become an attractive alternative to laboratory studies for QoE assessments because of its efficiency in time and cost, the easy accessibility of crowdworkers form different parts of the world, and the availability of commercial platforms for crowdsourcing. However, with the crowdsourcing approach the limitations of ACR scales are even more severe. The workers can be expected to have a wider range of behavioral patterns with respect to the rating tasks, cultural differences may strongly vary, and their reliability can be poor. Moreover, in crowdsourcing environments it is important to work with a low number of training sessions in order not to lose crowdworkers' attention as shown by Hossfeld et al. [38].

Advantages of Quality Estimation by Paired Comparison

A promising replacement for ACR tests in the crowdsourcing environment is provided by paired testing via CCR procedures. It eliminates offsets between different crowdsourcing campaigns (and laboratory tests, too) as proposed by Chen and Wu [9,109]. In the following we discuss this approach, its properties and advantages.

In paired comparison studies, participants simply express their preference for one or the other of two presented stimuli. If desired, the option for a tie or the degree of preference ('slightly better', 'better', 'much better') may be offered as well. Therefore, training procedures to properly align user ratings with an ACR scale (Bad, Poor, Fair, Good, and Excellent) in the context of a specific application like quality of speech synthesis are not necessary for paired comparison studies. Moreover, the response time yielding a preference for a given pair of stimuli can be expected to be significantly smaller than for a single absolute category rating as participants need not remember and recall the appropriate quality levels from the training sessions for each pair over and over again.

Another important advantage of paired comparisons is that checking for consistency in the answers of an individual as well as for a group of participants is straightforward, by use of the transitivity property. If stimulus X is regarded superior to stimulus Y, and Y superior to Z, then the judgment for the pair (X, Z) should be in favor of X, of course. Therefore, consistency can be expressed as the fraction of judgments that adhere to the expectation due to the transitivity rule, with a fraction of 1.0 giving perfect consistency. A consistency fraction below some threshold may be an indication that the results of the corresponding worker in the crowdsourcing study is not reliable. The notion of consistency can be generalized to the case where paired comparisons are repeated many times, as in a study with several participants, by the well-known concepts of weak, moderate, and strong stochastic transitivity as reported in Bossuty et al. [4].

Reconstruction of Absolute Ratings from Paired Comparisons

Lastly, and perhaps most importantly, there are ways to reconstruct an absolute rating from the relative ones provided by paired comparisons. The simplest such procedures are common scoring schemes as in round robin sport tournaments. Each player (or team) carries out a match with each other player (or team). In each match points are given for a win or a draw. Then after all possible matches have been carried out the players' respective teams can be ranked according to the accumulated scores, which can also serve as absolute measures of performance.

However, the most commonly applied models applied to the problem of assigning a scalar value to some object quality, based on paired comparison, are probabilistic or statistical in nature. Assume that the object qualities are (uncorrelated) continuous random variables ordered along a line. Then distances of their respective means reflect their relative qualities which can be assessed empirically by pairwise comparisons. Each of these random variables has a corresponding probability density function (PDF) and with such a linear model it is the task on hand to estimate their unknown means. A judge, asked to compare any two of the objects, respectively their qualities, say A and B, can then be modeled as follows. A sample is drawn from each of the two distributions and the larger sample drawn determines the winner of the comparison. Repeating this procedure yields $N_{A,B}$ preferences of A over B and $N_{B,A}$ preferences of B over A. The fraction $N_{A,B}/(N_{A,B} + N_{B,A})$ can be regarded as an estimate of $P(A > B)$, the probability that A is better (larger) than B. When we assume certain PDFs for the distributions of the random variables with unknown means we can in principle calculate this probability $P(A > B)$ as a function of the difference of the means. On the other hand, replacing the probability $P(A > B)$ by its empirical estimate $P_{A,B} = N_{A,B}/(N_{A,B} + N_{B,A})$ and applying the inverse of this function will yield an estimate of the distance of the means.

In the classical model of Thurstone-Mosteller [72, 100] the probability density functions are Gaussian, in the simplest case with equal variance. Here the estimate of the distance of the means simply is the inverse of the cumulative density function Φ of the standard normal distribution, applied to the empirical estimate $P_{A,B}$ of $P(A > B)$, up to a scale parameter that depends on the variance of the underlying distributions. Another popular linear model is the one of Bradley-Terry [6]. Here the logistic cumulative density function replaces the normal one, giving very similar results.

After deriving estimates for the distances $d_{i,j}$ between all the stimuli qualities, say A_i and A_j, we still need to reconstruct the linear ordering of all corresponding quality values A_i. This is a problem since a perfect one-dimensional embedding generally does not exist, as we cannot ensure that $d_{i,j} + d_{j,k} = d_{i,k}$ for all i, j, k. There are several approaches to define an appropriate ordering. The simplest one is given by the least-squares estimate, minimizing the sum of squared differences between the empirically estimated differences and the differences in the linear ordering, i.e., $\sum_{i,j}(d_{i,j}-(A_i-A_j))^2$. With the adjustment that the mean quality is zero, $\sum_i A_i = 0$, one obtains the solution $A_j = \sum_i d_{i,j}$ for all j.

Another approach is given by the maximum likelihood method that has been shown to have significant advantages over the traditionally applied least-squares method. For the linear model of Thurstone-Mosteller the likelihood that a sample of the random variable with mean A_i is larger than a sample of the j-th random variable is proportional to $\Phi(A_i - A_j)$. Therefore, if $N_{i,j}$ denotes the number times the i-th stimulus was judged to be larger than the j-th in a pairwise comparison, the log-likelihood for these observations is proportional to $\sum_{i\neq j} N_{i,j} \log(\Phi(A_i - A_j))$. The minimization of this quantity is a convex optimization problem and, thus, readily solvable by numerical methods. Note that it is necessary to add a constraint such as $\sum_i A_i = 0$ in order to ensure an isolated, unique solution. It may be of advantage to generalize this approach to a maximum *a posteriori* estimate, for example, by including a Gaussian prior, amounting to subtracting $\frac{1}{2}\sum_i A_i^2$ from the above log-likelihood.

We conclude this short exposition about paired comparison by giving pointers to some selected literature that describes further details of the methods, their theory, and some examples, and by discussing the limitations of the method of paired comparisons and how they can be dealt with.

Selected References

The most comprehensive treatment of the overall subject matter of pairwise comparison, including a large chapter on linear models, can be found in the monograph *The method of paired comparisons* [13] by H.A. David (1988). In the technical report [101] the authors Tsukida and Gupta provided a modern and short account of the theory and practice of the linear models of Thurstone-Mosteller and Bradley-Terry, including some of the proofs. Moreover, the report studies the different models and computational approaches for them by simulation and lastly lists MATLAB code for the routines for the method of Thurstone-Mosteller. Wickelmaier and Schmid [106] presented details for improvements of the Bradley-Terry model including corresponding MATLAB functions. Wu et al. presented a comprehensive study comparing crowdsourcing using paired comparison with Mean Opinion Score for QoE of multimedia content [109]. They also introduced a general, systematic input validation framework for crowdsourced QoE assessments. Lee et al. proposed an extension of the Bradley-Terry linear model to generate intuitive measures of confidence besides the absolute quality scores [65].

One of the main applications of subjective quality assessment is the comparison of the performance of different, competing (objective) quality assessment algorithms. For example, the correlation between the subjective mean opinion scores and objective scores can be used to judge different algorithms. Hanhart et al. propose that one may also use the results of (subjective) paired comparisons directly without reconstructing absolute scalar quality ratings beforehand [30]. This can be achieved by grouping responses for item pairs (A, B) into classes (e.g. $A > B$ and $A < B$) and then using a threshold t for any given objective quality measure μ to predict the corresponding classes for the same item pairs (A, B); i.e. (A, B) belongs to class $A > B$, if $\mu(A) > \mu(B)$. The performance of a quality assessment algorithm can finally be judged by classification error rates or the area under the corresponding receiver operator characteristic (ROC) curves (Area Under Curve).

Limitations of the Method of Paired Comparison

There are several problems with the method of pairwise comparisons that do not apply to direct absolute category rating.

The 0/1-Problem. When two stimuli presented in a paired comparison differ so strongly that all of the comparisons are in favor of one of them the so-called 0/1-problem occurs. Due to the infinite tail of the cumulative normal density function, the inverse of 0 or 1 will be infinite, yielding an infinitely large estimated distance between the stimuli qualities. One may simply ignore all such comparisons and base the calculations on such incomplete data. A better solution is to add a small amount (e.g. 1 vote) to the counts of the corresponding comparison outcomes. Still better yet is to apply the maximum likelihood method for the optimization as it does not apply the inverse of the cumulative density function and therefore does not require an artificial modification of the empirical data.

Scale and offset. The resulting values for the qualities A_i depend on an arbitrarily chosen scale (determined by the assumed variance of the corresponding random variables) and on an arbitrary offset (determined by the constraint $\sum_i A_i = 0$ or a similar one). Thus, for a comparison with some otherwise obtained ACR values an appropriate rescaling and shift must be carried out. For example, one may scale by equating the variance of the mean values A_i and shift to align the means of the means.

Complexity. Given N stimuli to be compared with each other there are $\frac{1}{2}N(N - 1) = O(N^2)$ pairs of stimuli to be compared. A worker has to make a binary decision for each of these $O(N^2)$ pairs in order to generate a complete data set for the analysis. In comparison, for a study based on ACR each worker makes only N decisions, however, these are multiple choice instead of simply binary. In the practice of studies based on crowdsourcing and even more so in a laboratory setting the quadratic complexity may drive the cost and time for the experiment above the given limits for the study. The obvious way to deal with this issue is to carefully select the most relevant comparisons that should be made avoiding those that are more or less redundant. The methods for the analysis of the resulting comparisons have to be properly adapted to the fact that the data is incomplete. Several methods for such complexity reductions exist [18, 66, 98, 110].

References

1. Alonso, O., Rose, D.E., Stewart, B.: Crowdsourcing for relevance evaluation. In: ACM SigIR Forum, vol. 42, pp. 9–15. ACM (2008)
2. Becker, M., Borchert, K., Hirth, M., Mewes, H., Hotho, A., Tran-Gia, P.: Microtrails: comparing hypotheses about task selection on a crowd sourcing platform. In: International Conference on Knowledge Technologies and Data-driven Business (I-KNOW), Graz, Austria, October 2015
3. Bhatti, N., Bouch, A., Kuchinsky, A.: Integrating User-Perceived quality into web server design. In: 9th International World Wide Web Conference, pp. 1–16 (2000)
4. Bossuyt, P.: A Comparison of Probabilistic Unfolding Theories for Paired Comparisons Data. Springer, Heidelberg (1990). doi:10.1007/978-3-642-84172-9
5. Bouch, A., Kuchinsky, A., Bhatti, N.: Quality is in the eye of the beholder: meeting users' requirements for internet quality of service. In: CHI 2000: Proceedings of the SIGCHI Conference on Human Factors in Computing Systems, pp. 297–304. ACM, New York (2000)
6. Bradley, R.A., Terry, M.E.: Rank analysis of incomplete block designs: I. The method of paired comparisons. Biometrika **39**(3/4), 324–345 (1952)
7. Callet, P.L., Möller, S., Perkis, A. (eds.): Qualinet white paper on definitions of Quality of Experience (2012)
8. Chen, K.T., Chang, C.J., Wu, C.C., Chang, Y.C., Lei, C.L.: Quadrant of euphoria: a crowdsourcing platform for QoE assessment. Network **24**(2) (2010)
9. Chen, K.T., Wu, C.C., Chang, Y.C., Lei, C.L.: A crowdsourceable QoE evaluation framework for multimedia content. In: Proceedings of the 17th ACM international conference on Multimedia, MM 2009, pp. 491–500. ACM (2009)
10. Cooke, M., Barker, J., Lecumberri, G., Wasilewski, K.: Crowdsourcing in Speech Perception. Crowdsourcing for Speech Processing: Applications to Data Collection, Transcription and Assessment, pp. 137–172 (2013)
11. Corriveau, P., Gojmerac, C., Hughes, B., Stelmach, L.: All subjective scales are not created equal: the effects of context on different scales. Sig. Process. **77**(1), 1–9 (1999)
12. Strohmeier, D., Jumisko-Pyykkö, S., Raake, A.: Toward task-dependent evaluation of Web-QoE: free exploration vs. who ate what? In: Globecom Workshops, pp. 1309–1313. IEEE (2012)
13. David, H.A.: The Method of Paired Comparisons. Griffin's statistical monographs, vol. 41, 2nd edn. Charles Griffin & Company Limited, London (1988)
14. Downs, J.S., Holbrook, M.B., Sheng, S., Cranor, L.F.: Are your participants gaming the system?: screening mechanical turk workers. In: Proceedings of the SIGCHI Conference on Human Factors in Computing Systems, pp. 2399–2402. ACM (2010)
15. Egger, S., Gardlo, B., Seufert, M., Schatz, R.: The impact of adaptation strategies on perceived quality of HTTP adaptive streaming. In: Proceedings of the 2014 Workshop on Design, Quality and Deployment of Adaptive Video Streaming, pp. 31–36. ACM (2014)
16. Egger, S., Reichl, P., Hosfeld, T., Schatz, R.: time is bandwidth? narrowing the gap between subjective time perception and quality of experience. In: 2012 IEEE International Conference on Communications (ICC), pp. 1325–1330. IEEE (2012)
17. Egger, S., Schatz, R.: Interactive content for subjective studies on web browsing QoE: A Kepler derivative. In: ETSI STQ Workshop on Selected Items on Telecommunication Quality Matters, pp. 27–28 (2012)

18. Eichhorn, A., Ni, P., Eg, R.: Randomised pair comparison: an economic and robust method for audiovisual quality assessment. In: Proceedings of the 20th International Workshop on Network and Operating Systems Support for Digital Audio and Video, pp. 63–68. ACM (2010)

19. Engeldrum, P.G.: Psychometric Scaling: A Toolkit for Imaging Systems Development. Imcotek Press, Winchester (2000)

20. ETSI: Speech Processing, Transmission and Quality Aspects (STQ); Reference webpage for subjective testing. ETSI Standard TR 103 256, October 2014

21. Fliegel, K.: Qualinet multimedia databases v5. 5 (2014)

22. Freitas, P.G., Redi, J.A., Farias, M.C., Silva, A.F.: Video quality ruler: a new experimental methodology for assessing video quality. In: 2015 Seventh International Workshop on Quality of Multimedia Experience (QoMEX), pp. 1–6. IEEE (2015)

23. Gardlo, B.: Quality of experience evaluation methodology via crowdsourcing. Ph.D. thesis, University of Zilina (2012)

24. Gardlo, B., Egger, S., Hossfeld, T.: Do scale-design and training matter for video QoE assessments through crowdsourcing? In: Proceedings of the Fourth International Workshop on Crowdsourcing for Multimedia, pp. 15–20. ACM (2015)

25. Gardlo, B., Egger, S., Seufert, M., Schatz, R.: Crowdsourcing 2.0: enhancing execution speed and reliability of web-based QoE testing. In: International Conference on Communications, Sydney, AU, June 2014

26. Guse, D., Egger, S., Raake, A., Möller, S.: Web-QoE under real-world distractions: two test cases. In: 2014 Sixth International Workshop on Quality of Multimedia Experience (QoMEX), pp. 220–225. IEEE (2014)

27. Hands, D., Wilkins, M.: A study of the impact of network loss and burst size on video streaming quality and acceptability. In: Diaz, M., Owezarski, P., Sénac, P. (eds.) IDMS 1999. LNCS, vol. 1718, pp. 45–57. Springer, Heidelberg (1999). doi:10.1007/3-540-48109-5_5

28. Hanhart, P., Korshunov, P., Ebrahimi, T.: Crowd-based quality assessment of multiview video plus depth coding. In: IEEE International Conference on Image Processing, ICIP 2014. Paris France, April 2014

29. Hanhart, P., Korshunov, P., Ebrahimi, T.: Crowdsourcing evaluation of high dynamic range image compression. In: SPIE Optical Engineering + Applications. International Society for Optics and Photonics, San Diego, CA, USA, August 2014

30. Hanhart, P., Krasula, L., Le Callet, P., Ebrahimi, T.: How to benchmark objective quality metrics from paired comparison data? In: Quality of Multimedia Experience (QoMEX), pp. 1–6. IEEE (2016)

31. Harris, C.: You're hired! an examination of crowdsourcing incentive models in human resource tasks. In: WSDM Workshop on Crowdsourcing for Search and Data Mining (CSDM), pp. 15–18 (2011)

32. Hirth, M., Hoßfeld, T., Tran-Gia, P.: Anatomy of a crowdsourcing platform - using the example of Microworkers.com. In: Workshop on Future Internet and Next Generation Networks (FINGNet), Seoul, Korea, June 2011

33. Hossfeld, T., Keimel, C., Hirth, M., Gardlo, B., Habigt, J., Diepold, K., Tran-Gia, P.: Best practices for QoE crowdtesting: QoE assessment with crowdsourcing. Trans. Multimedia 16(2), 541–558 (2014)

34. Hoßfeld, T., Seufert, M., Hirth, M., Zinner, T., Tran-Gia, P., Schatz, R.: Quantification of YouTube QoE via crowdsourcing. In: Symposium on Multimedia, Dana Point, USA, December 2011

35. Hossfeld, T.: On training the crowd for subjective quality studies. VQEG eLetter **1**(1), 8 (2014)
36. Hoßfeld, T., Egger, S., Schatz, R., Fiedler, M., Masuch, K., Lorentzen, C.: Initial delay vs. interruptions: between the devil and the deep blue sea. In: QoMEX 2012, Yarra Valley, Australia, July 2012
37. Hoßfeld, T., Hirth, M., Korshunov, P., Hanhart, P., Gardlo, B., Keimel, C., Timmerer, C.: Survey of web-based crowdsourcing frameworks for subjective quality assessment. In: 2014 IEEE 16th International Workshop on Multimedia Signal Processing (MMSP), pp. 1–6. IEEE (2014)
38. Hoßfeld, T., Hirth, M., Redi, J., Mazza, F., Korshunov, P., Naderi, B., Seufert, M., Gardlo, B., Egger, S., Keimel, C.: Best practices and recommendations for crowdsourced QoE - lessons learned from the qualinet task force "Crowdsourcing" October 2014. https://hal.archives-ouvertes.fr/hal-01078761, lessons learned from the Qualinet Task Force "Crowdsourcing" COST Action IC1003 European Network on Quality of Experience in Multimedia Systems and Services (QUALINET)
39. Hoßfeld, T., Schatz, R., Biedermann, S., Platzer, A., Egger, S., Fiedler, M.: The memory effect and its implications on web QoE modeling. In: 23rd International Teletraffic Congress (ITC 2011), San Francisco, CA, USA (2011)
40. Hoßfeld, T., Schatz, R., Seufert, M., Hirth, M., Zinner, T., Tran-Gia, P.: Quantification of YouTube QoE via Crowdsourcing. In: IEEE International Workshop on Multimedia Quality of Experience - Modeling, Evaluation, and Directions (MQoE 2011), Dana Point, CA, USA, December 2011
41. Hsueh, P.Y., Melville, P., Sindhwani, V.: Data quality from crowdsourcing: a study of annotation selection criteria. In: Proceedings of the NAACL HLT 2009 Workshop on Active Learning for Natural Language Processing, pp. 27–35. Association for Computational Linguistics (2009)
42. Huynh-Thu, Q., Garcia, M.N., Speranza, F., Corriveau, P., Raake, A.: Study of rating scales for subjective quality assessment of high-definition video. IEEE Trans. Broadcast. **57**(1), 1–14 (2011)
43. International Telecommunication Union: Methods for Subjective Determination of Transmission Quality. ITU-T Recommendation P.800, August 1996
44. International Telecommunication Union: Interactive test methods for audiovisual communications. ITU-T Recommendation P.920, May 2000
45. International Telecommunication Union: Vocabulary and effects of transmission parameters on customer opinion of transmission quality, amendment 2. ITU-T Recommendation P.10/G.100 (2006)
46. International Telecommunication Union: ITU-T recommendation e.800. Quality of Telecommunication Services: Concepts, models, objectives and dependability planning. terms and definitions related to the quality of telecommunication services. ITU-T Recommendation E.800, September 2008
47. International Telecommunication Union: Subjective video quality assessment methods for multimedia applications. ITU-T Recommendation P.910, April 2008
48. International Telecommunication Union: Methodology for the Subjective Assessment of the Quality of Television Pictures. ITU-R Recommendation BT.500-12, March 2009
49. International Telecommunication Union: Subjective Testing Methodology for web browsing. ITU-T Recommendation P.1501 (2013)
50. International Telecommunication Union: Subjective Methods for the Assessment of stereoscopic 3DTV Systems. ITU-R Recommendation BT.2021, July 2015

51. Janowski, L., Pinson, M.: Subject bias: introducing a theoretical user model. In: 2014 Sixth International Workshop on Quality of Multimedia Experience (QoMEX), pp. 251–256. IEEE (2014)

52. Jones, B.L., McManus, P.R.: Graphic scaling of qualitative terms. SMPTE J. **95**(11), 1166–1171 (1986)

53. Jumisko-Pyykkö, S., Hannuksela, M.M.: Does context matter in quality evaluation of mobile television?. In: Proceedings of the 10th International Conference on Human Computer Interaction with Mobile Devices and Services, pp. 63–72. ACM (2008)

54. Keelan, B.: Handbook of Image Quality: Characterization and Prediction. CRC Press, Boca Raton (2002)

55. Keelan, B.W., Urabe, H.: ISO 20462: a psychophysical image quality measurement standard. In: Electronic Imaging 2004, pp. 181–189. International Society for Optics and Photonics (2003)

56. Keimel, C., Habigt, J., Diepold, K.: Challenges in crowd-based video quality assessment. In: Forth International Workshop on Quality of Multimedia Experience (QoMEX 2012), Yarra Valey, Australia, July 2012

57. Keimel, C., Habigt, J., Horch, C., Diepold, K.: QualityCrowd - a framework for crowd-based quality evaluation. In: Picture Coding Symposium, Krakow, PL, May 2012

58. Keimel, C., Habigt, J., Horch, C., Diepold, K.: Video quality evaluation in the cloud. In: Packet Video Workshop, Munich, DE, May 2012

59. Korshunov, P., Cai, S., Ebrahimi, T.: Crowdsourcing approach for evaluation of privacy filters in video surveillance. In: 1st International ACM workshop on Crowdsourcing for Multimedia (CrowdMM 2012). ACM, Nara, October 2012

60. Korshunov, P., Nemoto, H., Skodras, A., Ebrahimi, T.: The effect of HDR images on privacy: crowdsourcing evaluation. In: SPIE Photonics Europe 2014, Optics, Photonics and Digital Technologies for Multimedia Applications, Brussels, Belgium, April 2014

61. Kraft, S., Zölzer, U.: BeaqleJS: HTML5 and JavaScript based framework for the subjective evaluation of audio quality. In: Linux Audio Conference, Karlsruhe, DE, May 2014

62. Kubey, R., Csikszentmihalyi, M.: Television and the Quality of Life: How Viewing Shapes Everyday Experience. A Volume in the Communication Series. L. Erlbaum Associates (1990). http://books.google.at/books?id=zk_Zg5fJSVwC

63. Laghari, K., Crespi, N., Connelly, K.: Toward total quality of experience: a QoE model in a communication ecosystem. IEEE Commun. Mag. **50**(4), 58–65 (2012)

64. Lebreton, P.R., Mäki, T., Skodras, E., Hupont, I., Hirth, M.: Bridging the gap between eye tracking and crowdsourcing. In: Human Vision and Electronic Imaging XX, San Francisco, California, USA, 9–12 February 2015, p. 93940W (2015)

65. Lee, J.S., De Simone, F., Ebrahimi, T.: Subjective quality evaluation via paired comparison: application to scalable video coding. IEEE Trans. Multimedia **13**(5), 882–893 (2011)

66. Li, J., Barkowsky, M., Le Callet, P.: Boosting paired comparison methodology in measuring visual discomfort of 3DTV: performances of three different designs. In: Proceeding SPIE Electronic Imaging-Stereoscopic Displays and Applications XXIV (2013)

67. Little, G., Chilton, L., Goldman, M., Miller, R.: TurKit: tools for iterative tasks on mechanical turk. In: Proceedings of the ACM SIGKDD Workshop on Human Computation, pp. 29–30. ACM (2009)

68. Mayo, C., Aubanel, V., Cooke, M.: Effect of prosodic changes on speech intelligibility. In: Interspeech. Citeseer (2012)

69. Mazza, F., Da Silva, M.P., Le Callet, P.: Would you hire me? Selfie portrait images perception in a recruitment context. In: IS&T/SPIE Electronic Imaging, p. 90140X. International Society for Optics and Photonics (2014)

70. Möller, S.: Quality Engineering - Qualität kommunikationstechnischer Systeme. Springer, Heidelberg (2010). doi:10.1007/978-3-642-11548-6

71. Möller, S., Raake, A.: Telephone speech quality prediction: towards network planning and monitoring models for modern network scenarios. Speech Commun. **38**, 47–75 (2002). http://portal.acm.org/citation.cfm?id=638078.638082, ACM ID: 638082

72. Mosteller, F.: Remarks on the method of paired comparisons: I. The least squares solution assuming equal standard deviations and equal correlations. Psychometrika **16**(1), 3–9 (1951)

73. Naderi, B., Polzehl, T., Beyer, A., Pilz, T., Möller, S.: Crowdee: mobile crowdsourcing micro-task platform - for celebrating the diversity of languages. In: Proceeding of 15th Annual Conference of the International Speech Communication Assocation (Interspeech 2014) (2014)

74. Naderi, B., Polzehl, T., Wechsung, I., Köster, F., Möller, S.: Effect of trapping questions on the reliability of speech quality judgments in a crowdsourcing paradigm. In: 16th Annual Conference of the International Speech Communication Assocation (Interspeech 2015), ISCA, pp. 2799–2803 (2015)

75. Ouyang, Y., Yan, T., Wang, G.: CrowdMi: scalable and diagnosable mobile voice quality assessment through wireless analytics. IEEE Internet Things J. **2**(4), 287–294 (2015)

76. Parasuraman, A., Zeithaml, V.A., Berry, L.L.: A conceptual model of service quality and its implications for future research. J. Market. **49**, 41–50 (1985)

77. Pitrey, Y., Engelke, U., Barkowsky, M., Pépion, R., Le Callet, P.: Aligning subjective tests using a low cost common set. In: Euro ITV, IRCCyN-Contribution (2011)

78. Polzehl, T., Naderi, B., Köster, F., Möller, S.: Robustness in speech quality assessment and temporal training expiry in mobile crowdsourcing environments. In: 16th Annual Conference of the International Speech Communication Assocation (Interspeech 2015), ISCA, pp. 2794–2798 (2015)

79. Raake, A.: Speech Quality of VoIP: Assessment and Prediction. Wiley, New York (2006)

80. Rainer, B., Waltl, M., Timmerer, C.: A web based subjective evaluation platform. In: Workshop on Quality of Multimedia Experience, Klagenfurth, AT, July 2013

81. Redi, J., Hoßfeld, T., Korshunov, P., Mazza, F., Povoa, I., Keimel, C.: Crowdsourcing-based multimedia subjective evaluations: A case study on image recognizability and aesthetic appeal. In: Workshop on Crowdsourcing for Multimedia, Barcelona, ES, October 2013

82. Redi, J., Liu, H., Alers, H., Zunino, R., Heynderickx, I.: Comparing subjective image quality measurement methods for the creation of public databases. In: IS&T/SPIE Electronic Imaging, p. 752903. International Society for Optics and Photonics (2010)

83. Redi, J., Povoa, I.: Crowdsourcing for rating image aesthetic appeal: Better a paid or a volunteer crowd? In: 3rd International ACM workshop on Crowdsourcing for Multimedia (CrowdMM 2014), Orlando, FL, USA, November 2014

84. Redi, J., Siahaan, E., Korshunov, P., Habigt, J., Hossfeld, T.: When the crowd challenges the lab: lessons learnt from subjective studies on image aesthetic appeal. In: Proceedings of the Fourth International Workshop on Crowdsourcing for Multimedia, pp. 33–38. ACM (2015)

85. Reichl, P.: From charging for Quality of Aervice to charging for Quality of Experience. Annales des Télécommunications **65**(3–4), 189–199 (2010)

86. Rerabek, M., Yuan, L., Krasula, L., Korshunov, P., Fliegel, K., Ebrahimi, T.: Evaluation of privacy in high dynamic range video sequences. In: SPIE Optical Engineering + Applications. International Society for Optics and Photonics, San Diego, CA, USA, August 2014

87. Ribeiro, F., Florencio, D., Nascimento, V.: Crowdsourcing subjective image quality evaluation. In: Image Processing. Brussels, BE, September 2011

88. Ribeiro, F., Florencio, D., Zhang, C., Seltzer, M.: CrowdMOS: an approach for crowdsourcing mean opinion score studies. In: International Conference on Acoustics, Speech and Signal Processing. Prague, CZ, May 2011

89. de Ridder, H.: Cognitive issues in image quality measurement. J. Electron. Imaging **10**(1), 47–55 (2001)

90. Rossi, P.E., Gilula, Z., Allenby, G.M.: Overcoming scale usage heterogeneity. J. Am. Stat. Assoc. **96**(453), 20–31 (2001). http://www.tandfonline.com/doi/abs/10.1198/016214501750332668

91. Rubino, G.: Quantifying the quality of audio and video transmissions over the internet: the PSQA approach. In: Design and Operations of Communication Networks: A Review of Wired and Wireless Modelling and Management Challenges. Imperial College Press (2005)

92. Sackl, A., Schatz, R.: Evaluating the impact of expectations on end-user quality perception. In: Proceedings of International Workshop Perceptual Quality of Systems (PQS), pp. 122–128 (2013)

93. Sanchez-Iborra, R., JPC Rodrigues, J., Cano, M.D., Moreno-Urrea, S.: QoE measurements and analysis for VoIP services. Emerging Research on Networked Multimedia Communication Systems, p. 285 (2015)

94. Schatz, R., Egger, S.: Vienna surfing - assessing mobile broadband quality in the field. In: Taft, N., Wetherall, D. (eds.) Proceedings of the 1st ACM SIGCOMM Workshop on Measurements Up the STack (W-MUST). ACM (2011)

95. Schatz, R., Hoßfeld, T., Janowski, L., Egger, S.: From packets to people: quality of experience as a new measurement challenge. In: Biersack, E., Callegari, C., Matijasevic, M. (eds.) Data Traffic Monitoring and Analysis. LNCS, vol. 7754, pp. 219–263. Springer, Heidelberg (2013). doi:10.1007/978-3-642-36784-7_10

96. Schnitzer, S., Rensing, C., Schmidt, S., Borchert, K., Hirth, M., Tran-Gia, P.: Demands on task recommendation in crowdsourcing platforms - the workers perspective. In: CrowdRec Workshop, Vienna, Austria (9 2015)

97. Shaikh, J., Fiedler, M., Paul, P., Egger, S., Guyard, F.: Back to normal? Impact of temporally increasing network disturbances on QoE. In: 2013 IEEE Globecom Workshops (GC Workshops), pp. 1186–1191. IEEE (2013)

98. Silverstein, D.A., Farrell, J.E.: Quantifying perceptual image quality. In: PICS, vol. 98, pp. 242–246 (1998)

99. Soldani, D., Li, M., Cuny, R.: QoS and QoE management in UMTS cellular systems. Wiley, West Sussex (2006)

100. Thurstone, L.L.: A law of comparative judgment. Psychol. Rev. **34**(4), 273 (1927)

101. Tsukida, K., Gupta, M.R.: How to analyze paired comparison data. Technical report, DTIC Document (2011)

102. Varela, M., Mäki, T., Skorin-Kapov, L., Hoßfeld, T.: Increasing payments in crowdsourcing: don't look a gift horse in the mouth. In: 4th International Workshop on Perceptual Quality of Systems (PQS 2013), Vienna, Austria (2013)

103. Varela, M., Mäki, T., Skorin-Kapov, L., Hoßfeld, T.: Towards an understanding of visual appeal in website design. In: 2013 Fifth International Workshop on Quality of Multimedia Experience (QoMEX), pp. 70–75. IEEE (2013)

104. Varela, M., Skorin-Kapov, L., Mäki, T., Hoßfeld, T.: QoE in the web: a dance of design and performance. In: 2015 Seventh International Workshop on Quality of Multimedia Experience (QoMEX), pp. 1–7. IEEE (2015)

105. Virtanen, M., Gleiss, N., Goldstein, M.: On the use of evaluative category scales in telecommunications. In: Human Factors in Telecommunications (1995)

106. Wickelmaier, F., Schmid, C.: A matlab function to estimate choice model parameters from paired-comparison data. Behav. Res.h Methods Instrum. Comput. **36**(1), 29–40 (2004)

107. Winkler, S., Mohandas, P.: The evolution of video quality measurement: from PSNR to hybrid metrics. IEEE Trans. Broadcast. **54**(3), 660–668 (2008). http://ieeexplore.ieee.org/lpdocs/epic03/wrapper.htm?arnumber=4550731

108. Wolters, M.K., Isaac, K.B., Renals, S.: Evaluating speech synthesis intelligibility using Amazon mechanical turk. In: 7th Speech Synthesis Workshop (2010)

109. Wu, C.C., Chen, K.T., Chang, Y.C., Lei, C.L.: Crowdsourcing multimedia QoE evaluation: a trusted framework. IEEE Trans. Multimedia **15**(5), 1121–1137 (2013)

110. Xu, Q., Huang, Q., Jiang, T., Yan, B., Lin, W., Yao, Y.: HodgeRank on random graphs for subjective video quality assessment. Trans. Multimedia **14**(3), 844–857 (2012)

111. Yu-Chuan, Y., Chu, C.Y., Yeh, S.L., Chu, H.H., Huang, P.: Lab experiment vs. crowdsourcing: a comparative user study on Skype call quality. In Proceedings of the 9th Asian Internet Engineering Conference, pp. 65–72 (2013)

112. Zinner, T., Hirth, M., Fischer, V., Hohlfeld, O.: Erwin - enabling the reproducible investigation of waiting times for arbitrary workflows. In: 8th International Conference on Quality of Multimedia Experiene (QoMEX), Lisbon, Portugal, June 2016

Erratum to: Crowdsourcing Versus the Laboratory: Towards Human-Centered Experiments Using the Crowd

Ujwal Gadiraju[1(✉)], Sebastian Möller[2], Martin Nöllenburg[3],
Dietmar Saupe[4], Sebastian Egger-Lampl[5], Daniel Archambault[6],
and Brian Fisher[7]

[1] Leibniz Universität Hannover, Hannover, Germany
gadiraju@L3S.de
[2] TU Berlin, Berlin, Germany
[3] Algorithms and Complexity Group, TU Wien, Vienna, Austria
[4] University of Konstanz, Konstanz, Germany
[5] Austrian Institute of Technology, Vienna, Austria
[6] Swansea University, Swansea, UK
[7] Simon Fraser University, Burnaby, Canada

Erratum to:
Chapter "Crowdsourcing Versus the Laboratory: Towards
Human-Centered Experiments Using the Crowd" in:
D. Archambault et al. (Eds.): Evaluation in the Crowd,
LNCS 10264, https://doi.org/10.1007/978-3-319-66435-4_2

The original version of this chapter contained an error in the third author's affiliation. The affiliation of Martin Nöllenburg was incorrect in the header of the paper. The author's affiliation has been corrected.

The updated online version of this chapter can be found at
https://doi.org/10.1007/978-3-319-66435-4_2

Author Index

Printed in the United States
By Bookmasters